The New Industrial World

The New Industrial World

Manufacturing Development in the Course of the Globalization Age

Livio Romano
Fabrizio Traù

Great Clarendon Street, Oxford, OX2 6DP,
United Kingdom

Oxford University Press is a department of the University of Oxford.
It furthers the University's objective of excellence in research, scholarship,
and education by publishing worldwide. Oxford is a registered trade mark of
Oxford University Press in the UK and in certain other countries

Published in the United States of America by Oxford University Press
198 Madison Avenue, New York, NY 10016, United States of America

British Library Cataloguing in Publication Data

Data available

Library of Congress Control Number: 2023943111

ISBN 9780192873736

DOI: 10.1093/oso/9780192873736.001.0001

Printed and bound by
CPI Group (UK) Ltd, Croydon, CR0 4YY

Links to third party websites are provided by Oxford in good faith and
for information only. Oxford disclaims any responsibility for the materials
contained in any third party website referenced in this work.

Contents

List of Figures   vii
List of Tables   ix
List of Abbreviations   x

Introduction   **1**

1. The Rise of the Globalization Age   **8**
1.1 A premise   8
1.2 Changing rules and economic development. A retrospective view   8
    1.2.1 A new paradigm   8
    1.2.2 Growth rates   11
1.3 International value chains, trade in tasks, diversification   15
    1.3.1 A new linkage   15
    1.3.2 An endogenous growth?   19
    1.3.3 Diversification   21
1.4 Multinationals and the control of the value chains   23
1.5 The road to industrialization ('the Rest' vs 'the Remainder')   26
1.6 The crisis   30
    1.6.1 The trigger   30
    1.6.2 Long-run trends   32
1.7 Trying to summarize   34

2. A New Landscape for World Manufacturing Production: Old and New Industrial Countries at the Dawn of the New Millennium   **36**
2.1 A premise   36
2.2 Output shares   38
2.3 Growth differentials   40
2.4 Size   42
2.5 Industrialization   45
2.6 Relative growth and international economic integration I: Old vs new industrial economies   51
2.7 Relative growth and international economic integration II: The 'Remainder' and the South–South competition   56
2.8 Conclusions   59

3. Heterogeneous Paths to Industrialization in the Post-War Years   **61**
3.1 Introduction   61
3.2 The political economy of industrial development   63

3.3 The 'Asian model'   68
   3.3.1 An overall view   68
   3.3.2 South Korea   72
   3.3.3 China   75
3.4 From import substitution to market openness in Latin America   78
3.5 What remains of planning. The advent of capitalism in
   former Soviet Union and Eastern Europe   82
3.6 The African issue   88
3.7 Conclusions   94

4. **Building a New Taxonomy of Manufacturing Countries**   **96**
4.1 Introduction   96
4.2 Defining industrial development   97
4.3 Identifying different tiers of manufacturers   101
   4.3.1 Which countries do belong to which tier   101
   4.3.2 The characterization of different tiers   103
   4.3.3 New and old taxonomies in comparison   106
   4.3.4 Evolution of the taxonomy over time   107
4.4 Institutional features   110
4.5 Conclusions   113

5. **The Role of External Demand in Manufacturing Development**   **115**
5.1 Some theoretical premises   115
5.2 Research hypotheses   119
5.3 Data and sample construction   120
5.4 Definition and characterization of the groups of countries   121
5.5 Structural change and industrial development: an
   econometric analysis   125
   5.5.1 Intra-sectoral structural change   125
   5.5.2 Inter-sectoral structural change   129
5.6 Industrial development and economic development   131
5.7 Conclusions   134

6. **The Fall of the Globalization Age**   **136**
6.1 Changing conditions   136
6.2 The slowdown of manufacturing growth   138
6.3 From external to internal demand   142
6.4 The comeback of distance   146
   6.4.1 Decoupling   146
   6.4.2 Back-shoring   147
6.5 From regionalism to multilateralism and back   151
6.6 The effects of the digital and the green transition   159
   6.6.1 Digitalization   159
   6.6.2 Going green   160
6.7 The twin shocks of the pandemic and the war   162

Conclusion   **165**

References   172
Index   187

List of Figures

1.1 World output growth rate, 1951–2015 (%)   15

1.2 World imports by broad economic categories as a percentage of GDP, current dollars   18

1.3 Relationship between per capita GDP and sectoral concentration of manufacturing value added (Gini index), 2015, current dollars   23

1.4 FDI outflows (Developed countries) and inflows (Developing countries), US dollars at current prices in billions, 3-year moving average   24

2.1 Cumulated world manufacturing output shares in the top 20 non-advanced economies in 2018, current dollars   40

2.2 Yearly average growth rates of manufacturing value added (%), constant dollars   41

2.3 Per capita value added in manufacturing, selected countries, United States = 100, current dollars   45

2.4 Yearly average growth rate of per capita value added in manufacturing, 1995–2018, constant dollars—selected countries   49

2.5 Per capita value added in manufacturing, 2018. Selected countries sorted by rank, current dollars   50

2.6 Manufacturing goods, degree of trade openness, and normalized trade balance for blocs of countries, excluding trade among countries within the same bloc, current dollars, three-year moving averages   53

2.7 Manufacturing goods, share of extra-area trade (left panel), and trade to output ratio (right panel) for blocs of countries, current dollars, three-year moving averages   56

2.8 Manufacturing goods, degree of trade openness, and normalized trade balance for different South regions, current dollars   58

3.1 Manufacturing growth between 1990 and 2018 against the degree of industrialization in 1990   62

4.1 Groups of manufacturing countries by manufacturing value added per capita in 2015, current dollars   104

5.1 Sectoral concentration and industrial development before the globalization's take-off, country averages 1980–83   124

5.2 Intra-sectoral structural change and industrial development, 1980–2011, constant dollars   126

5.3 Inter-sectoral structural change and industrial development, 1980–2011, constant dollars   130

5.4 Inter-sectoral structural change and economic development, 1980–2011, constant dollars, quadratic and non-parametric fits   133

6.1 Relationship between global trade and value added in manufacturing   137

6.2 Annual average growth rates of manufacturing gross output (constant dollars)   140

6.3 Average (left scale) and variance in gross output growth rates of individual countries at the world level (constant dollars)   141

6.4 Internal demand (apparent consumption) for manufacturing goods, 2007=100, constant prices   143

6.5 Manufacturing export to value added ratio, current dollars   144

6.6 Share of intermediate imports used by BRICs' domestic manufacturing (monetary values at current prices)   147

6.7 Domestic manufacturing inputs on total manufacturing inputs (%) by US industry, 2018, current dollars   150

6.8 Degree of regionalism (see note 24) in world trade, three-term moving average   156

6.9 World network of trade exchanges, manufactured goods, 2019   157

6.10 CO_2 emissions for dollar of manufacturing value added relative to EU (2018, EU average = 1), current prices   161

List of Tables

1.1 Percentage annual GDP growth rates (PPP) for some areas and countries 14

2.1 Structure and change of output flows in the long run (country shares of manufacturing value added in current dollars, %) 39

2.2 Yearly average growth rates of per capita value added in manufacturing by geographical area, constant dollars 48

4.1 Variables used to build a taxonomy of manufacturing countries 100

4.2 A new taxonomy of manufacturing countries, 2015 102

4.3 Characterization of the different groups of manufacturing countries (2015 mean values) 105

4.4 Comparing with the UNIDO taxonomy of industrial development 107

4.5 The taxonomy of manufacturing countries in 2001 (data in constant dollars 2015) 109

4.6 Institutional differences across different tiers of manufacturing countries (2015) 112

5.1 Selected indicators for individual countries, average 1980–83, current prices 123

5.2 Regression analysis of intra-sectoral structural change, 1980–2011, constant prices 128

5.3 The effect of trade on the intra-manufacturing structural change, 1980–2011, constant dollars 129

5.4 Regression analysis of inter-sectoral structural change, 1980–2011, constant prices 132

List of Abbreviations

ASEAN	Association of Southeast Asian Nations
BRIC	Brazil Russia India China
ECLAC (CEPAL)	United Nations Economic Commission for Latin America and the Caribbean
EU-15	European Union as to 1st January 1995 (Belgium, Denmark, Germany, Finland, France, Greece, Ireland, Italy, Luxembourg, Netherlands, Austria, Portugal, Spain, the United Kingdom and Sweden).
G7	Group of Seven (Canada, France, Germany, Italy, Japan, the United Kingdom and the United States)
G10	Group of Ten (Belgium, Canada, France, Germany, Italy, Japan, the Netherlands, Sweden, Switzerland, the United Kingdom, and the United States)
GATT	General Agreement on Tariffs and Trade
GDP	Gross Domestic Product
IMF	International Monetary Fund
ISIC	International Standard Industrial Classification of All Economic Activities
NAFTA	North American Free Trade Agreement
OECD	Organization for Economic Cooperation and Development
PPP	Purchasing Power Parity
UNCTAD	United Nations Conference on Trade and Development
UNIDO	United Nations Industrial Development Organization
UNSNA	United Nations System of National Accounts
USMCA	United States-Mexico-Canada Agreement
WTO	World Trade Organization

Don't do as the English tell you to do, do as the English did
(*Old American maxim*)

Introduction

This book is about industrial development in the years of globalization. In particular, it focuses upon a major phenomenon that in the last decades has completely re-shaped the economic landscape at the global level: namely, the spreading of manufacturing activities beyond the boundaries of 'advanced' economies.

Such a pathbreaking change has not come out of the blue, but has found its way through the reversal of the policy stance that, up to the early 1970s, had set the basis for the success of the so-called Golden Age of industrial economies. That is, the economic regime which—hinging on the Bretton Woods rules and on a high degree of regulation in internal and international markets—for a couple of decades ensured in those same countries, basically through the expansion of internal demand, a high and stable rhythm of growth.

In a handful of years, the logic of economic policy underwent a sharp change: as will be argued in the following chapters, by the late 1970s the impossibility for the old regime to come to terms with the twofold problem of slower growth and high inflation rates paved the way to the emergence of a new paradigm, calling for the abandoning of policy intervention and market regulation. The advent in subsequent years of what has been called the Washington Consensus (WC) marked the transition to an era characterized by the constant search for 'flexibility' and market liberalization all across the world. As will be shown, this set the premises for multilateral trade (i.e. for *international* demand) to eventually become, under the aegis of the WTO, the main driver of growth at the global level, and for market exchanges between different areas of the world to expand. So it came to the fore what in this book is called the Globalization Age, which became an outright regime in the same way as the Golden Age was, even if it was based upon quite opposite postulates (the latter hinging on strong regulation, the former on generalized liberalization), shaping something like a new world order.

As a matter of fact, the unfolding of the Globalization Age (GA) does coincide as to its timing with the aforementioned emergence of new manufacturing economies. Which is in itself the most noticeable event in contemporary economic history as to the real side of the economy, having completely upset

The New Industrial World. Livio Romano and Fabrizio Traù, Oxford University Press.

the way we have been looking at the relationship between the Global North and South ever since. The key feature of this phenomenon is that it has—for the very first time—linked together the former and (a part of) the latter on *productive* grounds, far beyond the 'traditional' exploitation of third-world commodities on the part of old-industrialized countries—therefore weaving into a common destiny developed and (formerly) underdeveloped countries through an unprecedented expansion of international trade. In turn, this has gradually brought about a radical change in the balance of powers at the global level, characterizing the 'new' industrial world as a polycentric entity.

The reasons and the ways whereby this could happen—and has happened in a relatively short time span—are widely discussed throughout the book. Here, however, we have to add that the emergence of new producers outside the walls of what still at the end of past century was the fortress under siege of the G10 has not been driven by the advent of the new paradigm as such. And that, consistently with this, it has concerned only a relatively limited number of underdeveloped economies.

In fact, it can be said that the countries that have emerged the most as new manufacturers in the course of the GA did not passively follow the prescriptions of the WC (macroeconomic policies aimed at controlling inflation and deficit spending, liberalization of trade and capital flows so as to exploit static comparative advantages, widening of the market boundaries through privatization and deregulation processes). Indeed, they followed quite a different strategy, principally consisting in the search for *dynamic* comparative advantages, i.e. the development of activities in which in principle the competitive advantages are still to be achieved and are to be pursued through active and selective investment policies (often on a conditional basis). On the one hand such policies were grounded on the knowledge and capabilities these countries had already been able to develop that far; on the other they were driven by the aim to emulate what already industrialized countries had done in the past as to their own development process. Such an approach—also requiring infant industry protection—has found its maximum expression in the East Asian context, where it culminated in the emergence of the 'Developmental State' as an entity explicitly oriented towards the purposeful building of strong competitive assets at the national level.

At the same time, it also has to be mentioned that, on the contrary, many countries that uncritically accepted the WC rules set forth by international institutions—generally imposed as a preliminary condition for getting access to financial aid—did instead perform quite worse, up to the point that when the mechanical introduction of the WC prescriptions was implemented without a previous building of adequate market institutions (as blatantly happened in the Russian experience) the system simply collapsed into default as soon as it was opened to market rules.

In this framework emerging economies found their way—in a manufacturing landscape which was already full of incumbents and entry barriers in almost every market—through explicit development strategies, trying to achieve a reasonably high degree of export competitiveness *before* opening to the market, and—at that point—by taking advantage of the worldwide market liberalization and the brakeless rise of multilateralism which the unfolding of the new paradigm pushed on. Hence, manufacturing growth in these countries has been export-led, by finding an extraordinary lever in the expansion of international trade: and in this sense—and within these limits—globalization has actually led to the diffusion of manufacturing into the underdeveloped world. Yet, according to the view set forth in this book, the GA has to be conceived as the fuel, but not as the engine, of the emergence of the new industrial world.

Anyway this is not the end of the story. Change, which is the normal feature of economic life, is happening again, and the GA has also come to an end. Why did this happen, and what is it going to bring about?

The basic argument put forth in this book is that the GA has primarily exhausted for endogenous reasons. Changes—extensively analysed in following chapters—cumulatively converge to the weakening of the relationship tying together advanced and developing countries through international trade, which had been at the root of the take-off of industrialization in the latter.

The new discontinuity was given way by the great financial crisis that hit the world at the end of the first decade of the 2000s, turning out into the shrinkage of demand in advanced countries and therefore into a lower demand from abroad (i.e. external demand) for the emerging economies, determining in following years a fall in the rhythm of growth of global market exchanges.

In the new framework emerging economies had to learn to do away with a relevant share of their exports towards the advanced world (especially East Asian ones, where the dependence on exports was peculiarly strong). For the largest emerging countries—which could rely on a wide size of the internal market—this has pushed towards a re-balancing between exports and the domestic market; more broadly, it has led to a wider process of decoupling, that in Eastern Asia has also involved a switch from the US to China in the role of importer for local producers, making deeper the intra-area productive linkages. In turn, the endogenous determinants of the decoupling have been buttressed by explicit changes—again—in the policy stance: namely, by the turning back of the US to protectionism, and more broadly to selective trade policies.

This means that, even if the degree of international economic integration is bound to remain sustained for long, its expansion will lack its historical driving forces, so that it should be expected to weaken. Above all, this should be furtherly enhanced by the upsurge, in later years, of important exogenous shocks, such as the sudden advent of the pandemic in the early months of 2020 and the outbreak of the war in Ukraine just two years later, which have contributed to raising the option value of relying on autonomous resources (commodities, and in particular energy; intermediates; even final goods, as has become critical in healthcare), therefore fostering an overall drift towards de-globalization. The totality of such trends has led in itself to a 'new normal', the basic features of which can be found in a slowdown of manufacturing growth rates, and in the comeback of geography and politics as key determinants of economic behaviour, against the idea—lying behind the multilateral view—according to which distance was simply to be taken for dead.

The arguments through which this story is explored are displayed in six chapters. Chapter 1, focusing on the long-run determinant of the rise of the GA, outlines a framework that can be divided into four intertwined blocks: (1) a retrospective analysis of the emergence of the new paradigm after the fall of the Golden Age; (2) a discussion of the determinants of manufacturing development in emerging economies; (3) an analysis of the logic of the integration of manufacturing systems at the global level through the creation of international value chains and the (related) expansion of direct investment flows, which has strongly re-shaped the organization of manufacturing activities all across the world; (4) a discussion of the origins and main implications of the crisis that struck the world economy at the end of the long expansionary cycle ending in 2008.

Chapter 2 contains a description of the actual changes that have occurred in the geographical distribution of manufacturing activity over the last thirty years, which have led to a new economic landscape at the global level and to an increase in capability of the new industrial economies to exert an influence on the global economy. The issue is analysed by looking at such changes from different points of view and providing some measures of the intensity of manufacturing growth and the rate of industrialization in emerging countries. Moreover, the chapter provides a measure of the degree of economic integration between 'old' and 'new' industrial economies through international trade.

Chapter 3 addresses the institutional determinants of industrialization in emerging economies. By comparing the different approaches followed by East Asian, Latin American and Former Communist countries to acquire and build endogenously productive knowledge, it is shown that the countries where industrial development has actually taken place did initially embrace infant industry protection policies and succeeded in creating comparative advantages in new activities. This also explains the failure of any attempt to set up policies aimed at favouring manufacturing development in the African continent, where this did not happen.

Chapter 4 tries to go a bit deeper into what industrialization is actually about by proposing a novel approach to the categorization of manufacturing development. It first addresses the way it can be defined in order to provide a measure of the overall degree of industrialization of different countries, suggesting some specific indicators to this end. On such a basis a new taxonomy of countries according to their degree of manufacturing development is proposed, accounting for the major global transformations that have occurred in the organization of industrial activities at the global level. It is stressed that this does not imply that countries are bound to follow, when developing, a mechanical path leading from one group of the taxonomy to another; in this respect, attention is paid to the fact that in the course of time countries can even move from one group to another in both directions.

Chapter 5 discusses the relationship between industrial development and structural change in the course of the GA. In particular, it sets within the same framework two stylized facts, i.e. that both the internal structure of the whole economy (i.e. the weight of manufacturing in the economic system) and the sectoral concentration of activities *within* the manufacturing sector do change in the course of industrial development. It is shown that both these phenomena are characterized by important differences among different groups of countries and such differences are claimed to depend upon the time at which industrial development has taken place. For late industrializing countries, in which the manufacturing take-off occurred during the GA, the inter and intra-sectoral structural adjustment has been on average, due to a structurally higher degree of competition from abroad, significantly faster as compared to that experienced by nations that built the foundations of their manufacturing system before the advent of the GA. This has involved an early increasing sectoral concentration of manufacturing activities and an earlier decline in the manufacturing share on the total economy, setting the premises for premature de-industrialization.

Chapter 6 provides an analysis of the long-run endogenous determinants of the exhaustion of the GA. It pays attention in particular: (1) to the

worldwide slowdown of manufacturing output growth that has characterized the post-financial crisis years, explaining the structural reasons behind
it; (2) to the fall of external demand, that has been the main driver of world
manufacturing development for the whole GA; (3) on the supply-side, to
both the decoupling of Chinese productions from global sourcing and the
emergence of back-shoring processes in advanced countries; (4) to the resurgence of regionalism in international trade and the economic consequences
of the advancements of the digital and green transitions; (5) to the expected
consequences of the (exogenous) twin shocks of the Covid-19 pandemic and
the war in Ukraine.

   The book is the outcome of some years of common work by its authors.
The bulk of the empirical research, here spread through the various chapters,
has been mainly carried out in the Research Department of the Confedera-
tion of Italian Industries (Confindustria), where both authors served for years
and where an explicit research programme on global manufacturing development was launched. The outcome of this activity has taken the form of a
series of papers, partially written in Italian (as far as they were related to the
production of institutional reports) and partially in English, some of which
have also involved other researchers in the same Department (see in particular Romano and Traù 2014, 2017, 2022; Traù 2016; Manzocchi Romano
and Traù 2020; Pensa, Romano and Traù 2020; Manzocchi and Traù 2022).
In this light, the authors wish to mention in particular Cristina Pensa and
Matteo Pignatti, who have been no less than their road companions along
this travel, having constantly shared with them the task of developing a view
about what was going on in the world economy, collecting data and following
the evolution of the related literature.

   Whenever possible, previous writings have been updated, and the whole
set of arguments has been reshaped accordingly, reflecting in some cases a
change in the way authors themselves have looked at the various phenomena
just as a consequence of the unfolding of their work. As far as the book owes
to such a background, its gradual development has benefitted in past years
from the comments to earlier drafts of the text by various referees; and even
more from the many discussions the authors have had the possibility to share
with various scholars, colleagues, and friends. We would like to remember
here at least Franco Amatori, Daniele Antonucci, Alessandro Arrighetti, Ser-
gio de Nardis, Gioacchino Garofoli, Anna Giunta, Lelio Iapadre, Stefano
Manzocchi, Valentina Meliciani, Fabrizio Onida, Francesco Paternò, Carlo
Pietrobelli, Mohan Rao, Francesco Silva, Annamaria Simonazzi, Tim Sturgeon, Lucia Tajoli, Hugh Whittaker. Thanks are also due to the participants
at the Workshop on 'Explaining Economic Change' held at the University of

Rome 'La Sapienza' in November 2014, at the XXXI Villa Mondragone International Economic Seminar on 'Capitalism, Global Change and Sustainable Development. The Future of Globalization' held in June 2019, and at the Annual Conferences of the Italian Society for Industrial Economics and Policy held in Ferrara in January 2018 and in Venice in January 2020, where single chapters of the book have been presented. Above all, the authors wish to acknowledge here their debt towards the members of the community of the Annual Workshop on the Dynamics of Industrial Systems, which has been held at the Antico Palazzo dei Vescovi in Pistoia since 2017, where the ideas expressed in the book have been gradually ripening. Special thanks are due to Chiara Puccioni, for excellent research assistance, and to two OUP anonymous referees, for their valuable comments.

The book is being published in the midst of an armed conflict at the doors of Europe which is likely to have far-reaching consequences in the years to come. Whereas the fall of the GA has *already* deprived the whole world of something like a global order, such an event may add in itself further reasons for the delay of the advent of a new order (whatever its actual configuration). What can be certainly said in this connection is that, anyway, coming back to the *status quo ante* is simply inconceivable. The 'world of yesterday' is gone.

1
The Rise of the Globalization Age

1.1 A premise

This chapter aims at tracing a course in the midst of the many issues that have contributed to making the last decades so tumultuous, setting facts within a framework that can be divided into four intertwined blocks: (1) a retrospective analysis of the emergence of a new paradigm after the fall of what has been called the Golden Age of advanced economic systems; (2) a discussion of the determinants of manufacturing development in the so-called emerging economies; (3) a measure of the integration of manufacturing systems at the global level via the creation of international value chains and the expansion of direct investment flows; (4) a discussion of the origins and main implications of the crisis that struck the world economy at the end of the long expansion cycle in 2008. No one of such issues is treated exhaustively. The goal of the chapter is simply to weave them into a comprehensive view of the paradigm that has shaped the last phase of world industrial development, which we will call the Globalization Age (GA).

1.2 Changing rules and economic development. A retrospective view

1.2.1 A new paradigm

Globalization, in the connotation it was given since it first came to the fore, developed on at least three different levels (UNCTAD 2016): (1) political, with the removal of barriers to the cross-border movement of goods, people, and capital; (2) economic, with the long-run increase of these flows and growing international integration of economic systems at the production level; (3) institutional (rules, norms, and organizations designed to oversee the huge development of international transactions). All these phenomena were backed by a vision of the functioning of the economy that radically overturned the previous approaches, providing a theoretical substrate to the idea that the development of economic systems was to be always and in any

The New Industrial World. Livio Romano and Fabrizio Traù, Oxford University Press.
© Livio Romano and Fabrizio Traù (2023). DOI: 10.1093/oso/9780192873736.003.0002

case entrusted exclusively to the operation of market forces. How did this happen?

At the very dawn of the GA, around the mid-1970s, international institutions were facing the rubble of a world which could no longer manage through regulation mechanisms—i.e. directly—the complexity brought about by the very success of their own policies. The successful catching-up of European countries as against the United States, their sustained growth in terms of per-capita GDP and wages, the attainment of full employment had eventually turned into rising inflation and output stagnation (the stagflation issue), asking for radical changes as to policy prescriptions. It was then easy to counterpose a 'simple' answer to 'the plethora of controls, regulations, and other restrictive practices in the domestic product, capital and labour markets' (Singh 1997: 14) that the Golden Age at its outset—i.e. the regime that had led the unfolding of the development process of industrial countries that far—was passing on to the generation of the 'boomers'. It was so simple that the transition between the two ages took no more than a handful of years (the second half of the 1970s).[1]

So, at the end of the 1970s the substantial impossibility of governing the 'new' problems of the economy with the instruments inherited from the regime of the Golden Age called for a radical change in the role of the state in the regulation process, and the abandonment of the interventionist approach. The shift was from a view according to which the coordination of production activities occurs outside of the market to a new one where the role of public choices consists in leaving the market forces free to adapt to a structurally changing environment. In this context, the key issue became the search for higher growth as the final goal of economic policy.

Beginning with the economic systems that had historically been more market oriented (United Kingdom and United States), the early 1980s witnessed the progressive assertion of a vision where the cornerstone of the development process was to 'free' individual initiative from the extensive public regulation inherited from the past. The deregulation and privatization of activities that had previously been under state control became the new intermediate goals of economic policy, and the import substitution industrialization (ISI) model—that had been at the root of the development of important developing countries (see Chapter 3 below)—became the

---

[1] The logic of the Golden Age—which has determined both its rise and its fall—has been analysed at length in Glyn et al. (1990) and cannot be summarized in these pages; yet it can be noted here that the phenomenon was driven on the one side by the expanding of internal demand (as Glyn et al. themselves wrote, 'the Golden Age growth could be regarded as primarily domestically based', 1990: 51), and on the other by strong regulation at institutional level. See also Kindleberger (1992), Singh (1995, 1997).

paradigm to be fought. This orientation received an important push also by the eruption of the so-called Latin American 'debt crisis' (opened by the declaration of default by Mexico in 1982). Gradually, it spread to the entire West; but in the meantime the political events also opened up the market to the entire block of former socialist countries (Chang 1997).

Starting from the early 1980s the spread of the new creed to the main international financial institutions (in particular the IMF and the World Bank), via the role played by the academic world and the most influential research centres, has led to the formulation of a *new* system of rules, commonly defined as the Washington Consensus (WC).[2] The economic policy of the WC can be summarized in three basic principles, that have become the new intermediate goals of economic policy: (1) macroeconomic stability, to be reached through policies aimed at controlling inflation and deficit spending; (2) liberalization of trade and capital flows; (3) an extension of the market boundaries to be obtained through privatization and deregulation processes.

The degree of attainment of these objectives by the individual economic systems ended up being the yardstick for measuring how 'virtuous' they actually were: on the one hand subjecting the delivery of international aid to the countries' compliance with the new rules; on the other, reducing the problem of development to the measurement of their aggregate performance (expressed in terms of GDP growth in the short term). 'Following the rules', in a framework where the need to make adjustments rapidly ended up in the mantra of 'structural reforms', entailed the abandonment of major government plans aimed at transforming society.[3] In the new perspective, the very problem of development as a *process* loses any meaning, as far as the governments of the different economic systems (whatever their degree of development) are all called upon to do the same things all the time ('one

---

[2] The term 'Washington Consensus' was proposed for the first time in 1989 in a paper by J. Williamson, prepared for a conference at the Institute for International Economics aimed at discussing the policies that had governed Latin America since the 1950s (see Williamson 2009). The paper suggested a list of 10 policies that—according to the author—'more or less everyone in Washington would agree were needed more or less everywhere in Latin America' at the time. They were: fiscal discipline; reordering public expenditure priorities; tax reform; liberalizing interest rates; a competitive exchange rate; trade liberalization; liberalization of inward foreign direct investment; privatization; deregulation; favouring the acquisition of property rights.

[3] It is worth pointing out that, at the same time, following the Millennium Summit held in New York in September 2000, the United Nations formulated the so-called Millennium Development Goals, putting a series of highly articulated development objectives at the heart of the world political agenda (among others: to eradicate poverty and hunger, achieve universal primary education, reduce child mortality, combat diseases, and ensure environmental sustainability). See on this United Nations (2000). In time, the pressure exerted by events (see below) was to lead to a partial softening of the more rigid version of the WC, that produced a new formulation including some partial elements of flexibility, that goes under the name of Institutional View of the IMF; see IMF (2012).

size fits all'), hence sterilizing the economy from any possibility of taking any nationally oriented direction:

> No longer was it a matter of governments selecting their industrial investments with the correct shadow prices. Governments were now adjured to divest themselves of state-owned industries and to liberalize comprehensively—in goods markets, labour markets, financial markets, capital markets and foreign-trade markets. They were encouraged to concentrate their efforts on law and order, education and health.
>
> (Toye 2003: 31)

In the new context what any given (specific) country is structurally characterized by does not matter any longer: what matters is simply the extent to which *all countries* do embrace the very same strategy by relying upon the very same (narrow) set of instruments that any one of them has at disposal.

1.2.2 Growth rates

The new paradigm did actually contribute to bringing about important changes in the organization of economic activities (in particular manufacturing ones) across the world. Yet, it started to show signs of strain as early as the 1990s (see below). At the centre of the stage has to be set the poor aggregate performance observed in the years following the introduction of the new policies, revealing a substantial failure of the fundamental assumption of the WC—according to which the new economic policy was expected to lead to higher growth, specifically in the economies which were lagging behind.[4] In practice, the expectations of a faster pace of growth following the trend towards a reduction in public intervention and lower commercial barriers were totally frustrated: as noted by Chang (2008: 11), 'the growth rates of the developing countries since the 1980s, when they abandoned the supposedly disastrous ISI policy and entered the "brave new world" of neo-liberalism, have been much lower than that during the "bad old days" of ISI'.

The phenomenon was indeed visible already in the last years of last century and it fuelled a progressive dissatisfaction with the provisions of the WC

---

[4] Among others, the point is documented in Weisbrot et al. (2006), also highlighting its consequences in terms of a decline in the rate of progress of major social indicators, including life expectancy and infant and child mortality.

by a growing number of observers.[5] In the wake of neostructuralism of the
ECLAC analyses (1990, 2000), that again questioned the dogma of the abolition of the ISI policies in Latin America,[6] and in the wake of the studies
analysing the development model of the fast-growing East Asian economies
(Chang 2006), the preconditions were informally laid for a 'Southern Consensus', oriented again towards the historic dimension of the phenomenon
of development (Gore 2000). In a matter of a few years, in the new century
a New Development Economics (NDE) emerged, setting the development
issue in laggard countries at the centre of the political agenda. The backwardness of such countries is viewed in this context as an outcome of market
failure, and as a problem linked first of all to a scant accumulation of manufacturing knowledge—thus restoring a central role to industrial policy (see
among others Singh 1994a; Amsden 2001; Chang 2002, 2003, 2006; Reinert 2007; Arestis and Eatwell 2008; Cimoli et al. 2009; Stiglitz and Lin 2013;
UNIDO 2009, 2013, 2016; UNCTAD 2016).

The distinctive feature of the NDE can be found in its realism (one
might say pragmatism) as opposed to the very idealism of the WC.[7] In
the outline suggested by Gore (2000), the fundamental traits are the idea
that the introduction of liberalized trade into a system should be pursued 'strategically' (and not in an unconditional manner); the importance
attributed to the creation of industrialization policies aimed at creating
dynamic comparative advantages;[8] a pragmatic attitude of the public institutions (also as to containing distribution imbalances within individual
economies).

On this basis, and in the presence of a WC still formally in the sad-
dle and vital (at least according to the declarations of the most prominent
international institutions), the world started to reorganize itself in practice, triggering a gradual shift in attention towards a more inward-looking
direction. The result was that

[5] Critical views about the mainstream approach to globalization emerged since the mid-1990s; see for
instance the contributions gathered in the books edited by Michie and Grieve-Smith (1995, 1996, 1997).

[6] 'Latin America represents, in this regard, an outstanding example of a region where the record of economic liberalization has not only been disappointing, but indeed has been considerably poorer than that
of State-led (or import-substitution) industrialization' (Ocampo 2005: 4). The point is widely discussed
in Chapter 3.

[7] 'The ideologues believe that such globalization promises economic prosperity for countries that join
the system and economic deprivation for countries that do not. It needs to be stressed that this intertwined
normative and prescriptive view of globalization is driven in part by ideology and in part by hope. It is
not borne out by experience' (Nayyar 2003: 68).

[8] 'In this forward-looking approach, the opportunities of current relative cost advantages are exploited
to the full, but efforts are made at the same time to promote investment and learning in economic activities
where comparative advantages can realistically be expected to lie in the immediate future' (Gore 2000:
797). See more widely on this point Chapter 3.

[b]y the mid-2000s, the Washington Consensus development model was already beginning to unravel. US hegemony was eroding and the large emerging economies, led by China and India, were altering the organization of production and how rules were made that affected the global economy. (...) When the global economic recession hit in 2008–09, this ended all prospects of a return to the old order.

(Gereffi 2014: 14–15)

But what continued to be missing was an alternative, widely shared development strategy, capable of replacing the WC—whose death sentence had not been pronounced by anyone. Indeed, individual countries proceeded in random order. The result in time was the disappearance of the idea of a totally interdependent world, and—after the failure of the 'Doha Round' of WTO in the course of the first decade of the new century—the ways for the multinational expansion of business and trade policies had to be entirely reconsidered (see Chapter 6).

The existence of a negative discontinuity in the rate of growth, represented by the watershed of the early 1980s, appears to be macroscopic even when seen from the perspective of today, i.e. when including in the data the period of general expansion of the early twenty-first century (Table 1.1).[9]

The comparison between the two great phases of development (pre and post WC) is immediate: with the exception of the East Asian area, all the areas of the world (and the world itself) recorded after 1980 a marked decline in growth rates. For the developing economies, excluding the Asian area, the comparison is harsh, and the transition from the first to the second 'model' coincided with a collapse of the annual growth rate from three to one per cent.[10] Of course the bad performance in the second period is affected by the crisis that stopped the expansion trend of the early years of the new century. But the crisis itself—as will be argued below—has to be considered wholly endogenous to the way development had taken place that far. From this point of view, the intensity of the growth in the years spanning from the explosion of the 'New Economy' bubble in 2001 to the crisis of the subprime loans in the United States in 2008 was fuelled by the accumulation of imbalances that were bound as such to explode, dragging with them the whole world economy (see below).

---

[9] In this chapter data exclude very recent years (characterized by a further fall in global growth rates), which will be explicitly addressed in Chapter 6.

[10] 'This is a particularly damning record for an economic doctrine that has prided itself in being single-mindedly focused on economic growth, on the grounds that "we first have to generate wealth before we can redistribute it"' (Chang 2003: 6).

Table 1.1 Percentage annual GDP growth rates (PPP) for some areas and countries

Economic Areas	1951–1980	1981–2015
Developed economies	3.5	1.8
United States	2.3	1.8
Developing economies	2.7	3.8
Africa	1.8	1.2
America	2.6	1.3
Asia	2.8	5.0
East Asia	3.0	7.1
China	2.3	7.7
South-East Asia	2.6	3.5
South Asia	1.4	4.1
West Asia	4.4	1.4
Transition economies	3.2	0.5
World	2.7	2.1
Memo items:		
Developing economies, excl. China	2.7	2.4
Developing economies, excl. East Asia	2.6	2.3
Developing economies, excl. East and South-East Asia	2.6	2.0
Developing economies, excl. East, South-East and South Asia	2.8	1.1

Source: UNCTAD (2016)

Indeed, if considered in a long-term perspective, the world growth shows a steady downward trend at least from the late 1960s (namely with the end of the Golden Age) to the end of the century (Figure 1.1).

In this picture the gradual inclusion of the emerging economies in the arena of growth had a compensating role, and in the early twenty-first century the world growth rate started to rise again—up until the 2008 crisis.

Therefore, as long as world growth was substantially determined by the advanced economies, the radical change in the logic of economic policy imposed by the WC did not affect the pace of its substantial decline.[11] Things started to change only when new *large* economic systems burst into the global arena, exercising an increasingly visible impact due to the combined effect of their size and the (exceptionally high) growth rates that physiologically

---

[11] It could be said that for these economies growth continued to slow down throughout the period, following the pattern highlighted in the literature since the late 1970s (see Matthews 1982). On the role that the persisting slowdown of the advanced economies played during the lost decades of the twentieth century in determining the slowdown of global growth—in spite of the dramatic turnabout in economic policy—see also Easterly (2001).

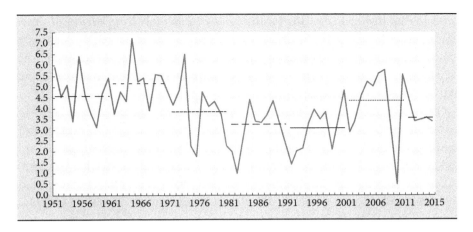

Figure 1.1 World output growth rate, 1951–2015 (%)

Source: UNCTAD secretariat calculations, based on The Conference Board, *Total Economy Database*, May 2015.

characterize early stages of development.[12] The point here is: how much did the above-mentioned globalization rules affect the uprise of such countries in the course of the GA, and if they did, in what way?

The next chapter pays attention on empirical grounds to the extent of growth in the emerging industrial world in the course of the GA; Chapter 3 provides a critical evaluation of the institutional factors (especially in terms of industrial policies) that have affected the behaviour of such countries over the same period. In the remaining pages of this chapter we will deal with the mechanism whereby, in the course of the GA, a major transformation of the geography of the industrial world—and a significant widening of its boundaries—did take place.

1.3 International value chains, trade in tasks, diversification

1.3.1 A new linkage

The issue dealt with in these pages is that differences in the degree of development reflect differences in the degree of industrialization and that the degree of industrialization comes from afar in that it is the result of a

---

[12] 'Average annual GDP per capita growth in the developing world during the 1980s and 1990s was actually lower than in the 1960s and the 1970s, with convergence resulting from economic slowdown in the developed economies and accelerating growth in East Asia' (UNCTAD 2016: 37).

process that has had the time to unfold over a suitably long period of time. A fundamental role in this process is played by the existence of adequate institutions and of manufacturing knowledge that emerged gradually in time (see Chapter 3); but of course without an increase in demand manufacturing activities cannot develop.

Given the fact that in laggard countries—even in the largest ones— domestic demand was bounded to a minimum up until the end of last century, the way out of underdevelopment had to come from abroad. From this standpoint, the great opportunity arose from the effects of what has been called the second 'great unbundling' (Baldwin 2006, 2013, 2014) that started the exploitation on a global scale of the so-called trade in tasks (UNIDO 2009; WTO—IDE-JETRO 2011).

In a nutshell, the knocking down of barriers following the spread of multilateralism has linked together the most industrialized and the less industrialized economies in the world. As far as this simple fact made it possible to exploit huge cost differentials, the conditions were created for a more or less extensive transfer of production stages—in general the more labour-intensive steps—from the former to the latter. In this connection an important prerequisite for unbundling to occur was the availability of technologies allowing the organization of economic activities to be managed at arm's length. This was made possible by the development of information and communication technologies (ICTs), which have been getting important advancements since the 1970s and more and more in the following decades.[13]

Indeed, a major point within this framework, usually neglected, is that, for unbundling to occur at the international level, industrial structure in the Global North had to be *already* fragmented along vertical lines. In this respect, a crucial role was played by the fact that many industrial countries had actually experienced a process of vertical disintegration in the course of the last quarter of the twentieth century, led by the search for flexibility in the face of higher uncertainty and rising competition. In those years, important changes affecting the macroeconomic environment brought about a radical change in the perception of the external context by business leaders, pushing towards a reshaping in the organization of production activities (Rosa 2000; Traù 2003). This led to the 're-emergence', as was then said (Sengerberger et al. 1990), of a specific way of 'solving the production problem' (in the sense suggested by Coase 1937). This happened through a high degree of division of labour *among* firms, rather than within them, led by outsourcing processes. The phenomenon reflected a major reversal with respect to what only thirty years earlier appeared as the only possible form of development

---

[13] See for example on the point Pekarčik et al. (2022).

of the industrial system: namely, the primacy of large business organizations characterized by a high degree of both vertical and conglomerate integration (Piore and Sabel 1984; Best 1990). It started developing within the national boundaries of advanced economies, but in a few years largely trespassed them (Feenstra 1998), partially transforming outsourcing into offshoring.[14] When did this happen?

It happened when a second condition did take place, that is the bursting onto the global scene (which is to say in world exchanges) of the East European economies, China, India, and other economies of the Asian area, which determined what has been called the 'great doubling of the labour market' (Freeman 2007), i.e. the creation of an 'industrial reserve army' in the sense suggested, after Marx (1867), by Lewis (1954). By paving the way to a widespread exploitation of potential worldwide (labour) cost differentials, this unprecedented one-off event encouraged an exceptionally intense cross-border transfer of manufacturing activities, translating outsourcing into offshoring and setting the conditions for the 'unbundling' of value chains on a global scale.[15] Through this type of cross-country diffusion of production activities supply chains became fragmented at the world level.[16]

On the whole the international fragmentation of the supply chains has determined an unprecedented demand shock from abroad for underdeveloped economies. The breakdown of (some) complex industrial processes into separate production phases was the channel through which many of them, that had not been capable of developing the technology required to accomplish the entire process, had the opportunity of being involved in the production of specific components,[17] thanks also to the simultaneous lifting of trade barriers.

This can be viewed as a release of the constraint highlighted by Bairoch (1971), according to whom in the final years of the nineteenth century—and

---

[14] It is worth stressing that this sorts of *vertical* fragmentation relates to a different issue with respect to the horizontal fragmentation (sub specie of intra-trade) that had long characterized the trade relations among industrialized countries, mainly—albeit not exclusively—involving *final* goods (Greenaway and Milner 1986).

[15] Whereas this type of investment was initially based on the advantages offered by enormous cost differentials, in many cases its relative profitability gradually waned. With reference to the European area in the light suggested by Freeman see also Eurofound (2016). Of course, the tumultuous growth of the IDE by the industrial countries was also fed by investments aimed at expanding their market size in final goods (that is, by the hope of selling the same things to a much higher number of consumers).

[16] The endless literature on Global Value Chains cannot be summarized here. Basic references include among others Gereffi et al. (2005), Sturgeon (2008), Nolan et al. (2008), Cattaneo et al. (2010), Sturgeon and Memedovic (2010), Gereffi (2014), and more recently Johnson and Noguera (2017), World Bank (2019a).

[17] According to Stigler (1951), the first condition for this to happen, i.e. for the division of labour to start, is the separability of cost functions, which may present marked differences between different industries. As a result, trade in tasks is likely to affect some activities more extensively with respect to others.

increasingly in the course of the twentieth—the important changes undergone by technology led to rising manufacturing complexity and therefore to rising entry barriers. In that view, the break with traditional techniques had been so sharp that, as a consequence, industrial activity in the underdeveloped world was discouraged, for laggard countries were cut off from the possibility to imitate early industrializers.[18] The advent of vertical disintegration changed the rules: in the words of the UNIDO Industrial Development Report, 'Potentially, trade in tasks ... simplifies getting started. Instead of needing to acquire the entire range of skills necessary to produce a product all at once, manufacturing can start with specialization in tasks most suited to the skills available' (UNIDO 2009: xiii, emphasis added).

The arrival of multinational companies or orders from abroad linked to specific production stages were the instrument through which it was possible for emerging countries to enter the markets for intermediates of advanced economies.[19] When measured in terms of the dynamics of the trade in intermediates (Figure 1.2), the degree of expansion achieved by global value

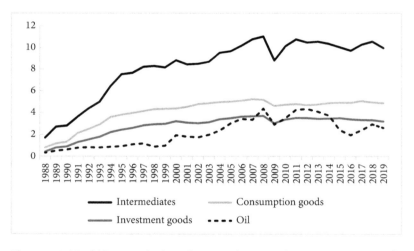

Figure 1.2 World imports by broad economic categories as a percentage of GDP, current dollars

Source: UN-Comtrade and UNCTAD, own calculations.

---

[18] According to Bairoch modern technology did require large scale which could not be set up by local producers, and this also displaced artisan production.

[19] The introduction of multinational companies within the context of developing economic systems is not at all a new phenomenon. The point here is the extent to which this time the presence of multinational companies in emerging countries succeeded in encouraging the activation of endogenous industrial activities.

chains (GVCs), starting from the late 1980s, is impressive. As a percentage of the world GDP, the level of trade in intermediates rose vertically in the first half of the 1990s, far more than the other goods categories, and kept growing up to the breakdown of the financial crisis (when it was more than five times higher than in 1988) in 2008. But then the index stopped rising and flattened.

1.3.2 An endogenous growth?

It is important to note that the creation of the GVCs was not enough as such to start an endogenous manufacturing development in the underdeveloped world. In fact, it is by no means obvious that trade in tasks *in itself* can trigger a widening of the supply matrix. Indeed, it may occur just the opposite: as suggested in UNIDO (2009), task-based production can encourage countries to specialize in a narrow range of industrial activities. Simply entering 'slices' of GVCs may not suffice to sustain an industrial development strategy, for the outcome of the process may be excessive specialization, which may have a very little impact on growth.[20] In order to take on the form of an *endogenous* process, once it has started development needs to be capable of triggering at the local level forward and backward linkages as they are defined by Hirschman (1958, 2013 [1977]):

> [D]evelopment is essentially the record of how one thing leads to another, and the linkages are that record. (…) [O]ngoing activities, because of their characteristics, push or, more modestly, invite some operators to take up new activities. (…) On the one hand, there are situations in which the same economic operators who are already engaged in the ongoing activity are impelled to undertake the new activity; this is 'inside linkage'. On the other hand, the push … might be carried on by indigenous economic operators. This is 'outside linkage'.
>
> **(2013: 169)**

This may occur either through the direct action of multinationals firms (i.e. firms physically coming from abroad), or as an effect of market demand coming from the outside and activating local supply. In both cases there needs to be a progressive interaction with the local economy.[21] Such vision,

---

[20] 'While the spread of supply chains has allowed more developing countries to participate in the international division of labour … that participation has been confined to a very narrow set of links in these chains and has rarely allowed them to diversify into higher productivity activities' UNCTAD 2020: 122.

[21] The existence of multinationals does not necessarily activate in itself an endogenous growth (if the United States were to actually 'withdraw' all their companies in current times, almost nothing would be left in Mexico). It is only through the activation of chains at the local level that endogenous development can be engendered.

which is very close to the idea of cumulative causation set forth by Perroux (1955), Myrdal (1957), and Kaldor (1981), and that—following Young (1928)—basically stems from Smith (1976 [1776], Book 1, Ch. 1), attributes to some 'ongoing activity' the task of activating a process of endogenous growth.[22] Therefore, in order to create an autonomous process of development there needs to be not only some productive activity, but also an activity that is capable of triggering other activities through the market.[23] The issue has been in more recent years envisaged in a very similar perspective by Rodrik (2005), according to whom the key point is that the growth dynamics is not linked to static comparative advantages, but on the contrary comes from the capability to gradually diversify investments into a range of *new* activities. In this view the most prosperous countries are those where new investments are being made in new areas.

Yet the matter is complicated by the fact that while globalization allows for the cross-country transfer of manufacturing activities, it nevertheless acts in the direction of forcing the recipients to specialize; in other terms, it makes the success of new initiatives subject to the *rapid* acquisition of a competitive advantage vis-à-vis other international competitors. As shown in Romano and Traù (2017; see here Chapter 5), in a context of open markets (i.e. the opposite to the situation of infant-industry protection), the countries that take the path to industrialization must come to terms with a global arena where market shares are already in the hands of incumbents. In other terms, the laggards who benefitted from unbundling had nevertheless a shorter time available to them to exploit the learning curves (increasing dynamic returns) of any given activity and to expand their supply matrix before it would be washed away by globalization. As they were compelled to seek competitive advantages right from the beginning of their industrialization process, the possibilities of diversifying their products were strongly restrained right from the start, thus determining for some of them a high concentration ahead of time (and, consequently, a phenomenon of early de-industrialization).

For a developing country, in a context of open markets the existence of a global foreign demand overpowers the domestic market, hindering the possibility for other activities to develop.[24] As a consequence, the greater the gap

---

[22] See on this point also Fujita (2007) and especially Berger (2009).

[23] Gonzalez et al. (2019) extend this point to the case for business services (also needing the existence of backward linkages to develop).

[24] For this not to happen the size of the country should be as large as to allow the internal demand to grow adequately. It may be noticed that the only one medium-sized laggard that has succeeded in developing leading firms in global markets is South Korea, where this has been achieved not due to the entry of new firms within specific market segments, but through direct public intervention. This was aimed at selecting industries and activities in order to build almost from scratch big vertically integrated *chaebols*,

between the size of the domestic economy and the size of the global market when industrialization is taking off, the earlier an upper bound of the industrialization rate is reached, due to the fact that industrialization remains 'thin' in terms of intersectoral linkages and sectoral span. Insofar as no explicit policies are set up (see Chapter 3), designed to gradually build competitive advantages in new activities, in such a context the supply matrix remains restricted—the more, the smaller the size of the country itself.

The issue can also be envisaged in the perspective of what has been recently called 'compressed' development (Whittaker et al. 2020), according to which manufacturing development happens faster than in the past (Felipe et al. 2012), but at the same time it tends to turn into de-industrialization earlier:

> [A]s a result of learning, licensing and investment from earlier developers[, r]elative to the UK, Germany and the United States grew rapidly, and Japan more rapidly still. Following Japan, South Korea and Taiwan experienced growth that was even more rapid, and, recently, mainland China, despite its vastness, has followed an even-more-rapid economic-growth trajectory. [...] There are, in fact, two intertwined phenomena within this trend. First, deindustrialization is commencing at lower levels of per capita GDP. Second, manufacturing is absorbing a smaller share of the total workforce, even at its peak. [...] This is because globalization throws sand into the wheels of the Kaldorian industrial upgrading process.
>
> **(Whittaker et al. 2020: 3 and 25)**

This means that the turning point in employment and/or output shares in manufacturing happens at lower levels of per-capita GDP and that the peak in the industrialization rate is correspondingly lower. This can be viewed as a process of premature de-industrialization (see also Rodrik 2016), which at a given point in time takes the place of a more prolonged phase of manufacturing development.[25]

1.3.3 Diversification

In the perspective outlined so far, it is therefore important the extent to which an economic system succeeds in making larger its supply structure starting

which have entered international markets only after having achieved the degree of competitiveness which was necessary to remain in the field. On this point see in particular Nathan et al. (2018).

[25] This may in itself give rise to a further problem: 'if the total desired export growth of the developing nations exceeds the absorptive capacity of the industrialised country markets, then the success of some developing countries in export promotion must come at the expense of failure for others' (Razmi and Blecker 2006: 2).

from an initial production core (see among others Lall 2003; Rodrik 2005; Hausmann et al. 2011; Kaulich 2012) and, in particular, the extent to which this articulation is paralleled by the accumulation of knowledge, allowing competitiveness to consolidate on endogenous foundations. According in particular to Hausmann et al. (2011), the backbone of the development process is—following Smith's view—the accumulation of knowledge induced by the division of labour. In this scheme the most important force that generates learning is not so much the development of already existing skills, but it is the creation—through investments—of new ones. As far as demand rises, labour may continue to divide, pushing towards new forms of specialization and hence new knowledge. In a condition of market openness, the width of the supply matrix (the range of the activities it has developed that far) measures at any one time the range (the amount) of the knowledge which an economic system can rely upon.

Yet, in order for the matrix to enlarge in the countries entering the trade in tasks model, it is necessary that the starting tasks are not too elementary: for very simple activities will not fuel a true division of labour and therefore will not trigger a learning process. In this perspective, the 'complexity' of the production structure of a country is bound by the level of knowledge it has been capable of accumulating up to that moment. The wider the range of supply, the greater the development potential.[26] The issue appears to be clearly stated in the same terms by UNCTAD (2016), arguing that the accumulation of new knowledge helps the introduction of new products, processes, and organizational forms, and that such new knowledge supports in turn further diversification of manufacturing activities, therefore requiring a wider range of capabilities. In the instance of an export-led development—which is the type of development activated by the trade in task process—what counts is that the exporting sector is able not only to raise its own productivity, but also to generate positive linkages with the rest of the economy.

An implication of the picture traced thus far is that, in general, a greater degree of manufacturing diversification should correspond to a relatively higher level of development, even among laggard countries. The correlation between the degree of concentration (Gini) and per capita output level bears this out (Figure 1.3). The scatter in the figure shows a direct relationship between the degree of diffusion of manufacturing activities and output: in the upper left-hand part of the diagram (low diversification and

---

[26] In Hausmann et al. (2011) the articulation of the supply matrix is approximated by exports, that directly measure the competitive potential of a country as far as they represent the share of output that has already overcome international competition.

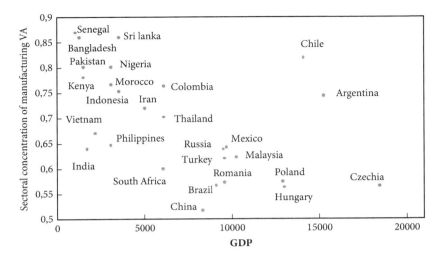

Figure 1.3 Relationship between per capita GDP and sectoral concentration of manufacturing value added (Gini index), 2015, current dollars

Source: IHS-Markit data, own calculations.

low manufacturing per capita output) there are the African Countries and the two less developed economies of Central Asia (Pakistan and Bangladesh), and in the lower right-hand side there are the East European economies[27].

1.4 Multinationals and the control of the value chains

As argued above, the development of the emerging world has been fuelled to a considerable extent by the flow of direct investments from abroad.[28] In particular, a considerable amount of the trading in intermediate inputs occurred through intra-firm exchanges, namely within the boundaries of multinational companies, and hence had an inherently 'hierarchical' nature. According to the evaluations made by UNCTAD (2013), in 2010 about 33% of international trade consisted of intra-firm exchanges; when considering the totality of exchanges that in any case involved the multinational companies in various forms (exchanges with other companies, contracts, licences, etc.) the share was estimated to rise to about 80%.

---

[27] Similar results are reported in UNIDO (2016, chapter 3).
[28] The role of multinational firms in the dynamics of what was then called the new international division of labour has been paid attention since the early 1980s (see for example Schoenberger 1988).

In quantitative terms, the profile of multinational activity in the GA is summarized in Figure 1.4, showing the dynamics of FDI world outflows of developed economies vis-à-vis FDI inflows of developing ones. Overall, from the early 1980s to the financial crisis in 2008—notwithstanding a short fall following the 2001 crisis—the outward FDIs of advanced countries skyrocketed from 200 billion to more than 1,500 billion, and then declined. As to developing economies, FDIs inflows show a steady increase in the years preceding the crisis, after which they seem to stabilize. This change in course—often described as the 'withdrawal' of the multinationals, such as to mark the return to a less interdependent world[29]—does not appear to radically alter the degree of global interdependence. Yet it is worth to stress that FDIs slowdown predates the arrival of the pandemic (and then of the war in Ukraine). The point will be more widely discussed in Chapter 6; here it can be simply observed that the slowdown in investments by multinationals must be considered to be largely physiological, and can be viewed as a consequence of the out-of-scale extent that offshoring had assumed prior to the crisis.

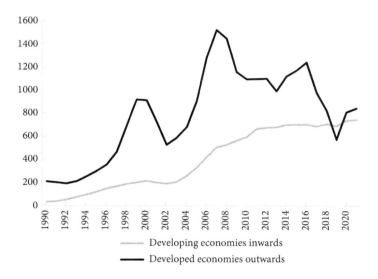

Figure 1.4 FDI outflows (Developed countries) and inflows (Developing countries), US dollars at current prices in billions, 3-year moving average
Source: UNCTAD, own calculations.

---

[29] The term has been suggested in a survey by the Economist (2017).

It has to be added that the cross-border extension of businesses does not consist merely of transferring activities abroad, but it also involves the management of trade networks among firms that operate through the market. It can be observed that it is precisely the above-mentioned logic of unbundling that has contributed in time to the expansion on a worldwide scale of inter-firm exchanges (even if under the substantial control of the multinational companies themselves). The literature has paid attention to this phenomenon since the mid-1990s, stressing that the governance of international production networks does not necessarily require direct ownership of productive assets, insofar as it can be based upon the power to coordinate activities performed by (quasi)-independent firms that are geographically and organizationally dispersed (Kozul-Wright 1995).

It was precisely the spread of value chains at the global scale that ended up determining new and different levels of governance of transactions along vertical lines of the chains. In the early twenty-first century the articulation of the phenomenon had already reached such an extent that it was possible to provide a taxonomy of the different types of such relationships.[30] The emergence within GVCs of firms taking the role of 'sub-system integrators' determines the consolidation at an intermediate level in the chain of new forms of market power. This means that some firms become able to affect the decisions of other companies at the production level far beyond the boundaries of mere ownership (control of assets). From this point of view it can be said that, in a wide range of business activities, the extent of conscious coordination over the surrounding value chain has actually increased, developing into a comprehensively planned and coordinated activity (Nolan et al. 2008).

In this sense the trade system has increasingly been influenced over the past decades by the strategic decisions taken by (multinational) enterprises, much more than by the 'free choices' expressed on the demand side.[31] Put in other words, as value chains have become global, the way they have been organizing has increasingly shaped the structure of trade patterns. The diffusion of production on a global scale has had the effect of directly influencing the evolution of trade flows, making a significant portion of world trade a

---

[30] According to the framework suggested by Gereffi et al. (2005), three intermediate levels between the market and the hierarchy can be identified: *modular value chains* (suppliers follow the specifications laid down by the clients but are responsible for the process technology); *relational value chains* (the interaction is complex and requires mutual dependence and a high degree of specificity of the assets); *captive value chains* (in practice suppliers depend on clients who are much bigger than them).

[31] The matter may be considered also according to the perspective suggested by Pitelis (1991), who, starting from Hymer (1976), argues that even in the case of exchanges between enterprises that take place on the market an asymmetrical relationship between demand and supply can be observed, so that the problem is simply to distinguish between market and non-market hierarchies.

function not of the dynamics of the demand for final goods (whether consumer or investment products), but rather of the very logic underlying the organization of production. Therefore, at the start of the new millennium, the profile of world trade has been more affected by the reasons underlying industrial development than by consumers preferences.

On conceptual grounds, in such a perspective it is not any more trade theory which can explain the whole of trade dynamics, but a theory of the firm capable of explaining the strategic decisions implemented by businesses (often influenced at the institutional level) that decide where and what to produce. In this framework firms' behaviour has to be reconceptualized from a passive process involving the reaction of independent actors to market signals (as in international trade theories) to a system-wide dynamics of coordination and control (Neilson et al. 2014).

1.5 The road to industrialization ('the Rest' vs 'the Remainder')

So far, we have argued that the globalization years coincided with the emergence of a series of new countries as manufacturers. In Chapter 2 the extent of the phenomenon will be widely documented on quantitative grounds and in Chapter 3 a description of the divergent behaviour of different economic systems in such respect will be provided. Yet what has to be stressed right from the start is that those laggards which succeeded in emerging during the GA had actually laid the foundations for their development long before the advent of globalization. In other words, they reached the appointment with globalization in conditions that enabled them to take advantage of what it had to offer: namely, to exploit the possibilities made available by the liberalization of trade.

The driving force of this process was their capacity to (previously) build the conditions for industrial development. Following Amsden (2001), it can be observed that the economies that were still lagging behind in the mid-XX century ('the Rest'), i.e. those that—unlike the first comers—had not succeeded in riding either the First or the Second Industrial Revolution, had to face a knowledge level which was beyond their possibilities to manage. The main barrier to access was the basic absence of crucial *proprietary* knowledge. The existence of a deep-rooted technological discontinuity between industrialized and developing countries put the latter in the condition of having to set up their development strategies on different foundations. This means that the entire architecture of the industrialization process was characterized right from the beginning by a radical peculiarity that marked the whole of its subsequent evolution.

The fact that in the years following World War II a portion of the economies lagging behind succeeded gradually in starting along the path of industrial development may be considered a function (1) of the amount of manufacturing knowledge they had built up in time, and (2) of the extent to which their institutions were capable of translating this capital into an industrialization process. As a result of the initial differences between the different areas of the developing world, in terms of their knowledge base and the role of the State, industrialization took place only in some of the developing countries and not in all of them.

In the wording suggested by Amsden (2001), 'the Rest' included China, India, Indonesia, Korea, Malaysia, Taiwan, and Thailand in Asia; Argentina, Brazil, Chile and Mexico in Latin America, and Turkey in the Middle East. As can be seen, these are countries where manufacturing take-off occurred at different moments in time (Korea 'started' in the early 1960s; the Latin American economies—except for Mexico—experienced their first stage of development via import substitution measures right in the aftermath of World War II). In addition, it is worth mentioning in this connection the economies belonging to the former Soviet bloc and their subsequent inclusion in a re-industrialization process (as well as their opening up to worldwide trade).

The development of such countries, that Amsden (2001, see in particular Chapters 4 and 5) illustrates through the review of a massive series of analyses relating to individual economies, takes on a different profile depending on the way in which the economies lagging behind acquired manufacturing knowledge (and, in particular, depending on the presence or absence of a prior colonial experience). In general, the countries that in the post-war period invested more in national enterprises and skills were those that had experienced a colonial presence in their territory, and that, through nationalization, directly acquired manufacturing 'know-how'; the others remained mostly linked to the presence of multinationals, with knowledge that remained mostly non-proprietary, and this substantially prevented the creation of a competitive national industry that could have access to foreign markets.[32]

Hence, at the dawn of globalization, the universe of the laggards was already divided into two groups: on the one hand 'the Rest' (namely a

---

[32] The first group includes among other countries China, India, Korea, and Taiwan; the second group includes Argentina, Brazil, and Mexico. In this sense, while the *existence* (or absence) of a previous manufacturing experience set apart the countries that emerged from those that remained still, the *type* of previous experience affected the nature and intensity of development where this happened.

group of countries already oriented, to a greater or lesser extent and with differing degrees in the implementation of the process, towards an explicit industrialization objective); on the other 'the Remainder' (without manufacturing knowledge and without adequate institutions). In this framework, the strength and the determination shown by public institutions in 'forcing' the industrialization process—culminating with the emergence of the so-called 'Developmental State' in South-East Asia—were the elements that enabled the latecomers of the first group to build in the medium term—and often from scratch—dynamic comparative advantages in different industries (see Chapter 3 below).[33] In such perspective the keystone of economic policy is not macroeconomic stability, but the acquisition of technological skills by domestic firms as the instrument for a constant competitive upgrading (viewed as the intermediate objective of economic policy) of the manufacturing system.

Therefore, well before the globalization process did take place, there was a group of countries potentially able to take advantage of an enlargement of demand from abroad: that is to set up an export-led model hinging upon previously accumulated manufacturing capabilities.[34] Here, however, divergent paths even within the very group of 'the Rest' did emerge, due to different institutional settings and policy options. In particular, East Asian economies stand out from the crowd. In this respect UNCTAD Reports (see in particular UNCTAD 2016) argue that in such countries the export-led growth model was oriented to maximize the developmental benefits of trade by setting up proactive industrial, macroeconomic, and social policies, including the pairing of export promotion with the protection of infant industries and import substitution. And that, indeed, this was the very same approach used by almost all of today's developed countries at some point in their industrializing history. A quite similar view is represented in other key reports by international institutions; according to the Department of Economic and Social Affairs of the United Nations,

Sustained rapid economic growth in a number of countries in developing Asia was held up in the 1980s and 1990s as exemplifying the success of the market-oriented, export-led development strategies advocated by the Washington Consensus. In

---

[33] Of course, also within the group of the 'Rest', the institutional framework differed from country to country, with important consequences on the intensity of the industrialization processes. For a comparison in particular between China and India see Saith (2008).
[34] 'Countries in "the rest" that industrialized rapidly after World War II had accumulated manufacturing experience in the pre-war period. This differentiated them from countries in "the remainder". Path dependence was such that no economy emerged from the blue as an industrial competitor' (Amsden 2001: 99).

reality, however, the development policies behind these growth successes, especially in their early stages, resembled much more the recipes associated with the
dirigiste paradigm of early development thinking and were not unlike the policies that had, in earlier times, promoted modern development in Western Europe
and Japan. These development policies involved, inter alia, agrarian reforms,
investments in human capital, selective trade protection, directed credit and other
government support for developing industrial and technological capacity while
exposing firms *gradually* to global competition.

(UN-DESA 2010: 9, emphasis added)

In this context it has to be mentioned the behaviour of a further group of
countries, which actually do not belong to 'the Rest': namely, those East
European economies that have also successfully switched to a market economy hinging upon previously accumulated manufacturing capabilities, even
if, properly, belonging to the world of *already* industrialized economies
(actually, it happened that these countries did exit from a previous industrialization path, and entered a new one). This is just what did not happen
in countries belonging to the former Soviet Union (including Russia), which
represent instead a spectacular example of the destructive consequences of
an ideological application of the provisions of the WC (see Chapter 3).

Indeed, starting a steady and stable development process has always been
a function of the capacity to dynamically build the foundations for a competitive manufacturing industry based on proprietary knowledge in a forward-
looking perspective.[35] This approach—that is deeply rooted in a wide range of
theoretical contributions in the history of economic thought—stands opposite to the idea according to which it is opening outside *as such* that provides
the preconditions for aggregate growth (through the exploitation of *current*
comparative advantages). The logic here is instead that of emulation. In the
words of a true expert in the subject:

Indeed England protected her manufacturing industry heavily for more than 350
years, the United States only for about 100 years, and Korea for only 40 years. (…)
[A]ll countries that have moved from being poor to wealthy have done so by going
through a period of emulation – of infant industry protection—in order to work
their way into the areas where technological progress is concentrated at the time.
This has been a mandatory passage point in human history.

(Reinert 2009: 81 and 100, emphasis added)

---

[35] On this specific point see also UNIDO (2016: 78): 'low-income countries … can overcome their
economic marginalization by acquiring skills and knowledge to diversify their economic portfolio rather
than by focusing on "what they do best".

Emulation brings about the progressive attainment of competitive advantages that did not exist before. This principle 'naturally' drives the industrial system towards a gradual widening of its supply matrix. The point—which has been masterly highlighted in the work by Chang (2002) and Reinert (2007)—is that the conditions for manufacturing development do not change in time, and the path followed by the economies that have succeeded in emerging is not the one laid down by the WC—as well as the industrial development of advanced economies themselves would not have been even imaginable in their time without an active role of economic policy.

The idea that huge development gaps could be bridged by denying this principle and merely following the WC rules (asserting that it was possible for the very first time in history to industrialize laggards through sheer market forces) has only had the effect of deepening the inequalities at the global level. This has kept out of the development process not only 'the Remainder', but even those countries belonging to the 'Rest' which did accept the prescriptions of the WC (such as Latin American ones), abandoning their former experience as Developmental States (see again Chapter 3).

1.6 The crisis

1.6.1 The trigger

The great financial crisis, which began in the last quarter of 2008, has assumed since its outset the shape of a change of pace. It was immediately clear that by no means it could be simply interpreted in a business cycle perspective, and, indeed, it gradually hardened into what has been defined as a 'new normal'. From this point of view it can be said that the intensity of the changes it brought about—which will be more widely dealt with in Chapter 6—finds its roots in the previous existence of problems that were already lying behind the very success of the globalization mechanism.[36]

The starting point can be traced back to the collapse in demand in some advanced economies that followed the long-lasting expansion of the 1990s and early 2000s, driven by a series of speculative bubbles (dot.com, housing) that for a long time had kept consumption at an exceptionally high level and, at the same time, fuelled the consolidation of huge (trade and fiscal) deficits in the United States. The crisis came from the financial side (from the collapse

---

[36] For a more comprehensive overview of the subject see Singh and Zammit (2010) and the references therein. For a fairly detailed reconstruction of the crisis mechanism see also European Commission (2009).

of the American subprime bubble to the Lehman Brothers' bankruptcy and
the so-called credit crunch). It caused—through the consequences of the contraction in consumer credit and the negative wealth effect brought about by
the crisis in the real estate sector—a vertical drop in household consumption
and demand in the building sector (fuelled till then by an unprecedented
expansion of liquidity), ending in a fall in investment demand:

> It is generally agreed that difficulties associated with the housing segment of the
> US house property market were the immediate cause of the crisis (…). Complex
> financial instruments that incorporated subprime house mortgages lost their value
> as the housing bubble burst following ten years of continuous price rises based
> on expectations of a continuation of such increases. (…) In brief, house prices had
> risen because interest rates were low and credit was easily available, and prices
> were expected to continue to increase, much as in the case of the classic tulip
> mania and bubble in the early 17th century when, at its peak, the price of a tulip
> bulb Holland was equivalent to that of a three-story town house.
>
> **(Singh and Zammit 2010: 1–2)**

In the presence of fully fledged global supply chains, the collapse in final
consumption and investment demand also instantly blocked the world trade
in intermediate goods—that had contributed to driving global exchanges so
high throughout the preceding phase of development.[37] The high import
content per unit of output entailed a larger contraction in trade than GDP.
After the recovery that immediately followed the crisis (see again Figure 1.4
above), elasticity remained low over the following years and translated into a
structural discontinuity with the pre-crisis period.[38]

This discontinuity has been attributed to the uprise of US protectionism,
leading to an increase in trade barriers and hindering world trade dynamics.[39] According to UNCTAD (2016: 18–19) assessments, however, even after
the crisis 'there [has been] little evidence that tariff changes explain[ed] the
prolonged sluggishness of global trade'. And on the other hand, the level
of tariffs, regardless of their dynamics, globally 'has remained considerably
and constantly below the corresponding level of the most favoured nation

---

[37] As was then observed, '[h]ence, the strong collapse in exports in the recent months is at least partly
driven by the same forces that allowed global trade to expand much faster than global GDP in the last two
decades, i.e. global production networks' (Godart et al. 2009: 123). On the same point see also Escaith
(2009), Milberg and Winkler (2010).

[38] The point is more widely treated in Chapter 6.

[39] See for example Haugh et al. (2106).

tariffs.'[40] Whatever the effects of the recent rise of a 'neo-protectionist' orientation at regulatory level, the current lower intensity of trade flows appears to be mainly linked to structural changes that predate the crisis. In this sense, the slowdown can be considered to be largely endogenous to the logic of manufacturing development in the course of the GA.

Here there are two relevant issues. The first one refers to the transfer of some portions of world production from advanced economies to the emerging world. The second refers to the out-of-scale ('aberrant'[41]) consumer boom starting from the 1990s, that offshoring—together with a practically unlimited supply of liquidity—fuelled in advanced countries as a consequence of the low price level of imported goods (be they final or intermediates). As will be more widely shown in Chapter 6, the combined outcome of these two issues, once the crisis did break out, was bound to be a structurally lower demand from the Global North for manufactured productions realized in the South. From this standpoint, it has been said that the process itself of de-location of manufacturing activities from the North to the South set the premises for the global economic turmoil at the end of 2008 to occur (Neilson et al. 2014).

1.6.2 Long-run trends

The slowdown in demand in the developed world takes on a more radical meaning if viewed in terms of a 're-entry' into a pathway of secular stagnation. The matter has been explicitly raised by Summers (2015), with an open reference to Hansen (1939), and is widely addressed in a book edited by Teulings and Baldwin (2014). The reasons suggested by Teulings and Baldwin as to the mid-2010s for supporting the hypothesis of stagnation take into account both the demand and the supply side and can be briefly summarized as follows:[42] (1) zero nominal interest rates along a fairly long time span (lasting up to the rise in inflation following the advent of both the pandemic and the Ukrainian war) have been coupled with the persistence of an under-employment equilibrium: if neither rates equal to zero are

---

[40] This means that the average tariffs actually applied globally remained between 1995 and 2014 systematically below the tariffs 'agreed' with the most favoured nations. Even if the orientation towards a higher degree of domestic market protection may also be expressed through a series of non-tariff measures, that undoubtedly have increased (see the Global Trade Alert periodical updates: www.globaltradealert.org), nevertheless this relates to mainly qualitative measures, introduced by different countries and difficult to compare, the actual impact of which is in any event hard to assess.

[41] On this particular point see Kaplinski and Farooki (2010).

[42] See in particular the essays by Summers himself, Gordon, Krugman and (in milder terms) Eichengreen.

enough to re-create full employment, the liquidity trap becomes the new normal; (2) in demographic terms, the exit of baby-boomers from the labour market, that has been accelerating over the past decade, and more generally the population's low growth rate entail a drop in aggregate demand (which is Hansen's theory); (3) the impact that the advent of mass schooling has had on productivity in Western countries as of the 1960s—regardless of its slowdown—needs to be considered as a no longer duplicable one-off event; (4) the move towards a polarization of incomes, exacerbated by globalization, has brought about a rarefaction in the ranks of the middle class and exercised a negative impact on final demand, by structurally lowering the propensity to consume;[43] (5) the burden of public debt in many Western economies limits the possibility to make use of Keynesian-like public demand policies.

Whilst points (1) and (5) have been completely upset by the arrival of the pandemic and the war in Ukraine, which—by determining a sudden rise in inflation and asking for income support—have drastically modified the political stance of governments both in the US and in Europe, points (2) to (4) are to be considered as still binding constraints. Indeed, they suggest an even more radical issue: overturning the point of view, it might be argued that what needs to be explained is not the current economic slowdown, but rather the exceptional growth rate that preceded it. As has been observed with reference to the United States (and similarly to what can be stated regarding other large Western economies):

> For decades, macroeconomists struggled to understand the post-1970 productivity growth slowdown. But in fact our entire generation has been asking the wrong question. Instead of wondering why there was a productivity growth slowdown after 1972, we should have asked: 'Can we explain the productivity miracle that occurred in the US economy between 1920 and 1970?'
>
> (Gordon 2014: 53)

In this regard, the entire problem could be reversed: what would the pace of growth have been during the twentieth century in the absence of World War II, the baby boom, the massive investments made for creating modern suburbia, the State building of welfare systems? In this perspective, no one can exclude that other future events of an exogenous nature might have a positive influence on the pace of growth in coming years, but no one can

---

[43] The emergence of growing income inequality within the advanced economies has become so evident that it has been paid explicit attention in an Outlook by the IMF, an institution that has traditionally been very supportive of the merits of globalization (IMF 2017, chapter 3).

state that this must happen either: indeed, according to information currently available, the chances appear to be relatively low.

1.7 Trying to summarize

The Globalization Age coincided with the development of manufacturing expanding beyond the G7's borders. This development, however, involved a relatively limited group of countries and, in any event, left out most of the economies that we used to call underdeveloped (and which today are sometimes defined as developing).

The liberalization of trade and capital movements played an important role in encouraging the transfer of manufacturing phases from the Global North to the South, including, through the so-called trade in tasks and the globalization of value chains, new countries within the perimeter of the industrial world. This process was considerably speeded up by the 'unfreez-ing' of large economic systems that still in early 1990s were sealed within a parallel world, outside of the area of market exchanges. Within an excep-tionally narrow period of time (little over a decade, from Deng's launch of the 'four modernizations' in 1978 to the re-entry of the main South Ameri-can economies into the area of representative democracy to the 'fall of the Wall'), new economic areas (and populations) simultaneously came to be part of the global world, alongside other lagging economies already included in the trade system. The outcome was a one-off event, unprecedented in industrial history, that opened up to the already 'emerged' world a new labour market characterized by an unlimited availability of labour at a very low cost. This new order, outlining a situation that is very similar to the one described in the Lewis–Kindleberger's model (extended to the global level), has made it possible—wherever some manufacturing know-how was already available—to launch an industrialization process triggered from the outside (i.e. via the export channel), avoiding for a long time any increase in prices.

But at the same time the globalization logic itself, by making the posses-sion of a comparative advantage essential, held back manufacturing to spread on a large range of activities. In this respect, the idea that the opening up of international trade (coupled with measures to liberalize and privatize domes-tic markets and a strict budgetary discipline) could be as such the driver of the development of manufacturing anywhere did find a limit. In a context of strong international competition, this has been represented by the difficul-ties (not to say impossibility) encountered by most laggards in achieving a degree of expansion of their supply matrix (and hence an industrialization rate) sufficient to trigger an endogenous development process.

In this regard the scale of the different economies is crucial: while smaller countries necessarily need to base their development strategies on specialization (few industries that are competitive at the international level), larger ones can benefit from a domestic market as a final destination for non-competitive domestic productions. But, in addition to the scale of countries, the orientation of the institutions is enormously important for launching and accelerating the industrialization process.

Anyway, the overview summarized in this chapter makes it possible to dismiss—or at least question—a number of clichés that have now become part of the mantra of political, as well as economic, jargon. To mention just a few: (1) the growth of the most successful emerging countries has not been driven just by the fact that they opened up to trade and it certainly did not take place in the presence of restrictive budgetary policies and the liberalization of capital movements (indeed, as will be showed in Chapter 3, one might say it took place in the presence of an opposite behaviour, such as the adoption of expressly selective policies that in some cases also strongly distorted competition, and in any case under strict public control); (2) trade in tasks has not in itself been enough to generate always and under all circumstances in the emerging economies a gradual extension of the supply matrix, and in many cases they have remained congealed around the initial specialization, generating early de-industrialization phenomena; (3) the explanatory power of the BRICs category, coined in the name of a similarity among the main emerging economies (mostly in terms of their size), appears to have already evaporated: as to industrial development, the differences nowadays seems to be more—and more significant—than the similarities; (4) The onset of the global financial crisis in 2008 is not on its own the event that altered the pace of development (and the relations between the North and the South): the way development took place in the years that preceded the crisis was the factor that determined its intensity and direction, creating the conditions for the ensuing impasse.

2

A New Landscape for World Manufacturing Production

Old and New Industrial Countries at the Dawn of the New Millennium

2.1 A premise

The early 2000s have witnessed a substantial change in the geographical distribution of manufacturing activity all across the world. The most striking feature of such a change is the emergence, at the very same time, of *several* new industrial economies, i.e. the fact that industrial development has been assuming in a few years a polycentric shape, spreading far beyond the narrow boundaries of the 'advanced' world. Even if the rates of growth of manufacturing activities—and therefore the industrialization rates—still appear to be characterized by sharp cross-country differences, it can nevertheless be said that—with the notable exception of most African countries—no one continent appears now excluded from the sphere of manufacturing activity.

As new productive systems have come to the fore—some of which are almost continental in size—an extraordinary catching-up process has happened of Emerging Economies (EEs) *taken as a whole* with respect to old industrial economies (OIEs). This has involved a conspicuous increase in their overall weight on world total output and, more generally, in their capability to exert an influence on the world economy. But it has also led, in many cases, to a remarkable transformation of their internal economic structure, setting them on the tracks of a new development path. This chapter is aimed at describing such transformations by looking at them from different points of view, providing some measures of the changes occurred and highlighting the important differences that can be observed in the behaviour of individual countries.

The whole matter can be looked at by focusing upon three main issues. First, several countries have entered, for the very first time, the road to manufacturing development, changing their international status as to their productive role. This is documented by their manufacturing output growth

The New Industrial World. Livio Romano and Fabrizio Traù, Oxford University Press.
© Livio Romano and Fabrizio Traù (2023). DOI: 10.1093/oso/9780192873736.003.0003

rates and is somewhat similar to what had already happened in the course of the 1970s, when the so-called 'new industrialized economies' (NIEs) also emerged as new manufacturers. The difference is that back then the process (1) involved just four small economies and (2) it was not fed by the offshoring mechanism described in Chapter 1 (as far as production in such countries largely concerned final goods). Second, this time manufacturing growth has also involved some quite large countries, so that it has brought about eye-catching consequences upon already industrialized countries, due to the absolute size of output flows coming from the emerging world. Third— as we have also anticipated in Chapter 1—the emergence of new industrial countries from the underdeveloped world has been anyway a *selective* process, and has left aside a conspicuous group of countries that still lie at the margin of the development process—thereby widening the variance of industrialization rates within the group of all those countries that at the beginning of the Globalization Age were still lagging behind. The following pages are aimed at providing some updated evidence about these features.

Before approaching the matter, it may be worth noting that the usual way of measuring the extraordinary widening of the role EEs have been able to gain so far has long been to look at their increasing importance as (net) exporters, i.e. at their world export shares. In a sense, this reflects the (implicit) idea— nurtured in the Washington Consensus approach—according to which the globalization process has been basically driven by international trade, that is—as is generally argued—by the sheer logic of comparative advantages. Be it true or not, this means to focus just upon *that* part of the overall output of such countries which has succeeded in winning the international competition beyond the national boundaries.[1] Yet, whereas this certainly provides a measure of their international competitiveness, it does not provide a measure of their actual manufacturing weight, that is of their ability to *produce*, for it can only take into account a fraction of total output—which, by the way, is far from being the same when comparing one country to another, due to strong differences in export propensities.

The point here, as will be better shown in Chapter 6, is that in the course of their development process, and in particular in more recent years, the rhythm of growth in some important EEs (most notably China) has been more and more tied to the widening of internal demand, which—by gradually substituting exports—has been fuelling domestic supply. Therefore, an effective measure of EEs output capacity needs to take into account overall output

---

[1] Actually, also firms producing (only or partially) for the internal market—provided it is not protected—undergo the competitive pressure by external producers.

flows. This means we should look at the production side of their development process rather than trade performance. In the following, therefore, countries' performance at the world level will be observed in terms of both gross and net output (e.g. manufacturing production and value added).[2]

2.2 Output shares

As shown in Table 2.1, the changes that have occurred from the end of the past century to the current date are no less than striking: the overall world share in manufacturing value added of the core European countries (EU-15), Japan, and the United States currently amounts to 41.3%, compared to 71.4% in 1995; just before the upsurge of the financial crisis in 2007 it was still 56.3%. In two decades, the industrialized world has lost more than 40% of its economic weight in manufacturing. The tendency appears most notably in Japan, shrinking by two-thirds of the share it held in the mid-1990s.[3]

Together, the seven largest emerging economies, that is the so-called BRICs plus Turkey, Mexico, Indonesia, now account for almost 40% of world total manufacturing value added, with China (28.4%) standing out of the group. Adding up more 'new' economies hardly changes their overall weight, so that the cumulated output shares rapidly flatten as the number of countries taken into account rises: in 2018, the top 20 Non-Advanced Countries account for about 44% of the world total (Figure 2.1).

The exceptionally high performance of a huge country like China (getting the top of the rank by the end of the first decade of the 2000s) involves the scaling down of all top industrialized countries, overturned from their previous position. In later years, the rank of some of them is also affected by the emergence among top manufacturers of the other Asian giant, India, as well as—quite impressively due to its relatively small size—of South Korea.

---

[2] The selected group of countries here analysed has been determined by the following steps: starting from the list of all the countries included in the UNCTAD data-set on manufacturing output and the World Bank data-set on population, a first group of countries affected by incomplete series has been excluded (namely, Curacao, Eritrea, Montenegro, Pacific Islands Small States, South Sudan, Timor-Leste). Then a further group of countries, characterized by an oil rent higher than 25% of the GDP according to World Bank data (https://data.worldbank.org/indicator/ny.gdp.petr.rt.zs) has also been excluded because of the overwhelming role that such a rent may have played in favouring industrialization. These countries include Angola, Azerbaijan, Dem. Rep. of Congo, Equatorial Guinea, Iraq, Kuwait, Libya, Oman, Saudi Arabia. Finally, Ireland has also been excluded, owing to the extreme volatility of Irish manufacturing output (which involves a well-known jump between 2014 and 2015), in order to avoid biases in the variability measures.

[3] The data analysed in this chapter do not include very recent years, due to the need to avoid the upswings and downswings tied to the arrival of the pandemic (and afterwards of the war), which starting with 2020 determine a complete loss of significance of the observed trends (fall and rebound).

Table 2.1 Structure and change of output flows in the long run (country shares of manufacturing value added in current dollars, %)

	Countries	1995	2001	2007	2013	2018
1	China	4.1	7.4	12.3	24.0	28.4
2	United States	22.2	26.6	20.1	16.7	17.0
3	Japan	21.7	16.2	10.6	8.2	7.2
4	Germany	9.0	7.0	7.6	6.1	5.8
5	South Korea	2.5	2.4	3.2	3.1	3.3
6	India	1.1	1.3	2.1	2.4	3.0
7	Italy	3.8	3.5	3.8	2.4	2.3
8	France	4.0	3.4	3.3	2.4	1.9
9	United Kingdom	3.5	3.7	3.2	2.2	1.8
10	Mexico	1.2	2.4	1.8	1.7	1.5
11	Indonesia	1.0	0.8	1.2	1.6	1.5
12	Russian Federation	1.3	1.0	2.1	2.1	1.5
13	Taiwan	1.2	1.3	1.2	1.2	1.4
14	Brazil	2.0	1.4	2.1	2.1	1.3
15	Canada	1.7	2.1	1.9	1.5	1.2
16	Spain	1.7	1.8	2.0	1.2	1.1
17	Turkey	1.0	0.6	1.2	1.3	1.1
18	Thailand	0.8	0.6	0.9	0.9	1.0
19	Switzerland Liechtenstein	1.1	0.9	1.0	1.1	0.9
20	Netherlands	1.2	1.0	1.1	0.7	0.7
21	Saudi Arabia	0.2	0.3	0.4	0.6	0.7
22	Poland	0.4	0.5	0.8	0.7	0.7
23	Australia	0.8	0.7	1.0	0.8	0.6
24	Malaysia	0.4	0.5	0.5	0.6	0.6
25	Austria	0.7	0.6	0.8	0.6	0.6
26	Sweden	0.9	0.8	0.9	0.6	0.5
27	Singapore	0.4	0.4	0.4	0.4	0.5
28	Belgium	0.9	0.7	0.8	0.5	0.5
29	Argentina	0.7	0.7	0.5	0.8	0.5
30	Philippines	0.3	0.3	0.4	0.5	0.5

Countries ranked according to 2018 value added. Ireland is excluded.
Source: UNCTAD World Statistics, own calculations.

Interesting enough, data show that, in the face of China's extraordinary performance, even important 'new' industrial countries like Mexico, Indonesia, and Turkey, although growing in absolute numbers (see below, Section 2.1.3), have been characterized in the last years by *falling* manufacturing *shares*; as to Brazil and Russia, the falling share between 2013 and 2018 is paralleled by negative growth. Overall, in the post-global financial crisis years the relative position of the different countries tends to stabilize (at least as

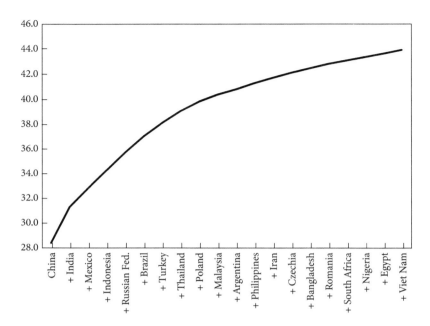

Figure 2.1 Cumulated world manufacturing output shares in the top 20 non-advanced economies in 2018, current dollars

Source: UNCTAD World Statistics, own calculations.

to the top of the rank), suggesting that the changes that have led to a new manufacturing landscape may have been exhausted.

2.3 Growth differentials

The dynamics of growth rates (Figure 2.2) help envisage the aforementioned changes from a different perspective. The overall evidence can be summarized as follows.

First, over the whole period spanning from 1995 to 2018, quite remarkable growth rates can be observed for countries of *any* size (among the top performers we can find largest, medium-sized, and small economies: China, Ethiopia, Cambodia) but not for OIEs, which in all sub-periods lie at the very bottom of the rank.

Second, as to the largest countries, excluding China, which can alter the landscape of world manufacturing most due to their very size (BRI+ in the graph), growth rates appear on the whole higher as compared to OIEs, but relatively low as compared to top performers (see below); they are anyway largely outpaced by China.

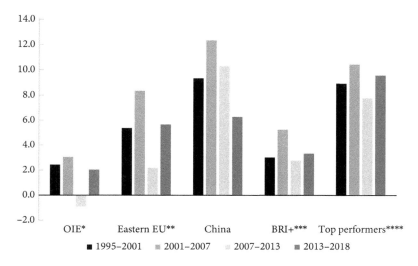

Figure 2.2 Yearly average growth rates of manufacturing value added (%), constant dollars

* Old Industrialized Economies, excluding Ireland.
** Bulgaria, Czechia, Hungary, Poland, Romania, Slovakia.
*** Brazil, Russia, India, Indonesia, Mexico, Turkey.
**** Bangladesh, Cambodia, Ethiopia, Lao, Liberia, Mali, Mozambique, Myanmar, Qatar, Viet Nam.
Source: UNCTAD World Statistics, own calculations.

Third, a group of top performers can be identified, showing growth rates *systematically* high, which also keep rising in the post-crisis years—when even China's performance is slowing down. Certainly the explosive rates of growth of some of these countries are simply due to their initial backwardness (i.e. to their low manufacturing output level in 1995), so that their overall share in world output at the end of the period is still very low (1.6%);[4] nevertheless, this testifies to the existence of some industrialization process (and policy) that needs to be taken into account when evaluating their growth potential.[5]

Fourth, even if they are far from the top of the ranking, it is worth mentioning those Eastern European countries that have successfully switched to

---

[4] On the one hand, moving from minimal values, the percentage variations in production levels are, by definition, exceptionally high; on the other, the initial stages of production activity are by their very nature characterized by sustained growth rates that cannot be maintained throughout all the ensuing stages of the process (due to the effects of structural change, which involve, beyond a given level of development, a gradual shrinking of the relative weight of manufacturing activities, and therefore a slowdown of overall growth). For a discussion of this point see Kruger (2008).

[5] See for example Perkins (2012), Chhair and Ung (2016), Gebreeyesus (2016), and Oqubay (2019). The group should also include Ireland, which however has been affected over the period by well-known problems as to the significance of its output measures on statistical grounds and has therefore been excluded from the group.

a market economy, innovating and developing a new manufacturing sector integrated at the international level (with Germany in particular). In such countries industrial development has meant exiting from a *previous* industrialization path and entering a new one. Due to their relative small size, the global weight of such countries still remains correspondingly small (1.8% in 2018); yet they represent a successful way to industrialization, in which the pre-existence of manufacturing knowledge has played a key role in driving a successful transition (see Chapter 3). This is documented below (Section 2.5) with reference to their rate of industrialization.

Fifth, overall, in most groups growth rates gradually slow down as compared to the years preceding the financial crisis. In the last sub-period (2013–18) they generally appear on the rebound; yet average data hide the new fall happening in the biennium 2018–19 (before the explosion of the pandemic on a global scale). The reasons for such a slowdown fall beyond the boundaries of the descriptive analysis proposed in this chapter and will be analysed in the following (see in particular Chapter 6).

2.4 Size

As noted above, a key role in the changing manufacturing landscape is played by the sheer size (in terms of population) of individual emerging countries—which, indeed, is just what gives still some significance to the BRIC category, referring in itself to quite different systems as to both their economic features and performance. The last decade of the twentieth century, and the early years of the 2000s, are the time window within which—for the reasons that have been outlined in Chapter 1—some billion people have almost simultaneously ceased to be excluded from mass industrialization.

This is different both from what happened in the course of the 1970s when the emergence of 'Asian tigers' did not at any rate change the balance of power between the Global North and Global South, and what is currently taking place with many fast-growing latecomers so small in size that the actual impact of their industrial development at the world level still appears negligible (see above). In this case, what matters is not the pace—albeit exceptionally fast—of growth, but the scale of manufacturing activities, which is unprecedented. The point is that even medium-sized economies in the Asian context had already in the past recorded growth rates comparable to China's, but '[t]ogether, Japan and Korea never exceeded 5 per cent of the global population. In 2008, China alone accounted for 20 per cent of global population, and together with India, for almost 37 per cent of the global total' (Kaplinski and Farooki 2010: 138).[6] From this point of view, even the (unavoidable) slow-down in the pace of China's growth does not alter the problem: a 5% annual growth rate in an economy with a GDP of almost 14,000 billion dollars traces a situation where every year it is as if a country larger than Poland were to enter into the world economic system.[7]

In such a perspective the reallocation of production shares at the world level that has occurred in the last decades simply reflects the physiological scaling down of the relative importance of some first comers (especially European ones), due to their relatively low weight in terms of population. This principle finds an exemplary synthesis in Cameron's words, referring to the fading away of British primacy in world markets at the end of the twentieth century:

> Britain could not retain its preeminence indefinitely, as other less-developed but well-endowed nations began to industrialize. In that sense, Britain's *relative* decline was inevitable. Moreover, in view of the vast resources and rapid popula-tion growth of the United States and Russia, it is not surprising that they would eventually overtake the small island nation in total output.
>
> **(Cameron 1993: 226, emphasis in original)**

This is a key point, which needs to be made fully explicit. The rank in world output shares obtained by relatively small economies such as the European ones in the course of 1970s, following a long development phase, has to be intended as a once-in-a-lifetime event: the very existence of the G7 or G10 has been the outcome of a historical phase in which the Global North had become the only area characterized by large-scale industrial development.[8]

Certainly, the origins of the economic development of advanced countries hark back to the Second Industrial Revolution, with which their take-off did coincide.[9] Yet this legacy received a further boost in more recent times— namely in the course of the Golden Age—when the economic systems of continental Europe were involved in catching up with the United States.

---

[6] The impact of the size of the two Asian Giants is widely discussed in Winter and Yusuf (2007) and Yusuf and Nabeshima (2010).

[7] In 2018 Chinese GDP amounted to 13,841 billion dollars, Poland's to 587 (World Bank, *World Development Indicators*).

[8] As already noticed, with the notable exception of Eastern European countries, then belonging to a different world.

[9] The topic is too wide to be more than merely evoked. About its general features, anyway, see at the very least Landes (1969). As to the differences in the behaviour of North Atlantic countries with respect to their European followers see also Chandler (1990), and Schroeter (1997).

This phase of world industrial development, having involved but a small fraction of world population, has to be considered as an outright *anomaly*. As stressed by Singh:

> In the long history of economic development in industrial countries the post-war quarter century of the Golden Age appears to be a historical aberration. Measured in terms of the rates of growth of output, productivity and capital stock, the period 1950–73 in advanced economies as a whole unquestionably represents a highly distinct deviation from the long-term trend values of these variables over the last two centuries. [... T]he length, steadiness, speed and spread of the Golden Age economic boom was such that they could not be accounted for by an accidental combination of favourable economic circumstances. Rather, the extraordinary economic performance of industrial countries was brought about and sustained by a unique historical conjunction which created a specific *economic regime*.
>
> **(Singh 1994b: 41, emphasis in original)**

If we take as a long-run benchmark the parity of per capita GDP among all world countries (in our case, manufacturing output), it follows that the economic (industrial) weight of a given country should converge to its world ranking expressed in terms of population. This means that *all* European countries, as well as the United States and Japan, are bound to gradually shift towards a lower position in every kind of ranking having to do with production, trade, or other economic flows.[10] As stressed in a report by the World Bank, in 2000 about three-quarters of world's GDP was concentrated in North America, Western Europe, and Northeast Asia; yet such a concentration was not new, for three centuries ago, China and India accounted for about two-thirds of the world's wealth as well. What was different then is that they also had more than half of the world's population, whereas the European Union (EU), Japan, and the United States have less than one-sixth (World Bank 2009).[11]

This said, the 'country size' effect that has been observed—leading to a more widespread allocation of manufacturing activities all across the world—does not mean as such that *all* (large) catching-up countries are experiencing a sudden uprise in their *degree of industrialization*. Output shares simply reflect the *absolute size* of output flows and do not entail that large emerging economies have actually achieved a degree of industrial development

---

[10] From this very same point of view, even the striking performance of South Korea as a manufacturer, or the indisputable success of German exporters in recent years, represent some sorts of anomaly having the prospect of assuming in the long-run lower relevance.

[11] Quite similar considerations can be found in Nayyar (2019).

comparable to that of advanced economies, for this takes time and asks for a deep transformation of the economic structure. The point is analysed in some detail in the next section.

2.5 Industrialization

An implicit measure of how the output performance of emerging countries is still mainly explained by their absolute size can be obtained by normalizing the output level with the size of population (that is, expressing it in per capita terms). Calculations reported in Figure 2.3, comparing for large EEs the ratio of per-capita value added in manufacturing to the corresponding value for the United States, help highlight several issues.

The first is that a huge manufacturer like China still hardly matches the (average) per-capita value added even of Eastern European countries; and, more than this, the strong improvement of the former over the period appears not too dissimilar from that of the latter. Then, countries showing enormous differences in terms of their importance as manufacturing producers may be characterized by both a similar degree of industrialization (per-capita value

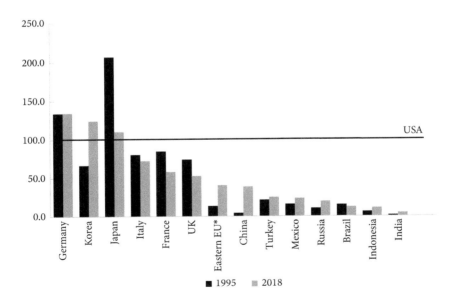

Figure 2.3 Per capita value added in manufacturing, selected countries, United States = 100, current dollars

* Bulgaria, Czechia, Hungary, Poland, Romania, Slovakia.
Source: UNCTAD World Statistics, own calculations.

added) and similar performances as to their speed in achieving it. Second, a small country like South Korea stands out in 2018 as the second manufacturing country in the world, having almost doubled since 1995 its degree of relative industrialization and left behind other large OIEs (with the exception of Germany). Third, India (sixth place in the rank of output shares) still lies, in terms of its degree of industrialization, far behind a laggard-like Indonesia.

Overall, these data mean that we are still at the very beginning of a process that—even if it may suffer a slowdown in the years to come—is supposed to continue. At the very same time, this implicitly highlights the economic—not to say environmental—consequences to be expected at the world level in the long run.

In order to understand what industrialization has really involved so far, we need to identify *which* laggards have experienced some discontinuity in their international status as manufacturing producers. 'Emerging' as a manufacturer, here, does not simply relate to rising importance in terms of output weight; indeed, it has first and foremost to do with the role that the manufacturing sector plays within any given country and the way it shapes its economic structure.

On methodological grounds, answering this question involves some arbitrariness in the choice of the variables to be taken into account. And, in fact, the economic literature—and documents by major international institutions—do provide a wide range of definitions about what, more generally, is meant for economic development (Nielsen 2011). A comprehensive evaluation of the specific features that characterize the 'passage' from one situation to another in the course of manufacturing development will be provided in chapter 4. Yet, before that, we can try to provide some measure of the industrialization process in the countries that were classified as underdeveloped before the globalization process took place.

As a starting point, the extent to which individual countries can be considered as emerging can be first of all measured, according to our previous arguments, in terms of the (manufacturing) output level relative to the size of the country, as measured by population. This means simply to follow the UNIDO approach (see Upadhyaya 2013), taking per-capita manufacturing value added as a measure of manufacturing development in the same way as per-capita GDP is usually taken as a basic measure of economic development by all international institutions. It has to be noticed that this way of measuring the phenomenon is different from evaluating the rate of industrialization in terms of manufacturing shares on total output (or employment). The point with output shares is that due to structural change they are bound to first rise and then fall over time *in any country*: so that it may happen that

OIEs themselves are characterized by *lower* manufacturing shares as compared to some (typically emerging) countries observed in the first phases of their development process.[12]

Following Reynolds (1983, 1986), a discontinuity in the course of the development process can be expressed in terms of the passage from 'extensive' development (global output growing at the same pace as population) to an 'intensive' one (rising *per-capita* output).[13] In the same way, we can assume rising per-capita value added in manufacturing as a measure of 'intensive' manufacturing development.

In this perspective, the way for distinguishing EEs in this work has been the following. First, a group of 'laggards' broadly corresponding to the IMF definition of 'Emerging and Developing Countries' has been identified.[14] Then, countries with fewer than one million inhabitants have been excluded, for in the perspective of the present analysis they are far from representing— both actually and potentially—anything like an economic system to be industrialized.[15] Last, as far as a positive dynamics in terms of growth is required in order to identify EEs, all countries characterized by negative growth in the period have also been excluded. Once this group has been identified, the following step has been to restrict the observation to the countries characterized by positive growth of *per-capita* manufacturing value added in the period 1995–2018.

Then these countries have been divided into eight groups, corresponding to the main economic areas of the world (Table 2.2). The results can be summarized as follows: (1) the years spanning from 2000 to 2007 are characterized, in all areas with the exception of Africa, by the highest increase in per capita manufacturing output. From this point of view it can be said that

---

[12] This is what typically happens when the rate of industrialization is measured in terms of employment or output shares in current prices, due to both demand and supply effects (i.e. Engel's law, involving non-homothetic preferences and therefore pushing towards a rising demand of services in the course of development; higher productivity growth in manufacturing compared to services, involving decreasing labour input in the former as well as decreasing relative output prices owing to higher competition in the tradable sector). Empirical evidence appears less straightforward when output shares are measured in constant prices; see in particular Rowthorn and Ramaswamy (1997), Herrendorf et al. (2014) and below, Chapter 5.

[13] Both such phases fall within the boundaries of the definition suggested by Kuznets (1973) of 'modern economic growth', according to which the transition to modern development is marked first of all by an uprise in per-capita output, paralleled by population growth and fast structural change. It seems difficult instead to find analogies with Rostov's (1960) definition of take-off (critically looked at by Kuznets himself, see Kuznets 1965). The whole matter is dealt with extensively in chapter 4.

[14] Other than the countries that have been dropped due to the incompleteness of time series and high oil rents (see above), this group excludes the Advanced Countries (AC) according to the IMF definition, encompassing Hong Kong and Taiwan (not included by IMF among 'Advanced *Countries*' for merely political reasons, but included among 'Advanced *Economies*'). AC do not encompass, in this case, the 'new' economies of Eastern Europe (Eastern EU), that for the abovementioned reasons have to be considered an important part of the emerging world.

[15] A quite similar solution is adopted by Page (2012).

Table 2.2 Yearly average growth rates of per capita value added in manufacturing by geographical area, constant dollars

Areas	1995–2001	2001–2007	2007–2013	2013–2018	1995–2018
Southeastern Asia	5.2	8.1	4.4	4.7	5.6
Eastern Europe	5.3	7.0	0.7	5.6	4.6
Ex Urss	4.1	6.4	3.1	2.6	4.0
Southern Asia	4.1	4.6	2.6	3.0	3.6
North Africa	2.7	1.8	1.8	1.7	2.0
Sub-Saharan Africa	2.7	2.0	2.0	1.3	2.9
Central and South America	0.5	2.6	0.8	0.2	1.1
Middle East	1.8	3.8	−1.3	−1.2	0.7

Source: UNCTAD World Statistics, own calculations.

the most intense phase of the globalization process (Chapter 1) has coincided with a general uprise of the industrialization rate; (2) nevertheless, Latin America appears lagging behind in all periods, showing in the years following the great financial crisis rates of growth even lower than Africa; (3) after 2013, Middle Eastern economies also appear to be affected by serious problems due to the Syrian civil war breaking out in the area, leading to negative growth rates; (4) all areas undergo a general fall in growth rates in the post-crisis years; as with Eastern Europe this only happens—with peculiar intensity—between 2007 and 2013.[16]

For each area, Figure 2.4 singles out the countries at the top of the ranking, sorted by their average growth rate in the whole 1995–2018 period. Unlike what happens in the Asian case, where China and India are top performers in their respective regions, no large economy ranks in the first positions in Latin America; in the same way, Russia is not displayed in the graph relative to former USSR economies. As to sub-Saharan Africa, the graph only includes—among the most important economies in the area ('the stars of Africa's growth turnaround', as defined by Newman et al. 2016)—Ethiopia and Mozambique.

But which distribution of industrialization *levels* has been determined by such trends at the end of the period? This can be viewed in Figure 2.5, reporting the per capita manufacturing value added in 2018 for selected countries of the overall rank.[17] It can be drawn from the graph that the first 20 countries in the rank, with the notable exception of Turkey, belong to no more than three

[16] A discussion about the slowdown of Eastern European countries in the post-crisis years can be found in Kattel (2010) and Åslund (2018).

[17] In order to reduce the noise due to some economies which do not actually represent anything relevant from the point of view of the emergence of a manufacturing system, five small countries strongly dependent upon oil extraction and a quite small island economy appearing near the top of the rank have

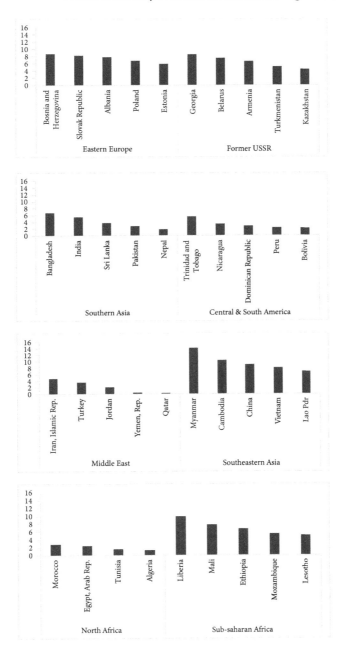

Figure 2.4 Yearly average growth rate of per capita value added in manufacturing, 1995–2018, constant dollars—selected countries

Source: UNCTAD World Statistics, own calculations.

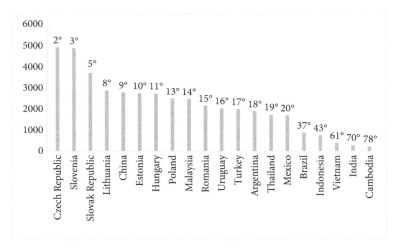

Figure 2.5 Per capita value added in manufacturing, 2018. Selected countries sorted by rank, current dollars

Source: UNCTAD World Statistics, own calculations.

areas of the world: Eastern Europe, Eastern Asia, and—far from the top—Latin America. That is, two areas where a previous round of industrialization had already taken place before globalization and the area that globalization has pulled the most out of the underdeveloped world as to manufacturing capacity. On the right side of the figure it can be noted that the index relative to Brazil is still half that of Mexico, and that India—burdened by a heavy population weight—appears just between Vietnam and Cambodia.

So, it can be said that, the current map of laggards' industrialization shows quite remarkable distances even among successful economies. There are several reasons for this, among which it has to be mentioned that emerging countries have entered the road to industrialization at different points in time so that their take-off is by no means simultaneous.[18]

Overall, industrialization in the underdeveloped world has been characterized by two different phases: first, up to the explosion of the financial crisis, in which several areas (but not all of them) have been able to take advantage of the globalization process; and second in which industrialization has kept deepening only in some regions. In this framework South-Eastern Asia and Eastern Europe stand out of the crowd. Hence, industrialization has not been

been excluded from the graph. The countries are Qatar, Bahrain, United Arab Emirates, Turkmenistan, and Trinidad and Tobago.

[18] This issue will be paid specific attention to in Chapter 4.

a worldwide phenomenon and appears to have been instead strongly selective. This will be discussed more widely in the next chapter; here, some more evidence about the consequences of the emergence of new manufacturing countries in the global economy follows.

2.6 Relative growth and international economic integration I: Old vs new industrial economies

The difference in the rhythm of growth of OIEs as compared to EEs relates to the degree according to which the slower growth—or even a negative growth—of the former has been endogenous to the meteoric rise of the latter. In other words, it relates to the extent to which a (more or less) substantial part of the production capacity of the Global North has been relocated in the Global South, determining a crowding out effect in the former.

In logical terms, the existence of a crowding out effect appears far from being straightforward. On the one hand, it cannot be measured in terms of any trends in world output shares (as we saw, they increase in EEs for quite physiological reasons); on the other, the results are rather ambiguous even when we refer to output dynamics in absolute numbers: what is the threshold beyond which EEs absolute growth determines a detrimental effect on OIEs? Besides, output growth differentials between the Global North and the Global South may be largely uncorrelated, as they may reflect different paths of expansion of domestic demand fed by domestic supply.

Inasmuch as the issue at stake is to see whether international integration involves a worsening of the capability of a given country (or block of countries) to face its consequences on manufacturing activity, a way of dealing with it may be to look directly at the dynamics of trade balances: in such case, crowding out (in the North) happens simply when growth in the South is paralleled by an increase in its net exports.

This approach is quite close on conceptual grounds to the view suggested by Singh (1977, 1987), according to whom for an open economy 'we may define an efficient manufacturing sector as one which (*currently as well as potentially) not only satisfies the demand of consumers at home, but is also able to sell enough of its products abroad to pay for the nation's input requirements*'. As Singh himself stresses, '[t]his is, however, subject to the important restriction that [...] [it] *must be able to achieve these objectives at socially acceptable levels of output, employment, and the exchange rate*' (1977, p. 128, emphasis in original). What matters here is that at the aggregate level an industrial system succeeds in (more than) matching the nation's imports through its sales abroad, independently of the nature of the goods that are exported and imported. The manufacturing sector is efficient when the international economic integration takes place in the absence of a fall of the (net) external demand (i.e. of a worsening of the manufacturing trade balance): when this does not happen, then de-industrialization is expected to follow. A weaker form of this relationship can be expressed by referring to *manufacturing's* imports, in which case the ratio becomes:

$$(X - M)_m / Y_m; \tag{2.1}$$

where X, M, and Y refer to export, import, and output respectively. Equation (2.1) can be rewritten in turn as the product of the degree of openness of the domestic manufacturing system and the corresponding normalized manufacturing trade balance:

$$(X - M)_m / Y_m = [(X + M)_m / Y_m] [(X - M)_m / (X + M)_m]. \tag{2.2}$$

Equation (2.2) helps highlight the economic mechanism by which import-led de-industrialization can follow economic integration, that is the effect of strong trade deficits coupled with high trade openness. By the same logic, it can be said that export-led industrialization occurs as a combination of strong trade surplus coupled with high trade openness.

In the following, this formula will be applied to two different groups of countries: the first one, we will call OIEs, includes the G10 and all Western European Union Member States; the second includes all the EEs—as they have been defined above—for which gross manufacturing output data are available along the entire period 1995–2018. This allows us to appreciate how the process of integration between the Global North and South has evolved asymmetrically in the last decades, and how it has contributed, in different ways, to the overall production flows of both groups.[19]

[19] The sum of the two groups does not coincide by definition with the whole global economy. The Asian Tigers, some non-EU European countries, the entire Oceania and most of the African countries have been left aside. However, in terms of their contribution to industrial output, such exclusion has a limited impact on the North–South relation (their inclusion would not significantly affect the results). Thus, to a large extent the flow of exports of OIEs can be interpreted as the flow of import by EEs and vice versa. To exclude that this analysis is driven by changes occurred in the oil market, refined petroleum products have been excluded from manufacturing production and trade data. All data are in current prices. For each group of countries only extra-area trade flows have been considered.

Figure 2.6 shows, in particular, that the degree of openness of OIEs towards the EEs has more than doubled during the last twenty-five years, but also that the intensity of the phenomenon was not constant over time: it grew slowly in the late 1990s, exploded at the dawn of the new millennium up to the burst of the global financial crisis, and then decelerated, at least up to 2018. Changes have been even more spectacular (and radical) when considering EEs, as their degree of openness towards the rest of the world first increased substantially and then, soon after the beginning of 2000s, turned back, so that at the end of 2018 it was well *below* its 1995 level. In these same years, the trade balance between the two blocs radically changed as well, passing from a strong extra-area surplus for the advanced economies in the mid-1990s to a strong deficit at the end of the period, which is mirrored for EEs by an initial strong extra-area deficit ending up in a surplus. How could this have happened?

In the mid-1990s, as the industrial world largely coincided with the boundaries of OIEs, most exchanges concerning manufacturing goods occurred *within* the North, while North–South bilateral trade was still scant in total

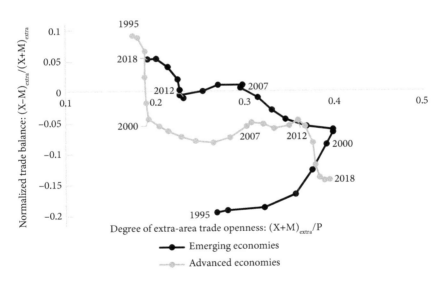

Figure 2.6 Manufacturing goods*, degree of trade openness, and normalized trade balance for blocs of countries, excluding trade among countries within the same bloc, current dollars, three-year moving averages

*Excluding refined petroleum
Source: World Bank, IHS-Markit, own calculations.

value. Thus, at the beginning of the period under scrutiny the manufacturing trade relationship of OIEs with the rest of the world was simply driven by the dynamics of exports, contributing to a positive normalized trade balance. The opposite was true for EEs, highly dependent upon manufacturing imports from OIEs and therefore showing a heavy trade deficit. As far as trade integration gradually intensified in the late 1990s, whereas exports from the North were structurally constrained by the low domestic demand of the South, exports from the latter could benefit from the high levels of domestic demand in the former. Therefore, the extra-area trade surplus experienced by OIEs rapidly eroded into a trade deficit as early as the beginning of 2000s, while at the same time the trade balance of EEs benefitted from the increasing international integration.

In the early 2000s a new scenario emerged. On the side of the OIEs, the accession of China to WTO, the enlargement of EU to the East, and more generally the surge in the process of vertical fragmentation of value chains on a global scale increased dramatically the import dependence of the North from South productions, contributing to boost its extra-area trade openness together with its trade deficit: i.e. the type of combination that is conducive to de-industrialization. The extra-area trade deficit of OIEs was only partially mitigated by two factors: the simultaneous emergence of some domestic demand in EEs—which also translated into higher manufacturing exports of the former—and the outbreak of the global financial crisis in 2008, which by depressing domestic demand in OIEs set a halt to their import flows.

On the side of EEs taken as a whole, the new millennium came along with rising production capacity. This progressively reduced their trade deficit and at the same time allowed them to satisfy an increasing (and increasingly diversified) domestic demand for manufacturing goods involved by raising standards of living. But, unlike the 1990s, when export flows were basically directed towards OIEs, the 2000s saw a remarkable *decrease* in the relative weight of extra-area trade for the South, corresponding to a sharp contraction in its trade dependence from the North. This does not mean that imports from and exports to Europe, North America, and Japan, were not still crucial for EEs to develop in these years, but simply that their importance progressively decreased as time passed. As will be more widely argued below (Chapter 6), the burst of the global financial crisis has accelerated such a 'decoupling' from the North, forcing EEs—starting with China—to find alternative and stable sources of demand for their manufacturing productions. In more recent years, the manufacturing trade imbalance between OIEs and EEs, far from stabilizing, has progressed even further: for the former the trade dependence from the latter has intensified and has been accompanied by a worsening of the trade deficit, while the opposite happened for EEs, where the degree of openness continued to get lower in the face of an extra-area trade surplus reaching historically high rates.

Further light on the structural changes (and determinants) that occurred in the global manufacturing landscape comes from the decomposition of the index measuring the extra-area trade openness (the first term on the right-hand side of Equation 2.2), which can be re-written the following way:

$$(X + M)_{extra-area}/Y = \{X_{extra-area}/Y\} + \{M_{extra-area}/Y\}$$
$$= \{[X_{extra-area}/X_{tot}][X_{tot}/Y]\}$$
$$+ \{[M_{extra-area}/M_{tot}][M_{tot}/Y]\} \qquad (2.3)$$

According to Equation (2.3) the degree of extra-area trade openness, for both exports and imports, can be divided into two terms, one capturing the relative importance of extra-area trade on total trade (that is the North–South orientation of trade flows), the other the relative importance of trade for domestic production.

By separately analysing the different terms of Equation (2.3) for both advanced and emerging economies, it can be appreciated how, starting from the beginning of the 2000s, the process of 'decoupling' of the South from the North has been twofold. On the one hand, EEs have been less and less relying on trade for domestic production (as shown by a lower trade to output ratio); on the other, they have increasingly re-oriented their trade relations towards themselves (as shown by a lower share of extra-area trade). Interestingly enough, this happened for both exports and imports, meaning that the South has become more independent from the North as to demand and supply, re-orienting its production towards domestic markets and intra-area transactions.

The opposite is true when looking at OIEs. In this case, an increasing dependence from the South has come through a higher weight of trade on domestic production (resulting in a higher trade to output ratio) and a decreasing role of intra-area trade (resulting in a higher share of extra-area trade). This can be observed on both the exports and the imports side as well

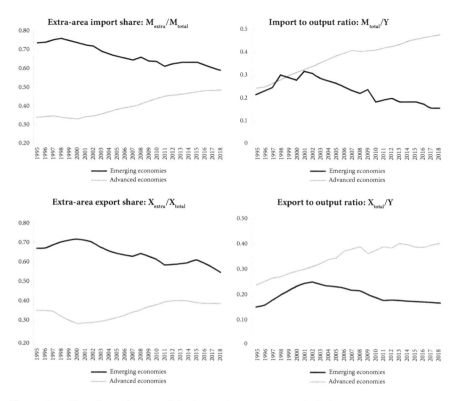

Figure 2.7 Manufacturing goods*, share of extra-area trade (left panel), and trade to output ratio (right panel) for blocs of countries, current dollars, three-year moving averages

*Excluding refined petroleum
Source: World Bank, IHS-Markit, own calculations.

(Figure 2.7). In other words, OIEs have become less and less self-sufficient, as to both manufacturing demand and supply, as against EEs.

2.7 Relative growth and international economic integration II: The 'Remainder' and the South–South competition

Hitherto, integration into the global manufacturing trade network of EEs has been analysed without isolating the contribution of its different regions. This simplification is useful to highlight the process by which the rebalance of industrial power between the North and South occurred in the last few decades, but it may induce us to overlook its selective nature, as industrial development has not occurred everywhere and has not revealed everywhere the same structural characteristics.[20] Indeed, the egress from underdevelopment of *some* countries (i.e. those able to enter the road to industrial development due to some previous knowledge and purposeful policies) has involved a permanent divergence of the industrialization rates *within* the whole group of laggards. That is, the sudden bursting onto the economic scene of new manufacturing systems has been accompanied by the persistent stagnation of a conspicuous part of the economies of the Global South (what in Amsden's 2001 terms can be defined as 'the Remainder').

Moreover, by focusing only on North–South trade relations an important part of the history of industrialization in the GA is neglected: namely, that involving the co-existence of different emerging countries *competing with each other*. In fact, by looking only at the extra-area trade relations of EEs we are (implicitly) assuming that economic integration has necessarily passed through their trade exposure with the North, and that no effects can be attributed to direct trade exposure *among* themselves. This is potentially misleading. In order to take into account this problem, it has been calculated—using the same formula presented in Equation (2.2)—the degree of openness of manufacturing and the corresponding trade balance against both OIEs and EEs for different regions of the Global South. Figure 2.8 shows the results of this decomposition, which can be summarized as follows.

Looking at manufacturing exchanges with OIEs, the picture shows that while all Southern regions contributed to the sharp increase in trade openness registered at the end of the 1990s, only some of them were responsible for its subsequent decrease, soon after the beginning of the 2000s. In particular, the stronger driver of change in trade openness towards OIEs came from Asia (in particular from China and, to a lesser extent, India), followed by South and Central America (which excludes Mexico), which registered a similar, albeit weaker, hump-shaped pattern. As to Africa and the Middle East, the reversal in trade openness with OIEs was marginal in intensity and transitional, while for Eastern Europe—in sharp contrast with the other emerging blocks—the 2000s saw a rising trade openness, pushed by the increasing economic (and in some cases political) integration with the European Union. Overall, the trade balance with OIEs generally improved for all Southern regions during the entire period, with the notable exception of

---

[20] Apart from what has been already observed in chapter 1, see on this point also Popov and Jomo (2018).

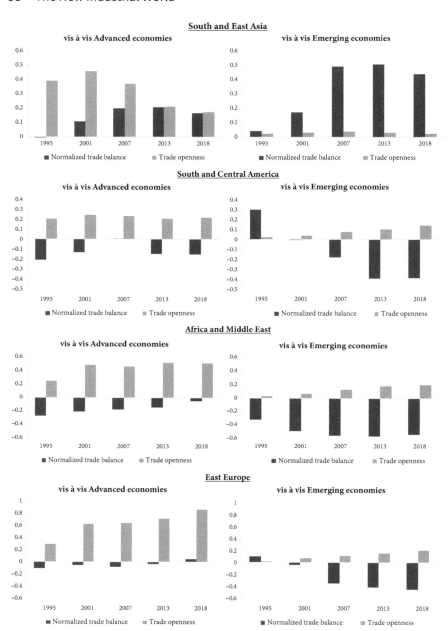

Figure 2.8 Manufacturing goods*, degree of trade openness, and normalized trade balance for different South regions, current dollars

*Excluding refined petroleum
Source: World Bank, IHS-Markit, own calculations.

South and Central America, for which the years following the financial crisis corresponded to a sharp deterioration of current accounts, impairing the significant improvements registered before.

Focussing on South-to-South manufacturing exchanges, it can be noted that all Southern regions excluding Asia have registered a worsening of their current accounts during the Globalization Age. This means that Asian emerging economies (first and foremost China) have become net exporters of manufacturing goods towards the rest of the world, putting competitive pressure not only upon the production systems of OIEs but also on those located in other underdeveloped areas in Africa, America, and Europe. That is, the increasing difficulties of many Southern regions in advancing their industrialization process cannot be read in isolation from the success of Asian economies in establishing themselves as global manufacturing actors.

2.8 Conclusions

The dynamics of industrial development in the last 30 years can be viewed first of all as a process of reduction of strong inequalities affecting the distribution of manufacturing activities at the world level. Such a process has led to a general increase in the manufacturing output share of what we have come to call emerging economies (EEs) viewed as a whole, and to a corresponding shrinkage of the share belonging to 'old' industrial countries (OIEs).

Such a phenomenon closely depends upon the very scale of *some* EEs, in the sense that it follows from the fact that—quite differently from what happened along the 1970s—among the countries that have succeeded in entering the road to industrial development in the course of the GA we can find economic giants. Whereas they have involved conspicuous shifts in the cross-country allocation of manufacturing activities, such changes have *not* involved, nevertheless, that EEs have *also* attained a *rate* of industrialization (as expressed by the ratio of manufacturing output to population) comparable to that of OIEs. This is true for both large and small EEs, even in the face of high *rates of growth*, over the last 25 years, of their per capita manufacturing output.

By its very nature, this process has led to a structural break of the 'model' of industrial development that had emerged in the course of the Second Industrial Revolution, passed through two world wars, and consolidated during the Golden Age, in which almost the whole of manufacturing production was concentrated within the walls of a handful of countries, corresponding to a small share of world population. The collapse of that model coincides with the end of a divergence between the Global North and South and paves the way to a totally different logic of manufacturing development, based upon a multipolar pattern of industrialization.

As far as it has been led by active policies, the simultaneity of manufacturing development taking place in different areas of the underdeveloped world can be envisaged in the perspective suggested by Alice Amsden, according to whom

> the herd or crowd effect, of a large number of latecomers all industrializing at once, probably made it easier *for each* to confront the North Atlantic's political and economic power. Synchronous development created more permissive conditions to deviate from the North Atlantic's market-driven model.
>
> **(Amsden 2001, p. 282, emphasis added)**

From this point of view the thesis itself according to which advanced countries have been partially 'crowded out' by EEs as to their manufacturing power appears in the end somewhat ill-posed: on average, what happened in the last phase of world development has simply been a process that has inverted the previous trend, leading towards a less unbalanced cross-country allocation of industrial activities in the long run.

On the other hand, in the same way as it has drawn a growing share of world population out of underdevelopment, pushing several countries towards an industrialization path, such a process has also made more dramatic the state of those countries which have not succeeded in making this passage, and are still lagging behind, therefore making even deeper the cleavage between what Alice Amsden has called 'the Rest' and 'the Remainder'. In this connection it has also to be mentioned that the strong expansion of manufacturing activity in Asia (driven in particular by China) has dramatically increased the competitive pressure on the production systems of the rest of the world, also affecting other underdeveloped economies in Africa, America, and Europe. As will be shown more fully in the next chapter, industrialization in the GA has been an inhomogeneous phenomenon.

3
Heterogeneous Paths to Industrialization in the Post-War Years

3.1 Introduction

According to the interpretive framework suggested in Chapter 1, the observed changes in manufacturing geography in the last decades basically start with vertical dis-integration *within* advanced countries (Rosa 2000, Traù 2003), followed by the 'unbundling' of the production process at the international level (Baldwin 2006), which—thanks to the 'great doubling' of the labour market (Freeman 2007)—translates into the unfolding of *global* value chains via the lever of the 'trade in tasks'. Such a mechanism is at the root of the advent of what we have called EEs as manufacturing producers.

This scheme, however, leaves out of the picture quite a large part of the underdeveloped world (mostly in the African continent), as well as an important group of countries that after World War II had already experienced an industrialization process, such as many Latin American ones, or Russia itself. In fact, the very mechanism of export-led growth, driven by the demand sourced by the North of the world, has only marginally affected these economies, and the group of laggards that succeeded in joining the development race were substantially limited.

As can be seen in Figure 3.1, showing the relationship between the level of per capita manufacturing output in 1990 and the increase in manufacturing output in the 1990–2018 period, when all economic systems are considered (and not just those in which a strong growth has already taken place) the relation between backwardness and (the speed of) development is by no means obvious. Among laggards, the graph shows the coexistence—in the face of similar levels of per capita output at the beginning of the period—of quite dissimilar rates of growth: minimal rates of industrialization correspond to both very high and very low rates of growth. In the same way, rising rates of industrialization—scattered along a quite wide range—are paralleled by very similar rates of growth.

Then, the very same international 'regime' (what we have called the Globalization Age) has produced highly varying, and even opposite, results in

The New Industrial World. Livio Romano and Fabrizio Traù, Oxford University Press.
© Livio Romano and Fabrizio Traù (2023). DOI: 10.1093/oso/9780192873736.003.0004

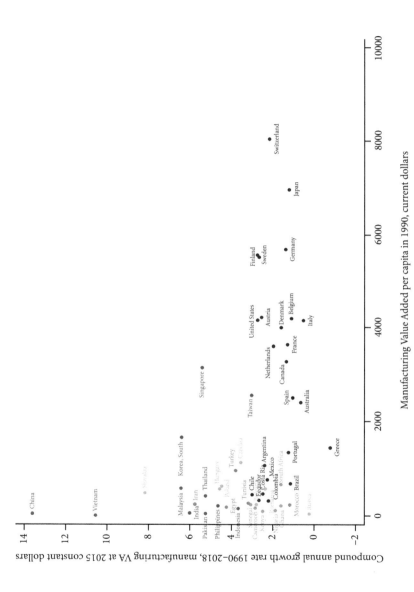

Figure 3.1 Manufacturing growth between 1990 and 2018 against the degree of industrialization in 1990

Source: UNCTAD and IHS-Markit data, own calculations.

different economic areas. The point here is twofold. On the one side, in general, economic development (and, in particular, manufacturing development) is not a mechanic issue—it is not something like an unavoidable destiny which sooner or later every economic system in the world has to come across. On the other, for the specific mechanism described above to unfold, as we have argued in previous chapters, some preconditions are required.

In this perspective a key role is played by what we usually call 'institutional factors', and in particular by public intervention in the field of industrial policy. As widely documented in a number of contributions, state-driven policies have always been at the root of industrial development, even in the case of OIEs.[1] From this point of view, the history of industrial development can be viewed as the history of the ways institutions have acted in order to accelerate, and even to guide, the constitution of their productive systems.

As we will show in this chapter the two pillars of this process were the explicit orientation of policymakers towards industrialization and—even prior to this—the determination to build institutions capable of managing its implementation. Indeed, the aim to set up policies oriented towards industrialization has been in the past a common feature of several underdeveloped economies; yet this has turned out into quite heterogeneous results in different areas. Why did these results differ, and how did it actually happen that some countries succeeded in reaching the status of emerging economy, while others continued to lag behind?

3.2 The political economy of industrial development

Before approaching the matter, we still need to clarify some basic issues. At any one time, the growth potential of an industrial system may be expressed in terms of its degree of accumulated productive knowledge, which in turn is the outcome of its previous history—thereby representing a 'localized' and path-dependent phenomenon. The set of capabilities developed by an economic system is the most relevant asset it has at its disposal to sustain an endogenous industrialization process. In a word, it is the key to development. In such a framework the most glaring phenomenon that the simple observation of facts puts in the evidence is that, in the course of time, the accumulation of productive knowledge has not been a universal phenomenon, as it has taken place only in some parts of the world. From this

---

[1] See among others Amsden (2001), Cimoli et al. (2009), Stiglitz and Lin (2013), Crafts and Hughes (2013), Szirmai et al. (2013), and in particular Reinert (1999, 2007, 2009) and Chang (2002, 2003, 2006, 2011). In a European perspective see Foreman-Peck and Federico (1999).

point of view the huge income gaps between rich and poor nations reflect correspondingly wide differences in productive knowledge amassed by different nations (Hausmann et al. 2011).

The point that needs to be stressed here is that knowledge is different from information, and that making profitable use of a given technology is different from its being available on the market. What matters from the point of view of endogenous growth is the ability to make use of available knowledge in the production process. But knowledge is embedded within people and organizations.[2] This feature closely depends on the tacit component of knowledge, which makes its transmission difficult, limiting its possibility to be universally adopted; up to the point that it can be said that this is one of the reasons why technological catching-up by developing countries remains so problematic even in the current era of free-information flows (Cimoli et al. 2009).

In our perspective, the first explanation for such evidence lies in the fact that those economies which were still lagging behind around the mid-twentieth century ('the Rest', i.e. those which, unlike first comers, had not succeeded in joining either the First or the Second Industrial Revolution)[3] had to face a world manufacturing context in which technological innovation had developed up to a degree which was totally out of their reach. They lacked proprietary knowledge, and they were not able to manage others' either. The emerging of a technological discontinuity—industrial revolutions are rare—created a structural difference in the premises for industrial development between OIEs and then underdeveloped economies. This pushed the latter to search for different strategies. As observed by Alice Amsden (2001), for the first time in history backward countries industrialized without *proprietary* innovations. In this sense late industrialization has to be viewed as a case of pure learning, meaning a complete dependence on technologies produced abroad in order to establish modern industries.

This is a framework in which—theoretically—the laggards could try to build upon what Gerschenkron (1962) defined as the 'advantages of backwardness' (evoked with reference to the catching-up, in the second half of the nineteenth century, of the European economies and the United States towards Great Britain): if you are not able to develop original technologies, then you can try to adopt technologies that have already been developed by

---

[2] We cannot delve here into the complex world of the theory of knowledge. As to its role from the point of view of the accumulation of capabilities in the context of economic development minimal references are Foss (1997, 2005), Loasby (1998, 1999).

[3] As we have seen in Chapter 1, following Amsden (2001) 'the Rest' includes China, India, Indonesia, South Korea, Malaysia, Taiwan, and Thailand in Asia; Argentina, Brazil, Chile, and Mexico in Latin America; Turkey in Middle East. A separate discourse has to be done about the countries belonging to the former Soviet Union, and their subsequent inclusion in a re-industrialization path (see below).

somebody else—which also means not having to cope with the sunk costs of older technologies to be dismantled and the risks associated with the process of research and development. Yet this is not an automatic issue, as far as pure learning is constrained by the actual extent of what the theory of the firm calls absorptive capacity (Cohen and Levinthal 1990), and development economics calls social capability (Abramovitz 1989): which, in the face of an unbridgeable gap of entrepreneurial and managerial capability to manage best practice technologies, becomes critical.[4] Therefore, what has happened in the end is that the whole architecture of the development process in the above-mentioned countries has been characterized since its very beginning in terms of a definite peculiarity.

At least until the watershed of World War II, the attempt to launch the development of a market-based competitive industrial system outside the boundaries of the North European and North Atlantic world has to be considered as a complete failure. And, actually, it has been necessary to wait for the opportunities offered by the Golden Age regime for the completion of the industrialization process even in two Western (relative) latecomers such as Italy and Japan. Between 1850 and 1950, while two industrial revolutions fed the industrial success of the Western World, 'the Rest' trudged along the low road of industrial growth. And albeit over such a long period some improvements in manufacturing capabilities can be observed, their speed and intensity were far lower than is required to attain some ability to compete at the world level. A negative role, in this situation, was also played by trade liberalisation, which determined a displacement of a modern manufacturing base in the Third World:

> Deindustrialization in developing countries predated the era of global integration; both in absolute terms and as a share of world manufacturing output, the position of the developing world declined sharply between 1830 and 1860 (…). But this process continued, and indeed, accelerated, during much of the period of global integration. Between 1860 and 1913, the developing country share of world manufacturing production declined from over one-third to under a tenth.
>
> **(Bairoch and Kozul-Wright 1996: 16)**

Along the whole nineteenth century (and at least for the first three decades of the following one) the world manufacturing production firmly remained in the hands of 'advanced' countries, and only after the colonial regime started unravelling and eventually came to an end did a mechanism of import

---

[4] See on the point also Amsden and Hikino (1994).

substitution begin to work among underdeveloped economies (Bairoch 1971). A key point, in such a framework, is that in this phase regulation in underdeveloped countries was still almost completely absent, so that it can be said that

[g]overnment policies in India, Latin America, China, and the Ottoman Empire before World War I ... provide a laboratory to study the effects of liberalism on attempts to industrialize *without world-class skills*. [The result is that] [a]fter almost one hundred years, there was no obvious, organic solution to 'the rest's' economic predicament. It was in this context of industrial growth without industrialization that the developmental state was born.

(Amsden 2001: 70 and 98, emphasis added)

Hence, it is the widespread awareness of a radical market failure that can be set at the very root, in lagging economies, of a discontinuity in the stance of institutions about the underdevelopment problem. Such a change of view has been buttressed by the birth of development economics as a specific topic: which finds its raison d'être in the belief that *the absence* of an economic policy has to be considered as the cause of the missed launch of endogenous industrial development in disadvantaged areas.

Starting with the 1940s, through the emergence of a series of important contributions—Rosenstein-Rodan (1943) with reference to the backwardness of Eastern and Southern European economies, Lewis (1954) about the whole underdeveloped world, and then Singer (1964) and more widely Prebisch (1970) specifically about Latin America—a new view gained ground according to which the causes of the failure to catch-up with OIEs on the part of laggards had to be find in the inadequacy of market forces. As a consequence, public intervention—as, indeed, had already happened in OIEs themselves—was called upon as the basic instrument for the empowerment of underdeveloped economies[5]. So, it is argued by Nayyar (2003) that in the post-colonial era (i.e. after the end of World War II) most underdeveloped countries radically changed their development strategies. On the one side, they tried to limit the degree of openness and integration with the world economy; on the other the State was assigned the role of actively promoting the development of manufacturing activities, insofar as market forces were not perceived as sufficient in themselves to lead to industrialization.

---

[5] 'It was the war-torn decade of the 1940s that saw development economics emerge as a sub-discipline of academic economics ... distinguished, above all, by its exploration of the problem of *government-engineered* economic transformation' (Toye 2003: 21, emphasis added). With specific reference to the industrialization issue, to the above-mentioned references we must add at least the key contributions by Myrdal (1957) and Hirschman (1958). It goes without saying that the attention paid to development finds an important support in the parallel spreading of Keynesian economics.

The appearance of the new view can be looked at as the will to provide an answer to problems the solution of which could not be delayed any longer; so that, in the words of one of the fathers of development economics written at the end of the 1950s,

> [D]etermination [is] one of the specific characteristics of the development process in today's underdeveloped countries, namely, the fact that they are latecomers. This condition is bound to make their development *into a less spontaneous and more deliberate process* that was the case in the countries where the process first occurred.
>
> **(Hirschman 1958: 8, emphasis added)**

It can be noted that such a change in the orientation of economic policies paralleled what had already been going on for decades—indeed, in far more radical terms—in the separate world of Soviet Union, where the industrialization process was directly driven by the State, and even trade exchanges were subject to controls (see below). It happened, then, that in the years following World War II a growing share of the industrial system at the international level became more and more conditioned by institutional forces as to the direction it was to take. These are the years in which what will be later called the 'Developmental State' (DS) emerges as a new lever of industrialization.

In particular, the notion of DS—suggested for the first time by Johnson (1982 and 1999) with reference to the Japanese experience ('miracle')—relates to the way East Asian economies faced the domination of North Western economies in the manufacturing field, inventing an 'idiosyncratic response' (Woo-Cumings 1999) which was to be shared in sequence by South Korea, Taiwan, and other 'New Industrial Economies' (NIEs), up to its adoption by China itself (see below). The key feature of the DS can be found in its attempt to establish a new paradigm between a 'planning' State controlling both ownership and management, and a 'free-market' one not controlling either ownership or management (both in private hands). The aim of the DS, in this scheme, was to find a way to keep together private ownership with State guidance.

But the latter requires, as such, a state which is able not only to cope with the problem of moving towards an optimal condition given the choice set, but also with 'that of formulating the choice set itself' (Chang 1999: 194). Put in other words, this means a State being able to identify the range of activities that can be developed by building dynamic (potential) comparative advantages, i.e. activities in which the advantages are still to be achieved, going far beyond the boundaries of static Ricardian comparative advantages. As will be better argued in the following (Section 3.3), in East Asia public intervention has been implemented in particular through original policies aimed at ensuring conditional incentives to the private sector, subject to the achievement of given targets consistent with government long-run strategies. More widely, the outcome of active industrial policies is a function of the ability to outline the instrumental set of variables to be put in place in order to meet the desired goals. The best results are achieved by those countries which succeed in making their industrial systems more and more competitive at the international level, therefore gaining growing export shares, in a context in which it becomes crucial 'how vigorously and rapidly exportables [are] extracted from a sequentially rising number of import substitution sectors' (Amsden 2001).

In the remainder of this chapter four different institutional contexts are analysed in order to provide a comparative assessment of the logic that has characterized, in the course of post-war history, different attempts to set up an industrialization process. The first one, which represents the most successful industrialization project in modern times, is that prevailing in East Asia, where the building of an adequate institutional setting predates the laying down of industrial policies conducive to building dynamic comparative advantages in new production areas. The second is Latin America, where the approach to industrial development has shifted from the so-called ISI policies (favouring a first wave of industrialization in several countries) to a market-friendly approach (after the failure of ISI policies in fuelling a sustained growth since the 1970s), which however did not lead to any effective results in terms of (re)industrialization. The third is the aggregate of the Euroasian transition economies, which also (and suddenly) shifted from centrally planned policies aimed at forcing industrial development to a complete vaporization of any attempt to regulate market forces, leading to rapid de-industrialization—especially in former USSR. The fourth is Africa, i.e. perhaps the only area in the world where a real industrialization process on endogenous grounds has not taken place at all.

3.3 The 'Asian model'

3.3.1 An overall view

Manufacturing development in the Asian area has emerged gradually, passing along a continuum that has involved different economies at different points in time. This can be appreciated looking at the—more and more visible—export performance of individual countries, starting with Japan, followed by the so-called 'Asian tigers' (or NIEs: South Korea, Taiwan, Hong Kong, and Singapore), and then by the economies of the 'second tier', i.e. Thailandia, Malaysia, and Indonesia. The advent of China has introduced in this world a new key variable, that is the size of the economic system, which—as we have shown in Chapter 2—has played a crucial role in re-shaping manufacturing development at the world level. Later, it has gained ground—even if on a quite different scale—the emergence of two further laggards such as Vietnam and Cambodia.

The continuity of the industrialization process in the area—resembling something like a baton exchange in a sprint relay—has triggered a spate of studies aimed at identifying the common traits—beyond national specificities—of the phenomenon (see below). This section tries to provide a brief account of this work, looking in particular at the role played by public institutions.

Before approaching the topic, it is worth recalling a key point that has marked the debate about industrialization in the Asian continent since the post-war years, harking back to the analysis of the rationality of capitalism by Max Weber (1968 [1922]), according to whom 'modern capitalism' (shaped by the search for profits and the rational organization of labour) is but a specific feature of Western economic systems.[6] The issue, in particular, lies at the very root of the monumental study carried out by Gunnar Myrdal (1968) about the 'Asian Drama': that is the description of the failure of Asian countries—with the notable exception of Japan—to enter a development path in the course of the nineteenth century, vis à vis the rapid catching up of European countries as against the United States. Even if it has to be stressed that Asian Drama did not pay attention to what were to become the most dynamic countries in the whole area (Japan, Korea, Taiwan, Hong Kong, Singapore, and China itself) and was mainly centred on Southern Asia (India in particular, where a large part of the book was written), the position of Myrdal was undoubtedly pessimistic. As highlighted by Nayyar (2019), this view stemmed from the conviction—to be envisaged in the perspective of Myrdal's circular and cumulative causation theory—according to which economic development is not simply a matter of economic variables, but is instead strongly affected by institutional factors that, as such, can only be changed in the long-run[7]. The point is that institutional change was

---

[6] A quite similar view is expressed by Landes (1969), in his introduction to one of the most important books on the history of industrial development.

[7] At the methodological level Kanbur (2019) emphasizes three elements in Myrdal's view: the need for making explicit the values underpinning economic research (instead of pretending they can be bypassed

then hard to imagine, so that nobody could think at the time that in some fifty years things would have changed so sharply: and as recently observed, '[i]n 1968 the answer as to whether the twenty-first would be the "Asian Century" almost certainly would have been clearly negative' (Findlay 2019: 98), so that '[Myrdal] cannot be blamed for not being able to foresee how reality would unfold in Asia over the next fifty years' (Nayyar 2019: 10).

Still at the end of the 1960s, then, the picture was one of a persistent economic stagnation of a continent which a couple of centuries before was instead at the top of the wealth in the world,[8] and which, starting with the Industrial Revolution in Great Britain, had constantly been losing ground, originating what has been called the 'Great Divergence' and marking the end of 'a polycentric world with no dominant center' (Pomeranz 2000: 4). So, the important results obtained by emerging Asia (even by India, where as we have seen in Chapter 2 manufacturing output growth averaged 5.4% between 1995 and 2018) appear clearly at odds with what only a few decades ago was a consolidated view. How was such a sharp change of perspective possible?

We can begin by paying attention just to the 'cultural specificity' issue, according to which—*against* Weber's arguments and Myrdal's conclusions—the current success of East Asian economies would be the outcome of a set of cultural factors (a bent towards hard work, a strong propensity to saving, a habit of accepting authoritarian behaviour of public powers), more or less ascribable to Confucianism. Which in turn would imply—as argued by mainstream economists—the impossibility to 'export' the model outside its original boundaries, towards other economic systems lacking by definition a similar cultural background.[9]

In such respect it can be observed that the principle according to which, due to their very nature, the so-called cultural factors are exogenous and—as far as they are path-dependent—cannot be influenced at the political level is far from being straightforward. And just in the archetypical case of Japan, representing the paradigm of the 'Asian model', the achievements in terms of the extent of the industrialization process and of manufacturing competitiveness have to be considered, first of all, as the result of the elaboration of an explicit industrialization programme hinging upon the purposeful behaviour of the

by 'scientific' analysis); the necessity of going beyond economic principles in order to understand the transformations of society; the need to find a balance between state and market.

[8] 'Until around 1750, Asia accounted for almost three-fifths of [the] world population and world income, while China and India together accounted for one half of the world population and world income' (Nayyar 2019: 10).

[9] For a description of the reasons at the roots of such thesis and an attempt to test it on empirical grounds see Liang (2010). On the actual relevance of 'idiosyncratic' factors in facilitating economic development in East Asia and the 'replicability' of the model outside its boundaries see Chang (1995, 2006, ch. 4).

state. In this framework, the 'economic environment' itself has been *built*, as it is but the outcome of a project that has been rationally pursued. As observed by the father of the notion of 'Developmental State' himself,

> The famous Japanese consensus, that is, the broad popular support and willing-ness to work hard for economic development … is not so much a cultural trait as a matter of hard experience and of the mobilization of a large majority of the population to support economic goals. (…) The priorities of the Japanese state … are in this sense a product not of culture or social organization or insularity but of rationality.
>
> **(Johnson 1982: 307)**

In the whole Asian context, actually, the 'quality of bureaucracy' is far less the result of a tradition than that of the deliberate acquisition from abroad of institutions suited to the promotion of industrial development, that have been imported, assimilated, and adapted to the national context—just in the same way as this has been done at the technological level. As far as Japan in particular is concerned, the construction of its 'modern' institutional shape (which has called for a massive import of organizational models from Europe, see Westney (1987) and the launching of industrialization (calling for the import of technologies, see Morris-Suzuki (1994) can be both set within the years of the Meiji era (1868–1912).

What happens in the face of such facts is simply that cultural factors—that certainly do exist—are quite often evoked ex post in order to explain phe-nomena they are not related to at the causal level, up to the point that it is well possible to interpret their role according to utterly opposite perspectives.[10]

In general, the final goal of the economic policy of the Asian Developmen-tal State has been to pursue industrial development, and not macroeconomic stability (even less—with the notable exception of Taiwan for historical reasons—the control of inflation).[11] The definition of such an objective has involved a constant search for the upgrading of the industrial system, to be achieved through a policy of resource allocation oriented towards investments (including selection at the sectoral level) and a concomitant compression—at least in relative terms—of consumption. The cornerstone

[10] 'Confucian culture has been there for centuries but did not lead to development earlier. Indeed, until the 1950s, many people blamed Confucianism for holding East Asia back' (Chang 2003: 119).

[11] 'When they were faced with external shocks … adjustments were not simply seen as an exercise in getting short-run macroeconomic balances right, but seen *as a step within a continuous transformation of their economic structures towards high-technology industries*' (Chang 2006: 125, emphasis added). Just as an example, it can be recalled that the average rate of inflation in South Korea has been since the 1960s around 17%, almost reaching 20% in the 1970s.

of such a policy lies in the aim to acquire proprietary knowledge in strategic activities. In many cases—especially in Japan and South Korea—this goal has been pursued by *discouraging* investments from abroad and financing the import of new technologies via the extra profits obtained in the internal market. A specific feature of this policy—which sharply differentiates the Asian model from those of other emerging economies—is that the development of an endogenous internal supply certainly reflects the logic of import substitution but is first of all explicitly oriented towards the growth of exports.[12]

Having said this, what sorts of instruments have been put in place in order to get the final (and intermediate) goals of the Developmental State? In general, it can be noted that the stance of the authorities, as well as their reliability, has been grounded upon a peculiar cornerstone: i.e. the building of a substantial independence from the influence of lobbying groups, and the simultaneous conditionality of incentives, to be provided subject to the attainment of pre-defined targets in terms of economic performance. This approach has been made possible by a political realism which has allowed to select, at any one time, the industries to be privileged on the basis of economic criteria (i.e. their market potential and the actual capabilities attained by national industry) and to monitor the effects of the adopted policies—so as to introduce corrections where appropriate. Even if in the outlined framework a wide spectrum of different solutions has found place, the basic features of the approach are common among the single economies of the area. In the following a brief account is given about two important emerging industrial countries such as South Korea and China.

3.3.2 South Korea

The Korean case is perhaps the most impressive in the whole area, both in terms of the degree of determination in pursuing the industrialization process and in terms of the results that have been actually achieved. Following Chang (1994, ch. 4; 2006, ch. 2), the head start of the whole process can be found in the coups d'état by General Park Chung Hee, leading to his coming

---

[12] In this sense, '[i]mport substitution was the mother of export growth' (Amsden 2001: 171). The orientation towards an export strategy characterizes the development of manufacturing in these countries since the very beginning, as is testified by the setting up of institutions like the Japanese Supreme Export Council (which in more recent times has been reproduced both in South Korea and China). See Johnson (1982), Wade (1990), Amsden (2001), Chang (2003, 2006).

to power in 1961.[13] The advent of such a leader (who maintained his role at the top of the state for almost 20 years until his assassination in 1979, strongly limiting the civil rights in the country) created an unprecedented situation, insofar as it brought about the setting up of a series of measures designed to channel the resources of the economic system towards a massive development of new industrial activities. Such measures included (Chang 1994): (1) the complete nationalization of the banking system (which was partially re-privatized only in 1982), and consequently a total control of the direction of financial flows; (2) the centralization of the power in a single ministry (Economic Planning Board) joining together both the side of taxes and that of expenses (so as to eliminate any frictions between the two levels); (3) the imprisonment of many important businessmen, and their release in return of the promise to 'serve the nation through enterprise', that is to commit themselves to build new plants in the industries indicated by the state; (4) the mobilization of the public opinion through the idea of a 'Renaissance of the Nation', according to which workers were defined 'industrial soldiers' and businessmen were given medals for their achievement of targeted results (especially in foreign markets); the centralization in the State hands of the propriety of enterprises belonging to the sectors that were deemed to be strategic (energy, fertilizers, steel).[14]

The key role attributed to the industrialization strategy, and the coherence with which it has been maintained for such a long time, reflect a view strongly influenced by Japanese corporatism. In this framework the fundamental variables to be kept under control by the policy maker are first of all the capital accumulation at the national level (i.e. excluding investments from abroad) and the attainment of economies of scale in manufacturing. In particular, the South Korean industrialization model is explicitly grounded upon the centrality of large firms. Such a focus is quite consistent with the logic that had characterized the development of manufacturing in advanced industrial countries along the 1960s. Yet in the Korean experience this trait has been persisting far beyond the period of the take-off, whereas in the latter it has been followed, as we have argued in previous chapters, by a gradual fragmentation of the industrial structure along vertical lines.

---

[13] General Park was brought up in the Japanese army during the occupation of Manchukuo, and gained visibility within the military world in the course of the Korean War (1950–53).

[14] As can be seen, this is a policy that can be conceived only within the boundaries of an authoritarian regime. But it is worth to note that authoritarian regimes have also characterized other economic systems (often much more heavy-handed), which were not able to develop anything similar as to the development of a competitive industry.

The aim to channel financial resources towards capital accumulation was paralleled by the penalization of domestic consumption, to be obtained through all available instruments—public banks were prevented from providing credit to consumption, personal taxes were kept high, the import of consumption goods was discouraged by high tariff barriers).[15] This led to an exceptionally intense structural change in terms of the manufacturing output share. Between 1963 and 1972 the South Korean manufacturing annual average rate of growth was astonishingly high (18.3%); in the wake of a programme called 'Heavy and Chemical Industrialization' (HCI), growth rose to 24.7% in the following five years, in the face of the quite apparent slowdown in growth rates that affected the whole industrial world.[16] The weight of the industries included in the programme rose from 22.8% in 1961 to 39% in 1974, and then to 44.5% in 1978 (Wade 1990). In this connection it is worth mentioning the amazing performance of the shipbuilding industry, created from scratch by a personal decision of Park, that in slightly more than a decade (between 1973 and 1986) raised its world output share from zero to 21.6% (Chang 2006).

The identification of different strategic sectors according to the various phases of manufacturing development is a constant feature of the targeting process implemented by the Economic Planning Board, through a series of five-year plans. The idea behind such a strategy is that in an underdeveloped economy, even if an industry may not be profitable at a given point in time, this does not mean it cannot succeed in becoming profitable. Whilst it involves a limitation of the role played by market forces at the 'local' level, this approach pays attention to the conditions that can enable a strong presence in the market in the long-run:[17] in this sense the key feature of the Korean State's view of the market economy lies in a dynamic view of comparative advantages, whereby the centre of the stage is taken by technical change and learning rather than allocative efficiency (Chang 1994).

The key to the functioning of the model lies in the conditional character of incentives (broadly defined), which is grounded on the credibility of the government as to its capability to withdraw them (even for important economic

---

[15] 'Given such a clear … anti-consumption bias, Korean macroeconomic policy can be more appropriately understood as "investment management" rather than as "aggregate demand management"' (Chang 2006: 76–77).

[16] Data are taken from Chang (1994). About the slowdown of growth in advanced countries in the early 1970s see Matthews (1982).

[17] The White Paper of the Economic Planning Board in 1968 emphasizes that 'excessive competition can result in social waste'. Again in 1984 it stresses—at a relatively advanced stage of manufacturing development in the country—that 'the market mechanism cannot be entirely trusted to increase the competitiveness of Korean industries'. Both quotations are reported by Chang (respectively, 1996 and 1994).

actors) in the face of a failure to meet the assigned objectives. This stance survived the death of Park himself (an Industrial Development Law was still issued in 1986), and was abandoned only in the early 1990s, making room for a growing opening of international exchanges and capital flows. The point, however, is that at that time the capability of the Korean industrial system to stay in international markets had become competition-proof, so that trade openness could only make its performance better.

3.3.3 China

A possible starting point to provide a description of the role played by institutions in the Chinese case—i.e. in the country which is at the same time the latest in having joined a development path, by far the larger, and possibly the best performer, at least as to the speed of the process—is to evaluate its evolution as compared to the other Asian giant, that is India. From this point of view it can be said that, even if their advent took place almost simultaneously (India got independence in 1947, communist China was born in 1949), at the end of the 1970s the two countries were already diverging as to the substance of their industrial activities—as is testified by an industrialization rate that in 1980 was in India about half of China's.[18] It can be easily inferred that such a gap is not just a function of market openness in China (which only took place in following years), but has to be evaluated in light of what happened in the years that predate the advent of China's reforms. A key point about such a difference lies in the missed transformation of agriculture in India, vis à vis the complete disruption of Chinese agriculture in the aftermath of the revolution, which completely erased the feudal world.

The first push to industrialization comes just from the reorganization of the agricultural system; but it is the whole institutional framework of the newborn republic that—shaped by a 'perennial … search for institutions that seek

---

[18] In 1950 the economic structure of the two countries was still quite similar: per capita GDP was 65 US dollars (prices of 1960) for China and 62 for India; agricultural employment shares were 77% and 72%, respectively, and industrial employment shares were 7 and 11%. In 1980 industry share as to GDP had reached 49% in China, but was still at 22% in India, and the distance did not shorten in following years (in 2003 the shares had become 53% and 26%, respectively). For a wider account about such data, including an evaluation of the role played by public intervention in the two contexts see Saith (2008). As to the slowness of India manufacturing development (and the limited rate of industrialization it reached, which led to talk of early de-industrialization), see Basu and Maertens (2007), Kambhampati (2016), and above all Dasgupta and Singh (2005) and Singh (2009), who underline that during the mid-1990s the growth pattern had begun to diverge from the one set out by Kuznets, showing an exceptionally strong expansion—for that level of development—of the services' share. Measures obviously differ depending on their being referred to the whole industry or to manufacturing only (and above all on their being calculated at constant or current prices). A comparison between the two countries with reference to industrial policies can also be found in Dahlman (2009).

out, release and exploit new potential sources of accumulation and growth'
(Saith 2008: 34), and taking advantage of the institutional vacuum created by
the revolution itself—points to the building of a governmental organization
functional to a development strategy.

In general, the very authoritarian nature of the state involves as such an
unconditional ability to direct the economic system through the implementation of administrative measures. Yet the goal of industrial development in
China has been pursued by the recurrence of all the canonical instruments
of public intervention that had already been used by OIEs: public property
of firms, selective allocation of credit flows (allowed by a credit system that
was in public hands as in South Korea), tax benefits for targeted industries,
barriers to imports, public procurement, and special attention paid to the
role of large firms (Dahlman 2009). In the years that followed the opening of
the market introduced by the launch of the 'four modernizations' set forth
by Deng Xiaoping (in 1978), the planned economy was gradually flanked
by a market economy, mainly constituted by the so-called Town and Village
Enterprises (TVEs) owned by municipalities. TVEs were mainly concentrated in the labour-intensive industries, so as to take advantage of the main
resource of the country at the time. In the same period the State Owned
Enterprises (SOEs) also underwent a restructuring process (but they were
not privatized due to the absence of an adequate capital market). The first
state document to explicitly use the term 'industrial policy' was the seventh
Five-Year Plan (1986–90), which was followed by a series of plans aimed
at enhancing industrialization through the promotion of 'pillar industries'.
But it was only starting with the tenth Five-Year Plan (2001–05), that 'industrial policies in the spirit of selective intervention were put into practice on a
systematic scale' (Lo and Wu 2014: 315).

A peculiar trait of the Chinese variety of the East Asian model is the special
relevance attributed to foreign direct investment (FDI) flows from abroad
(which, as we have seen, on the contrary had been discouraged the most
in Japan and South Korea). The main problem of FDI inflows—that is, the
possible crowding out of local supply—was bypassed by simply concentrating them within the walls of Special Economic Zones (SEZs) opened to free
trade, unlike the rest of the economy which was opened later, and binding the
investors to export the whole output produced in the area.[19] Foreign multinationals interested in the internal market were forced instead to set up joint
ventures with national firms, thereby favouring (also through coercion) technology transfer from abroad. In the course of the 1990s the plan economy

---

[19] The constraint was gradually relaxed as far as the SEZs started including national firms as well.

faded away, and there was an increase in the financial resources allocated to firms by way of focused incentives. Employment growth in the private sector compensated the shrinking in the number of firms and employees in the public sector, while the SEZs increased in number and growth. This phase ended up with the decision to join the WTO (December 2001).

Based on qualitative evidence, and surveying previous empirical research, a book edited by Watanabe (2014) argues in this framework that the development of Chinese manufacturing has been largely favoured since its beginning by policies facilitating a 'vigorous entry' of new small suppliers. That is to say it has been characterized, especially in durables, by economies of specialization. Even if this does not exclude a parallel search for scale economies, especially in heavy industries,[20] such a view suggests that the development of markets for intermediates (of 'supportive value chains') has played an important role in reducing fixed costs, fostering the emergence of upstream and downstream linkages. In this sense China's industrialization model departs from that of South Korea, and shows some similarities to that of Japan, where economies of specialization tying small and medium-sized firms into a close array of inter-firm linkages have played an important role in shaping the evolution of industrial structure (Whittaker 1997).

As will be better argued in Chapter 6, after the great financial crisis in 2008 the slowdown of demand from the US, EU, and Japanese economies has set a constraint on exports as an engine of growth, pushing the whole emerging East Asian world—where the dependence on exports was especially strong— towards a new centrality of domestic demand, and the deployment of explicit strategies of Domestic Demand Led Growth. This has assumed peculiar relevance for China, where, after decades in which consumption had fallen in favour of capital accumulation, between 2006 and 2015 the manufacturing industry's propensity to export (exports as a percentage of production) dropped from 35 to 13%. At the same time, import penetration (imports in relation to apparent domestic demand) also dropped from 22.6 to 8.3%, i.e. imported inputs (to be re-exported as components of assembled goods) have been replaced by inputs produced domestically, also serving the domestic market. The sum of the two tendencies outlines a situation in which Chinese development begins gradually to move away from an export-led logic, and behaviour that is typical of developed economies of (very) large size begins to gain ground.[21]

---

[20] Nolan (1996: 27) suggests in such respect that 'large-scale, state-owned, predominantly heavy industrial sector, was at the heart of China's growth in the 1980s'.

[21] This is paralleled by the widening of the supply matrix; a survey of the results obtained by Chinese manufacturing in different manufacturing sectors is provided by Yang and Yu (2011).

More recently, active industrial policies have furtherly fostered internal supply. In 2015 the plan 'Made in China 2025' has defined ten-year targets aimed at getting a gradual independence from imports of intermediate goods, and at enhancing investment in selected industries. A second plan, spanning from 2026 to 2049 (centenary of the revolution) explicitly aspires to make China a leading country at the world level in the field of technological innovation (Sampaolo et al. 2021).

3.4 From import substitution to market openness in Latin America

Starting from the 1930s and till the beginning of the 1980s the development process in Latin American countries hinged upon a process of Import-Substitution Industrialization (ISI), that is on the purposeful construction— guided by the state—of an industrial system aimed at substituting manufacturing imports with domestic production.

Such a strategy was inspired by a nationalistic sentiment—in particular, the will to reduce the political and economic influence of the United States in the area—but was also motivated by economic reasoning, given the historical high dependence of Latin American economies from the primary and mining sectors. More specifically, the idea known as the Prebisch-Singer hypothesis became popular, that industrialization was the only way to escape from a long-run economic decline caused by a progressive reduction of the commodity prices relative to those of manufacturing goods, which would have caused the terms of trade of commodity-based economies—like those of Latin America—to deteriorate in favour of more advanced (and industrialized) ones.[22]

The policy instruments used to implement the ISI strategies largely coincided with those observed in the same years in Korea and Taiwan (Baer 1984).[23] They included import tariffs and quotas to discourage imports of manufacturing goods that were also produced domestically; direct involvement of the state in strategic productions (heavy and military industries); favoured access to bank lending through public credit; attraction of foreign direct investments to import technologies and know-how in new industries. Yet, while instruments were similar in Latin America and East Asia, policy targets differed substantially (Jenkins 1991; Bruton 1998).

---

[22] See Singer (1964). For a detailed analysis of the Prebisch–Singer hypothesis and of its sophistication in the following decades, see Ho (2012).
[23] As argued above, however, neither Korea nor Taiwan (differently from China) have relied on foreign direct investment as an ingredient of their industrialization strategies.

First of all, while Asian industrial policies were ex-ante selective in the choice of the targets, not only between sectors but also among firms within the same sector, protectionism in Latin America was basically indiscriminate, as import substitution was not meant as a way to build dynamic comparative advantages—in order to temporarily protect infant strategic industries—but to favour local production per se. Moreover, while protectionism of infant industries in Asia was part of a long-term development strategy focused on exports, with the goal of building internationally competitive productions able to intercept foreign demand coming from the advanced economies, the Latin America ISI strategy was inward-oriented, with domestic productions serving the domestic demand, and with inflows of foreign direct investments and imports of machinery and equipment providing the technologies that were beyond the possibility frontier of local producers. Finally, in contrast with the Asian Developmental State, the Latin American experience was characterized by the absence of binding intermediate targets that local companies had to reach to remain eligible for public support. In other words, protectionism in Latin America came without conditionality, which reflected the difficulty of building public institutions independent from powerful vested interests.

Although already in the 1960s an attention to foreign market gradually emerged, through intra-area trade agreements and export subsidies,[24] no substantial change in the process of industrialization in Latin America emerged before the sudden change in the economic regime that occurred in the 1980s as a result of the burst of the debt crisis which, starting from Mexico in 1982, affected all countries in the region (Ocampo 2014).

The crisis has to be considered as endogenous to the inward-oriented development strategy. Decade after decade this strategy resulted in a growing balance of payments deficit, as the increasing volumes of imports (of basic inputs, starting with oil and capital goods) instrumental to the expansion of the domestic production capacity were not mirrored by a sufficient increase of exports, which remained structurally weak. The high stock of foreign debt accumulated became unsustainable at the beginning of the 1980s, when macro-economic conditions at the global level worsened. On the one hand, the slowdown of the advanced economies reduced even further the export

---

[24] In 1960 Guatemala, Honduras, El Salvador, and Nicaragua established the Mercado Comun Centroamericano, which was abolished in 1969 after political tensions among member states. In the same year South American countries and Mexico established a similar agreement, known as Asociacion Latinoamericana de Libre Comercio (ALALC). Its failure in delivering the expected reduction in trade barriers among member states pushed some of them to establish in 1969 the Grupo Andino. In 1982, ALALC was replaced by the Asociation Latinoamericana de Integracion (ALADI). In 1991 Argentina, Brazil, Uruguay, and Paraguay established the free trade agreement MERCOSUR, while Mexico signed in 1994 a trade agreement with USA and Canada (NAFTA). All these issues are further documented in Chapter 6.

performance of Latin American countries; on the other, the sharp increase in interest rates decided by the Federal Reserve to control US inflation caused an outflow of financial capital from Latin America and a jump in the cost of foreign debt.

In the two final decades of the century the ISI strategy was totally disman-tled in favour of a free-market system. The reforms that were introduced steered policy in precisely the opposite direction, with the objective of increasing efficiency in existing sectors rather than developing new sec-tors, pursuing static comparative advantages—in this case, abundance of unskilled labour and natural resources. The radicality and direction of the institutional change make the Latin American experience similar to what, more or less in the same years and under the same ideological paradigm— the Washington Consensus—occurred in Eastern Europe and even more drastically in the Soviet Union (see below).[25] As for the transition out of the communist regimes, also in the case of Latin America domestic productions were suddenly exposed to international competition, through the abatement of import quotas and tariffs and through complete market de-regulation. At the same time state-owned companies, including those in the banking sector, were privatized. Moreover, tight controls to monetary and fiscal policy were imposed to bring public spending (and deficits) under control. Differently from the Asian experience, therefore, market liberalization did not come after a strategic repositioning of domestic productions towards the export markets, but was itself the means through which international market openness was realized.[26]

The radical change in the political economy approach (partially) con-tributed to address some of the structural weaknesses of Latin American development, that is a low export-orientation of the domestic economy and high volatility of domestic prices associated with persistent high inflation. Competitive pressure from imports, new inflows of foreign direct invest-ments attracted by a more stable macroeconomic framework and by the dismissal of state-owned assets, and a stronger economic integration with the more advanced economies partially reshaped the sectoral specialization. At the same time, the control of exchange rate fluctuations—often through fixed exchange rates with US dollar—and restrictive fiscal policies brought inflation under control, at least in the short run.

---

[25] In most of the cases, the liberalization was imposed as a pre-condition to access debt relief mea-sures and receive assistance by IMF and World Bank. See Edwards (1995) and United Nations (2017, chapter 3).

[26] In Chile the process of liberalization had already begun in the 1970s (starting with the coup d'état in 1973) but did not prevent the country from suffering a debt crisis in 1982. See Singh et al. (2005).

On the other hand, these same reforms forced a (premature) de-industrialization in the entire region, which returned to be strongly dependent on natural resources, as non-competitive manufacturing industries, left alone in confronting imports, were abandoned. Manufacturing was often seen by the local political élites who came to power in those years as the 'illegitimate son of protectionism and state-interference: symbol of the worst "vices" of the previous development model' (Palma 2019a: 946; authors' translation).[27]

Hence, the economy of Latin America downgraded in terms of sectoral specialization—from manufacturing to extraction industries—and in terms of technological know-how, as what remained of manufacturing was to a large extent linked to either processed agricultural and mineral products (as in the case of Argentina, Brazil, Chile, Uruguay) or to intermediate assembly of inputs imported from abroad (as in the case of Mexican *maquilas* close to the US border) under strict control of foreign multinationals (Shaffaedin 2005, Dingemans and Ross 2012). The result was a weak capacity of endogenous technological upgrading and a marginalization of Latin American economies in the international trade network (Palma 2009).[28] At the same time, the reforms implemented in the 1980s in order to liberalize the economies in Latin America, while favouring exports, also induced a strong increase in imports, generating new tensions on the balance of payments which resulted in new financial crises in the mid-1990s and early 2000s. This disequilibrium came from the asymmetric effects of the policy measures, which eliminated barriers to imports without actively supporting exports[29]

---

[27] See also Palma (2019b) for a reflection on the theoretical premises of economic policy in Chile (and other Latin American economies).

[28] According to Oreiro et al. (2020), in the Brazilian case premature deindustrialization was due to the consequences of real exchange rate overvaluation which has occurred since the early 2000s and by the reduction of the economic complexity of the industrial system (in the sense suggested by Hausmann et al. 2011). As to the effects of the Washington Consensus policies in Brazil see also Nassif et al. (2020), and about their consequences in terms of 'regressive specialization' Nassif e Castilho (2020). Similarly, in Chile between 1974 and 1982—during the first wave of liberalization policies—about 16% of manufacturing companies went bankrupt (Kats 2001). An empirical exercise aimed at determining the possible causes of deindustrialization in Colombia, Brazil, Ecuador, Chile, Uruguay, Bolivia, Mexico, Costa Rica, and Argentina shows that deindustrialization in the region is related to the fall in tariffs (following the requirements of the Washington Consensus) and to a Dutch disease process (Hoyos López 2017). A further empirical analysis of de-industrialization in Argentina, Brazil, Chile and Mexico can be found in Castillo and Neto (2016). About premature deindustrialization in developing countries see also Tregenna (2013).

[29] According to Ernst (2005), during the 1990s Argentina and Brazil registered an average annual growth of exports of 8.5% and 6.0% respectively, while imports grew in the same period by an average of 25.2% and 11.8%. Differently from the other Latin American economies, in Mexico (manufacturing) exports were prioritized by the Government. However, the *maquila* model of industrialization did not solve the problem of trade imbalance: according to Palma (2005), between 1991 and 2000 exports from *maquilas* grew by 301% and imports by 319%.

and caused a real appreciation of local currencies, which made exports less attractive and imports less expensive.

Overall, the years following the dismantlement of ISI delivered poor results in terms of income and productivity dynamics, with economic growth during the 1980s either negative or very weak (the so-called 'lost decade') and its recovery in the 1990s being modest—indeed, even lower than the dynamics observed during the ISI decades (Ocampo and Martin 2003, Ocampo 2005, Palma 2003a and 2009, Cimoli and Correa 2005).

The early years of the new century marked a significant improvement in the economic and industrial performance in Latin American countries. However, despite a partial return of selective (sectoral) policies in Argentina, Mexico, Chile and Brazil (Peres 2013), this did not bring about a substantial change in the regional development path, which remained highly dependent upon the exogenous variation of commodity prices in international markets—boiling down to a basically extractive-export model (Grazzi et al. 2016, ch. 1; Gorenstein and Ortiz 2018). Indeed, the expansionary phase which lasted till the mid-2010s was mostly driven by the boom in the prices of agricultural products and minerals, which generated an increase in income and in domestic consumption, with positive effects for local productions serving the domestic market. Looking in particular at manufacturing, it has been noted (Correa and Stumpo 2017) that market signals have not favoured structural changes in manufacturing, but on the contrary they have fostered a lock-in situation where the incentives for channelling investments into new sectors were very weak.

Overall, opposite to what happened in East Asia, this translated into a fall of labour productivity in relative terms (expressed as a percentage of US productivity) in the largest Latin American countries (Argentina, Brazil, Mexico) after 1980 (Palma 2019b), taking them 'into the quicksand of a middle-income trap'.[30] This situation resembles what happened in the same period to Russia and other countries formerly belonging to Soviet Union, which, abundant in natural resources, after the collapse of their industrial system still do struggle to diversify their economy away from extraction industries.

3.5 What remains of planning. The advent of capitalism in former Soviet Union and Eastern Europe

As has been recalled above (Section 3.1), in the course of history state intervention has been, under any sky, at the root of every attempt to pursue industrialization. But, in this context, a peculiar trait has characterized the

---

[30] On the definition of 'middle-income trap' see in particular Kharas and Kohli (2011).

development of the industrial system in the Eurasian former communist bloc, where the industrialization strategy pursued since the early 1930s, after the fading away of the NEP[31], and more and more after World War II, was marked by the aim of radically solving the problem of market failures by replacing market signals with central planning. This obviously gave the state a key role in the building of a domestic production system, and—from this point of view—the Soviet model can be viewed as a special type of Developmental State. In this sense, it shows many features in common with the other models we have considered so far, and in particular with the East Asian one.

Similarly to what happened first in Japan and then in other Asian emerging economies, the growth process under the Soviet guidance was driven by a state actively promoting an increasing accumulation of fixed capital (capital deepening) in the economic system (Easterly and Fischer 1994).[32] At the same time, however, in no other industrial development experience the public control of the means of production was so exclusive and long-lasting (resisting, without substantial changes, up to the mid-1980s). It was grounded on a chain of command that, starting from GOSPLAN (the State Planning Committee), could reach the single factories, determining quantities, the value of exchange, and the destination of output.[33]

The logic behind the central planning of production was functional, on the domestic side, to forcefully orient the consumption choices according to the political priorities set by public authorities. At the international level, the goal was to design a coordinated division of labour among communist economies into the different production activities, so as to build a self-sufficient economic system (largely) isolated from capitalism. In this respect, the establishment in 1949 of the Council for Mutual Economic Assistance (COMECON), which dissolved in 1991 after the collapse of the Soviet Union, can be read as the communist alternative to the European Economic Community (born with the Treaty of Rome in 1957).

In this world the push towards sectoral specialization among the different economies belonging to the same integrated area did not come from the market-based logic of comparative advantages, but was shaped from the top, with a complex set of bureaucratic arrangements including bilateral or multilateral specialization and cooperation agreements, through which some

---

[31] The Novaja Ekonomičeskaja Politika (New Economic Policy) was a state-oriented mixed economic policy put in place by Lenin in the early 1920s.

[32] Indeed, the industrialization process in Russia had already taken its first steps in the last decade of the eighteenth century, strongly driven by an explicit industrial policy as well (see Gerschenkron 1962).

[33] See here Kaser and Zielinsky (1970) and Hackett et al. (2017). The central planning approach followed in Communist regimes has been interpreted differently depending on the specific country under scrutiny. It was—and remained—stricter in Soviet Union and Romania as compared to the other Socialist Republics, as for instance Hungary, which as early as in 1968 adopted some forms of market socialism where the central planners were no longer to set obligatory production targets and some prices were even set freely.

COMECON members agreed to supply given volumes of specific commodities, intermediates or final goods (investing in the related process of research and development) while others agreed to absorb such volumes via their domestic demand.[34]

The central planning mechanism for governing industrial production resulted in a hybrid system in which the pattern of sectoral specialization was partially influenced by the natural resource endowments and technical and organizational capabilities of the different economies. At the same time, it was constrained by the control and discretion exerted by national political élites and especially by the Politburo in the USSR, through a tight coordination of the (multiannual) economic plans and the strict control of the values of exchange of the different products (which rarely reflected those prevailing at the global level).

Such a hybrid system, focusing upon capital accumulation, struggled to maintain a sustained output growth since the 1970s, both because it became increasingly difficult for central planners to balance input and outputs firm-by-firm and sector-by-sector in a world of increasingly complex products (requiring different technologies including the new-born ICTs), and because the access to the technological frontier reached by the more advanced capitalist economies was very limited if not prevented at all (IMF et al. 1991).

Export bans on key-technologies prevented COMECON members from purchasing sophisticated products made in Western Europe, USA, and Japan, and at the same time the low quality of COMECON productions made then not suitable for exchanges with the advanced economies, which in turn limited the amount of hard currencies available for import purchases.[35] Furthermore, the central planning system and the Cold War tensions between USA and USSR did not offer strong incentives for foreign investors (from the advanced economies) to establish local productions, as they were constrained to serve local demand and were subject to stringent non-market rules. It should come at no surprise, then, that at the end of the 1980s more than 90% of production in the Soviet Union was centrally planned by state-owned enterprises (IMF et al. 1991), and that two-thirds of the trade flows activated by COMECON members remained within the COMECON area.

---

[34] A detailed description of such agreements as well as an evaluation of their (actually weak) effectiveness in fostering economic integration among COMECON members can be found in Crane and Skoller (1988). Further information on COMECON can be found in various works that can be found in the US Library of Congress, available at: www.Countrystudies.us.

[35] From 1950s Western countries established the COCOM (Coordinated Committee for Multilateral Export Control) to put an embargo on COMECON countries for key products and technologies.

In such a context, the sudden transition from central planning to a pure market-based system, which abruptly followed the fall of the Berlin Wall in 1989, caused a huge drop in output in the whole area (of about 40% between 1989 and 1994; see Fischer et al. 1996). In fact, the collapse of the Soviet Union was accompanied not only by a change in the political regime (from single party to democracy, at least nominally), but also by a single burst of change in the institutional setting, the so-called all-out approach to government reforms, which forced a total reset in doing business. These reforms 'include[d] rapid price and trade liberalization, accompanied by a determined stabilization program [...]; a quick move to current account convertibility; the immediate opening of markets to entry by new private businesses; [...] privatization of state-owned companies, demonopolization of industry [...]' (World Bank 1996: 9).

It has to be stressed that in this case the simultaneous implementation of such policies without building up market institutions beforehand entailed, other than a long-lasting recession, the vanishing into thin air of the whole productive system, and a massive dissipation of human capital that was unprecedented in modern history (Chang and Nolan 1995; Lo 1995; Stiglitz 2002).[36] As observed by Lin (2009), for such a violent shock to have stimulating effects on the industrial structure, it would have required that the 'weak' part of the production system should have been relatively small—and not the largest component. In fact, the all-out approach involved:

[not only] [a] huge deterioration in … human rights for most people, including the right to live safely, to employment, to decent food, to a decent education housing and health service, … [but also that] [t]he enthusiasm of post-communist 'capitalist triumphalism' … may have caused a major mistake in assessing not only the desired speed of the transition, but also the desirable economic functions of the state over an extended transition period[,] … in which private agents tend, more than under other circumstances, to look towards the short-term and speculation rather than towards longer-term investment, so that the gap between private and social benefits may have been especially wide.

(Chang and Nolan 1995: 4 and 39).[37]

---

[36] The most evident counter example—as we have documented above—is the maintaining of public property and control over domestic financial flows and capital movements in the Chinese case, and in general the set of strategies pursued by the East Asian economies: 'China, Vietnam and other east Asian transitional economies did not follow the Washington Consensus and adopted a dual-track, gradual approach—referred to by some economists as the "Asian approach"' (Lin 2009: 51).

[37] It may be worth recalling in this connection that in the early 1960s the USSR registered one of the lowest death rates in the world, whereas 30 years later life expectancy did fall back to the level of middle-income countries (see again Chang and Nolan 1995).

The point here—contrary to what rests implicit in the all-out approach—
is that the market system is not a 'natural' institution. And this involves the
fact that it is not easily transplantable in a context that did not experience it
before.[38]

The negative shock spared no country involved in the transition, but the
intensity and length of the recession varied greatly. On the one hand, the
majority of the countries formerly belonging to the Soviet Union (first and
foremost Russia) suffered a prolonged period of contraction in industrial output and production capacity, which lasted for more than a decade, up to the
beginning of 2000s. On the other hand, the economies of Poland, Hungary,
Czechia, and Slovakia, already in the second half of the 1990s experienced
a resurgence in manufacturing activity and a strong increase in export volumes, largely re-oriented away from former COMECON members towards
Western Europe.[39] The difference in (industrial) fortune between these two
blocs of transition economies was reflected in the inflows of foreign direct
investments, which since the early 1990s were attracted mostly by Eastern
Europe to finance projects in the manufacturing and trade sectors, while the
modest share of capital flows directed towards the former USSR served to
finance almost exclusively investment projects in the mining (including oil
and gas) industry (Meyer and Pind 1999).

The reasons behind this divergence in the paths of industrial development
are many. Partially, they are rooted in the different quality of the institutional
framework and, in particular, in the high degree of State capture especially in
former USSR, which limited the extent to which private businesses independent from political ties could emerge in Russia and neighbouring countries
(Hellman et al. 2000; Johnson et al. 2002). Partially, the divergence can be
traced back to the geographical and cultural proximity of Eastern Europe
to the Western part, favouring its rapid inclusion into the process of political and economic integration within the EU, which meant—among other
things—large inflows of public and private funds to sustain the transition.
But a further explanation has to do with the pre-existence of cross-country
differences in the trajectories of industrialization within the COMECON
area since the decades of central planning, involving that Eastern European

---

[38] A fundamental reference about this point at the theoretical level can be found in Polanyi (1944).
With reference to the Soviet Union history, the point is explicitly raised by Chang (2006: 145): '[T]he
mainstream economists tend to believe that market-oriented economic systems are easily transplantable,
(...). This view is behind the widespread adoption of the Big-Bang reform models in the former Communist countries during their transition period, and led to systemic collapses and massive falls in living
standards in most of these countries.'

[39] Romania and Bulgaria were in between these two extremes, together with most of the Balkan
economies. See World Bank (1996) and EBRD (various years).

countries were structurally advantaged to overcome the difficulties of the transition to the market.

In fact, the distribution of production activities was not homogeneous within the COMECON area: while Eastern Europe had become increasingly specialized in manufacturing, with a significant share of light industries (Rodrik 1994), taking advantage of the stock of knowledge (capabilities) inherited from their pre-communist past—especially in Eastern Germany, Czechia, and Hungary—the Soviet Union—a laggard in the history of industrialization—had concentrated its efforts mainly in the supply of raw materials (minerals, fuels, foodstuffs) which were abundant, of basic intermediates (chemicals, metals) and in the development of the defence and aerospace industry—in which, on the other hand, it had achieved quite brilliant results, competing directly with the United States (Lavigne 1979).

Such inherited difference in the sectoral specialization entailed that the transition process in the 1990s had different effects in Eastern Europe and USSR. In particular, transition was relatively easier in the former, where existing manufacturing assets were (at least partially) converted to intercept the increasing offshoring of intermediate productions from Western Europe (especially from Germany).[40] In the latter, technologically outdated productions in vertically integrated capital-intensive industries were either rebuilt from the ground up or just dismantled, and productions related to the defence and aerospace industry struggled to survive as military expenditures were structurally scaled back.[41]

Despite a strong rebound of manufacturing production in Russia (and other former USSR economies) starting from the early 2000s, the difference with Eastern Europe in the industrial development paths persisted. Manufacturing in Czechia, Slovakia, Hungary, and Poland expanded along the European value chains attracting foreign direct investments with an increasing business-friendly environment and a relatively qualified but low-wage workforce, even succeeding in some cases in increasing their direct contribution to medium- and high-tech productions (Damijan et al. 2018).

Yet, some concerns about the solidity of this export-led way to industrialization—regarding in particular the quality of the forward and backward linkages activated by foreign direct investments—do emerge. In fact, more recent years have witnessed a relocation of manufacturing

---

[40] See Klapper et al. (2002). The restructuring of industry in Eastern Europe was substantial, though. FDIs from the West were relatively capital intensive and labour saving and many plants—especially those specialized in heavy industries—were forced to shut down. See Naudé et al. (2019) for further details.

[41] According to United Nations (1992), in 1991 about 90% of Soviet machinery and equipment in the oil and gas industry was obsolete.

activity away from these economies, as well as a premature narrowing of their supply matrix (especially as to the automotive industry) and a—quite related—excessive dependence from Germany as a trade and investment partner.[42] On the other hand, re-industrialization in Russia is not related to an increase in the international attractiveness of the domestic production system, but it is, to a large extent, driven by the commodity prices boom, which started in early 2000s and lasted for more than a decade. In fact, Russian manufacturing simply benefitted from an exogenous increase in the domestic demand made possible by the high quotations of commodities which boosted Russian exports of primary goods. Overall, the condition of the Russian economy today

> […] is indeed close to what it was a few years after the USSR collapsed. Russia's rapid growth in 2000s was predominantly driven by the oil market boom of the early twenty-first century as well as manufacturing and services expansion in response to increasing oil income inflows. Such expansion, however, was chiefly inward-oriented and therefore had no substantial impact on export complexity. That Brazil and South Africa, two more BRICs members, exhibit a similar stagnant complexity of their economies can hardly be a consolation for Russia.
>
> **(Lyubimov 2019: 195)**

In the case of Russia, therefore, current concerns are not related to the excessive dependence of local productions from the investment strategies of foreign multinationals, as in the case of Eastern European economies, but—similarly enough to what happened at the times of the Soviet Union—to its excessive degree of specialization in natural resource exploitation, basic inputs and military-related productions.

3.6 The African issue

The African continent is characterized by an enormous heterogeneity as to the history, the size and the specific experiences of individual countries.[43] This section attempts anyway to draw a broad sketch about some general traits of the industrial policies it has been interested by over the years. In fact, many governments in several African countries did set up in the years

---

[42] On the limits and threats to Eastern European industrialization see Naudé et al. (2019), Filippetti and Peyrache (2013).

[43] In this connection quite peculiar features are shown by South Africa, marked by remarkable expectations as to the development of a strong manufacturing sector, and a strong determination to adopt pro-active policies to this end.

following World War II explicit programmes aimed at favouring the development of manufacturing activities. And, more than this, such programmes in most cases brought about, initially, visible effects in terms of manufacturing growth. Yet these effects only endured for short periods and did never translate into the establishing of an endogenous growth process. Why did this systematically happen in various countries? And how did different sorts of industrial policies come and go in the course of different decades?

As a first issue, it has to be said that, historically, the colonial past of almost all African countries has never favoured the development of an industrialization strategy. The reason is simple and has to do with the absence of any incentives, for European economic systems, to encourage industrialization in their colonies given the role they played as a market for their manufactured goods and as suppliers of cheap raw materials.[44] Put in other words European countries did not think that manufacturing would generate profits big enough to justify a change in activity (Mendes et al. 2014).

Hence, in order to take off, industrial development in most African countries had to wait for independence, which happened only in the course of the second half of the twentieth century. On such premises Africa, and in particular sub-Saharan countries, entered the 1950s almost deprived of manufacturing experience. More than this, they were heavily affected by the lack of any sorts of institutional environment apt to encourage the development of manufacturing activities, in terms of human resource endowments, natural resource endowments, and physical and social infrastructure. Probably the main exceptions to such general pattern are South Africa and the then Rhodesia (now Zimbabwe). Both countries were indeed forced to adopt an import-substitution strategy during many years of apartheid, and this contributed to build a local manufacturing sector able to produce a variety of intermediate products and spare parts. Moreover, South Africa has always benefitted from a large domestic market with a reasonable purchasing power and also from a regional market through the various regional integration agreements (see Chapter 6), now unified into the Southern African Development Community (SADC).[45]

With these exceptions, on such premises—and in the presence of long-run declining terms of trade for primary goods—the need to exit from the exploitation brought about by the colonial heritage implied that since the

---

[44] This often also reflected a logic of specialization, where each country was called to produce a specific commodity or natural resource of interest of the colonial powers (which contributed to hinder the process of local diversification and manufacturing development).

[45] In South Africa, among the many policy instruments used the Government has often imposed local content requirements to foster the development of local manufacturing, for example in sectors such as railways and mining (Anzolin and Pietrobelli 2021).

very beginning the road to development had to be marked by an anti-colonial ideology and the will to end the foreign capital experience. This translated into the search for new endogenous production activities in non-primary sectors (namely in manufacturing); so that the new African governments, confronted with the calamitous situation of their countries and in the face of the apparent success of Latin American policies, concluded that they needed to adopt import substitution strategies. Indeed, this approach did not exclude completely foreign investments, due to the basic shortage of domestic savings; so that a series of instruments were also deployed to encourage private investments (tax exemptions, preferential access to credit, favourable exchange rates). At the same time it was the state that played a pivotal role in the building of the manufacturing sector, mainly through the setting up of state-owned enterprises (SOEs) in strategic activities (heavy industries, infrastructures).

Overall, this translated into a capital-intensive technology, at the expenses of labour-intensive industries. Be that as it may, quoting from Pearson (1969), Mendes et al. (2014: 128) conclude that at the beginning of the 1960s 'the countries of the East African Union—Kenya, Uganda, and Tanzania—already had very diversified manufacturing'. A similar picture is provided by Newman et al. (2016) with reference to a wide range of sub-Saharan economies, showing that along the 1960s manufacturing grew substantially faster than overall output in most countries.

A key point in this framework, however, is that the import substitution process required a great deal of machines, parts, and other intermediate inputs for production, which the local manufacturing sector was not able to produce at the time in spite of the rising demand; as a consequence, such goods had to be imported, thus determining a growing pressure on the balance of payments. But ISI policies also required the availability of skilled labour, which could not be found within the boundaries of these same countries in the amount which was needed. It also happened that many foreign businesses preferred importing synthetic inputs, produced in industrial countries, to using natural domestic inputs (e.g. rubber). This behaviour, pushing towards the search for upstream goods abroad, thwarted the thickening of inter-firm linkages at the local level, breaking the connections among sectors, and therefore hindering endogenous growth and preventing the natural expansion of the economy.

Overall, it was clear that foreign capital and market forces would not provide in themselves the economic transformations needed to overcome underdevelopment effectively. And, paradoxically, import substitution—instead of relieving the external constraint—by determining an increase in the need for imports of capital-intensive technologies—ended up in a further deterioration of the balance of payments. These difficulties were enhanced by the first oil shock in 1973, and when the economies were further hit by the second shock in 1979, foreign indebtedness skyrocketed and manufacturing growth rates fell far below expectations. In 1983, after 25 years of attempts to develop through import substitution, the African manufacturing sector was just a small enclave in the economy of the region, accounting for only 7.5% of GDP. In several countries, the manufacturing share in GDP, compared to that in the 1960s, had even decreased (Mendes et al. 2014). Moreover, the diversity and sophistication of the manufacturing sector in the region—in the sense suggested by Hausmann et al. (2011)—had declined (Page 2012).[46]

Then, unlike what had happened in Latin American countries, Africa's industrialization strategy failed on the whole due to strong structural constraints both in the domestic market and in the external context: the amount of physical and human capital available in sub-Saharan Africa was much smaller than that of other underdeveloped countries; the same has to be said about the literacy rate, which was quite low, the lack of basic skills in the labour market and the substantial shortage of experienced management. And the institutions themselves were too fragile to sustain a development process: Africa's elites, often driven by self-interest, did not play a supportive role, and governance rules were extremely weak (by far weaker than in successful East Asian economies).

Given these premises, when in the 1990s the whole world was involved in the spreading of globalized value chains, driven by the offshoring of manufacturing activities and the establishment of trade in tasks as a new paradigm, African countries failed to enter the road to industrialization, due to the fact that their manufacturing experience still lay below the critical level which could have allowed them to actively participate in the process. Therefore, even in the face of an increase in the value added brought about by the participation to GVCs (from 6 to 24 billion between 1990 and 2011 for least developed countries, according to UNCTAD estimates), sub-Saharan economies were mostly integrated as suppliers of resource-based products (Sanpath and Ayitey 2016), so that for the majority of the population agriculture still remained the most relevant source of employment and income. On the other hand, even the (quite narrow) manufacturing activities involved in

---

[46] Similar figures are recalled in Signé (2018), who also stresses the high degree of spatial concentration of manufacturing activities (in 2017 almost 70% of African manufacturing value added was produced by four countries: South Africa, Egypt, Nigeria, and Morocco in descending order). See also de Vries et al. (2015).

the trade in tasks mechanism were confined to low value added segments, so that no system effects, in terms of innovation, could take place.[47]

It has to be stressed in this connection that—as argued in Section 3.2 above—the missing link between trade in tasks and endogenous industrialization has a definite explanation. In principle, even resource-based products *can* provide a basis for the development in the medium term of high value added activities (mining, for example, asks for a wide range of suppliers in other sectors), potentially activating many backward linkages at the local level. Yet for this to happen, deliberate governmental policies have to be implemented (as happened in the East Asian context), whereas at the institutional level—in the years following the failure of the ISI policies—the African environment was on the whole characterized by a substantial absence of explicit policies aimed at encouraging learning and upgrading (Lall and Pietrobelli 2002, 2005; Kaplan 2016). In this sense, dynamic comparative advantages were not pursued effectively, with well-designed and strongly implemented policies.

Indeed, such a context has also been affected by the policy prescriptions set forth since the 1980s by international institutions (namely the IMF and the World Bank), which had to be accepted in order to gain access to financial aid. The view behind such prescriptions was that the major reason for the difficulties encountered by African countries in their attempts to industrialize had to be found mainly in government intervention (distorting markets and encouraging import-substituting industry at the expense of agriculture). This fostered the tendency to pursue competitiveness through the static comparative advantages based on each country's natural resources, running against the idea according to which opportunities are created, and not inherited (which had been the key to success for East Asian countries) and playing an active role against the possibility to build an industrialization strategy (Stein 1992). In fact, as far as these recommendations have included liberalizing foreign exchange, removing protectionist barriers, and reducing the role of the government through privatization, their main consequence has been a persistently large agricultural sector, that has remained the main source of income. This contributed to keep internal demand weak, limiting the size of the domestic market for manufactured products and acting as a further significant constraint to growth.

So, as showed by de Vries et al. (2015), whilst the early period of economic development (roughly from 1960 to 1975, called the Golden Age of

---

[47] Early studies had already noted how the whole notion of an 'innovation system' was largely absent in the African continent, and that at best some traces of useful 'technology systems' could be detected (Lall and Pietrobelli 2002, 2005)

African development) saw an increase in the manufacturing employment share, reflecting a Lewis-type dual economy model (where workers move out of subsistence agriculture and are absorbed in modern manufacturing), when growth rebounded during the 1990s—in the absence of any sorts of industrial policy—structural change took the shape of a fall of manufacturing employment share (from 8.9% in 1990 to 8.3% in 2010). In this case it happened that workers moving out of agriculture were instead absorbed in market services sectors, in particular in distribution services (characterized by lower productivity as compared to manufacturing).[48]

The development of some other new activities outside manufacturing— namely agro-industry, tourism, and business and trade services (including transport and logistics)—has been recently called for as an example of what has been termed as 'industry without smokestacks' (Newfarmer et al. 2018), i.e. a potential new (complementary) path towards structural transformation not involving manufacturing development.[49] Yet it appears hardly conceivable that such a range of activities can actually play the same role historically played by manufacturing in structural change: and in the view of the African Development Bank itself (Opoku and Kit-Ming Yan 2019), economic transformation is deemed not to be feasible without industrialization—especially as it sets the ground for exports, i.e. for expanding market demand. From this point of view, a major role could be played in the future by the institution of the African Continental Free Trade Area, founded in 2018 (signed by 54 out of the 55 African Union nations), potentially leading to larger markets and economies of scale in production (McMillan and Zeufack 2022). By fostering regional economic integration, this could also help reverse the neo-colonial dependence that the development of GVCs has de facto determined through liberal engagements with the advanced economies (Rekiso 2017).

In this overall framework, a specific problem arises as a simple consequence of the success of other laggards, which over the last decades have become major global manufacturing players (and exporters): from this point of view, Africa today has to face a very different challenge, as to industrialization, from that faced by earlier developing countries (the 'Rest') which succeeded in entering the road to manufacturing. The challenge is twofold: on the one side African countries, given their specialization (especially in

---

[48] 'Market-oriented policy reforms in the 1990s likely increased demand for wholesaling and retailing services. For example, trade liberalisation facilitated the imports of numerous consumer goods and investment good parts, and stimulated the expansion of foreign retail chains through FDI. More recently, driven by increasing incomes, a relatively larger share of domestic demand is shifting towards consumption of services' (de Vries et al. 2015: 679).

[49] In terms of what has been argued in Chapter 1, this can be considered something like a premature deindustrialization.

clothing industry, furniture, basic metalworking), have now to compete with
a wider spectrum of (large) economic systems, both on the foreign and the
domestic market; on the other they are strongly constrained by such systems
as to the possibility to diversify their supply matrix. Overall, this translates into a crowding-out effect, that is a displacement of internal supply, by
emerging countries, and particularly on account of China (Giovannetti and
Sanfilippo 2009; Sandrey and Edinger 2011).[50]

3.7 Conclusions

The entry of the 'emerging world' into the global industrial system has happened within a quite short time span (between the second half of the 1980s
and the first half of the 1990s), driven by the almost simultaneous wearing off
of the seclusion of some very large economic systems. International economic
integration, under the guidance of the WTO, has played quite an important
role in fuelling manufacturing development in these systems. But development has only unfolded as far as they have been capable of setting up active
industrial policies, aimed at building dynamic comparative advantages.

   A key point in this context is that—as already argued in Chapter 1—all the
economic systems here considered were initially characterized by a basic lack
of proprietary technologies, for their development began after the big technological discontinuities of the second half of the nineteenth century did take
place.[51] Such being the case, not only had these systems to rely upon public
intervention in order to pursue industrial development, but they also had to
assign to the state the specific role of building a catching up process, in the
face of an unbridgeable gap with respect to first comers. This was especially
difficult, for one thing is to help private enterprises to emerge in a world still
dominated by agriculture, quite another one is to translate into explicit targets
the aim to become an industrial country in a world in which manufacturing
markets are already dominated by incumbents holding in their hands best
practice technologies.

   In this chapter four different ways of coping with the task of developing a manufacturing sector, emerged in the course or post-war history, have
been recalled. The results obtained in the different contexts appear extremely

---

[50] The very same problem has also affected Latin America (see Jenkins and Dussel Peters 2008), even in
terms of the dynamics of FDIs diverted towards East Asia (and China in particular). In the case of Mexico
a massive reallocation of 'maquila' firms into China has taken place since the early 2000s (Palma 2003b).
   [51] This holds also for the Soviet Union (Russia is just the case study for lagged development in Gerschenkron's analysis, see above), which had already attained an extremely high degree of technological
knowledge before globalization did take place.

uneven, even if the globalization process over the last decades has offered all of them, in principle, the same opportunities. Results basically differ according to the role played by two main factors: the amount of manufacturing capabilities achieved before international integration; and the capability to build institutions apt to lead the industrialization process by setting up conditional policies designed to get competitive advantages in foreign markets in the medium term. As to the latter, the following features appear most relevant: (1) the capability of not being 'captured' by the various stakeholders in the system; (2) the setting up of *selective* policies (indiscriminate ISI policies do not lead to the development of comparative advantages); (3) the idea according to which the manufacturing sector has to be built with the aim to enlarge the potential market through a growing capability to export.

Indeed, it can be said that such features are to be borne in mind by policy makers even in already industrialized countries, inasmuch as all industrial systems—in a globalized world—need to constantly re-define their set of competences, so as to maintain a wide range of comparative advantages.

4
Building a New Taxonomy of Manufacturing Countries

4.1 Introduction

Major changes affecting the organization of industrial activity all across the world along the Globalization Age (GA) have led to an unprecedented degree of productive interdependence at the country level. As shown in Chapter 2, this has linked together countries originally characterized by strong differences in their degree of industrialization and determined the emergence of new manufacturing systems.

Not only has the bursting onto the economic scene of these players brought about some downsizing of manufacturing production within the Global North, but it also has been accompanied by the persistent stagnation of a conspicuous part of the economies of the South (involving in turn an increase in inequality within the whole group of laggards). This has determined an overall reshaping of the landscape of global manufacturing, making obsolete the view according to which the world was sharply divided into two parts, largely unrelated to each other: on the one side the industrialized countries (basically Europe, North America, and Japan); on the other the South—i.e. almost all other economies.[1]

In the face of such radical transformations we still lack a metrics which can account for the changes occurred in the relative 'distance' among all countries involved in manufacturing activity, and therefore to return a consistent picture of what global manufacturing has actually become. In fact, the way the degree of industrialization of different countries is classified according to standard taxonomies is still largely rooted in the North-South dichotomous way of thinking about development, and appears increasingly at odds with reality.

In this chapter a novel approach to the categorization of countries is illustrated, which rests on economic theory and empirical research in order to

---

[1] As already noticed, this framework has set apart for many years, as a separate group, the ensemble of the East European countries, characterized by a strong role of the industrial sector in the economy.

The New Industrial World. Livio Romano and Fabrizio Traù, Oxford University Press.
© Livio Romano and Fabrizio Traù (2023). DOI: 10.1093/oso/9780192873736.003.0005

build a multi-dimensional metrics for measuring the degree of industrialization. By applying cluster analysis to a set of complementary structural economic indicators it is possible to account for the increasing cross-country heterogeneity and to shed new light on the different directions undertaken in the last decades by manufacturing development worldwide, putting into evidence the conditions for industrial development to happen and the reasons for heterogeneous paths to emerge. First, it will be addressed the way manufacturing development can be defined in order to provide a measure of the degree of industrialization of different countries (Section 4.2); then it will be described the methodology employed to define a new taxonomy of manufacturing countries and the specific features which characterize each of the resulting tiers (or groups) of manufacturers (Section 4.3). Attention is paid in this connection to the fact that in the course of time countries can—and usually do—move from one manufacturing tier to another, and more specifically to the role played by institutional factors in explaining different degrees of development.

4.2 Defining industrial development

The Globalization Age has coincided with the development of manufacturing expansion beyond the borders of the G10. The emergence of the four 'Asian tigers' since the 1970s set something new somewhat in between the North and the South, but this fact did not translate into a rethinking of the idea according to which the world was to be divided into two blocs, until the emergence in the new century of large manufacturing countries such as China (and, to a lesser extent, the other BRICs) did actually alter the whole mechanism of industrial development at the global level. As we have seen, this happened due to the very size of the new emerging countries (whose impact became suddenly visible), and the fact that their development has been hinging upon an increasing division of labour on a cross-country basis, creating a widespread flow of exchanges on productive grounds between the two sides of the world.

The point, in this context, is that—as we have seen in the previous chapter—the different areas of the underdeveloped world have followed rather heterogeneous paths, due to different approaches to the problem of industrialization, especially in terms of the policies they have been able to set up. Such heterogeneity has involved that the overall outcome of the above-mentioned changes has been a general blurring of the usual way of grouping countries according to their degree of development. Here the issue is twofold:

on the one side, in spite of the still widespread habit of conceiving the world in dichotomous terms,[2] the very success of 'emerging' countries definitely sets something new—characterized by its own identity—between the North and the South. On the other, the sharp distinction between 'industrial' and 'emerging' countries itself seems in fact not to hold that much, in a context in which important differences seem to emerge within these same groups. Put in other words, new differences and similarities may lead to characterize the shape of the industrial world in a different (more articulated) way as compared to the past.

This is not simply a matter of classification of economic systems: this is first and foremost a conceptual issue, insofar as it has to do with the definition of what industrial development actually is about. The point here is that the transformations we have discussed so far have changed the relative distance among all the countries belonging to the group of manufacturing producers (be they 'old' or 'new'). But how do we measure such distance, i.e. the degree of development of different countries?

As has been done in Chapter 2, the degree of industrial development can be first expressed in terms of manufacturing per capita value added.[3] Yet, despite its straightforward interpretation, this indicator cannot suffice to the purpose of identifying different paths of industrialization, because along the continuum of the distribution it is virtually impossible to identify the critical output thresholds according to which the whole population of countries should be divided into relatively homogenous groups.

The solution proposed by UNIDO, as recalled in Upadhyaya (2013), is to group countries according to a mix of alternative rules. These rules do alternatively pay attention to the level of manufacturing per capita value added (by using aprioristic information about the historical evolution of manufacturing

[2] 'The literature is replete with competing terminologies; examples include poor/rich, backward/advanced, underdeveloped/developed, North/South, late comers/pioneers, Third World/First World, and developing/industrialized' (Nielsen 2011: 1089).

[3] Other economic institutions (IMF, World Bank, WTO, and the like) dealing with the problem of defining a rank of individual countries according to their degree of development, for operational as well as analytical purposes, shape their definitions on the basis of the characteristics that matter for their specific institutional role (Nielsen 2011). Hence, the IMF pays attention to the developing of financial markets, the United Nations Development Programme to the country's achievements in terms of longevity and education, and so on. For all institutions, anyway, the basic measure to refer to is generally per capita income. Basically, this means that country grouping boils down to identifying the critical (absolute or relative) thresholds of per capita income according to which the whole population of countries can be divided, taking into account *in some ways* also some other variables. In this framework, however, nothing is said about the rationale for the choice of thresholds themselves. And, in some cases, grouping is simply based on judgement, as happens in the World Bank's classification system. In such system, in order to identify industrialized countries, in 1978 it has been used as a distinguishing feature the OECD membership, and in the following years the placement of some countries has been arbitrarily changed—setting them alternatively outside or inside the same group without giving any formal explanation about such a choice.

share in GDP) and to ad hoc assumptions about the levels of per capita GDP and countries' share in world manufacturing value added. The overall result is the classification of countries into four groups (Industrialized economies, Emerging Industrial Economies, Other Developing Countries, Least Developed Countries—the fourth referring to countries which have never actually industrialized). Yet by using different identification criteria with reference to different countries, it becomes impossible to determine to what extent countries assigned to the same group are actually homogenous in terms of their industrial development level.

The view set forth in these pages is that, in order to identify from the ground a taxonomy of manufacturing countries, the challenge is to build metrics which can capture the multidimensional, complex nature of the industrial development process. Such a process—other than the sheer expansion in the size of the national manufacturing sector—does involve important changes as to the relative specialization of the entire economy, the range of manufacturing activities, their technological content (both in the sense of cross-sectoral shifts and of intra-sectoral upgrading processes), and their degree of international competitiveness. All such transformations are historically determined, knowledge-based and path-dependent, and can be viewed as an evolutionary process in the course of which a given country changes by moving (developing) through different phases of growth.

It is important to stress that this has not to be intended as a mechanical sequence of stages, but simply as the logic to be followed by countries in the course of their development process. The literature on the stages of growth has been developed with reference to both economic systems (as in Rostow's analysis, see Rostow 1960) and firms (mostly in management theory, see for all McMahon 1998). The approach followed in this chapter differs from such a way of interpreting the development process in that it challenges the idea of a unique pattern of development to be applied to all countries, in light of the thought of Gerschenkron (1962), Fuà (1978), Piore and Sabel (1984), Amsden (2001).

From this point of view it may be argued, for example, that laggards must come to terms with global markets that are already structured, and market shares that are already in the hands of the incumbents, so that they have to rely upon different strategies with respect to first comers, as we have repeatedly stressed. Or that industrialization may take place in quite different forms as to the organization of production activity (hierarchies vs markets), and so on. Even more, as will be clear in the following, in this view countries can move along the development path (passing from one group to another) in *both* directions—i.e. no achievement can be taken for granted indefinitely.

What is meant here by phases of growth, therefore, has to do with some passages that economic systems go through, but that at the same time may be implemented in different ways in many respects (as well as they may even turn out into a reversal of the path).

When classifying countries according to their degree of (manufacturing) development, the key issue then becomes to identify the variables (indicators) which characterize such different states.[4] To this end, the present analysis has been carried out by considering, in addition to the well-established manufacturing value added per capita, four other indicators. Each of them is chosen on the basis of specific theoretical premises and has to be intended as complementary to each other in characterizing an industrial system (Table 4.1).

Two of the variables included in the table are commonly referred to in the literature on structural change: the share of manufacturing value added in total value added (pioneered by Fisher 1939, Clark 1940, Fuchs 1968, and Kuznets 1973, and recalled in Kaldor's 1966 analysis of increasing returns, hinging on Verdoorn's 1949 contribution); and the intra-manufacturing concentration of output (pioneered by Imbs and Wacziarg 2003). The former is

Table 4.1   Variables used to build a taxonomy of manufacturing countries

Variable	Mean 2015	S.d.	Mean 2000	S.d.	Source
Manufacturing value added per capita (log, real dollars)	7.81	1.03	7.51	1.20	UNIDO
Manufacturing value added on GDP (real dollars)	0.16	0.06	0.15	0.05	UNIDO
Gini index of intra-manufacturing value added (4 digit, real dollars)	0.62	0.10	0.59	0.11	Oxford Economics
Share of Medium&High-tech manufacturing value added (real dollars)	0.49	0.19	0.47	0.17	UNIDO
Manufacturing trade balance, normalized by the sum of export and import (current dollars)	−0.05	0.15	−0.04	0.18	ComTrade, OECD

---

[4] In empirical terms, capturing these different dimensions is not straightforward, as far as information about some indicators of interest may be non-existent (in particular for non-OECD countries), or, even when available, it may happen that the way information is collected affects cross-country comparability due to methodological differences. Therefore, the choice of the indicators that have to be taken into account needs to balance, in a way which is consistent with the final objective, the scope of collected information as to the variables to be included with the number of countries which can be actually compared.

meant to capture the relative direct contribution of manufacturing to GDP, the latter to measure the dynamics of sectoral concentration over time, that is the evolution of the national supply matrix. The third variable is the normalized manufacturing trade balance (difference between exports and imports divided by their sum), taken as a proxy for the 'efficiency' of the manufacturing sector in the face of trade openness, in light of Singh's (1977 and 1987) definition. The fourth variable is the share of manufacturing valued added produced by medium and high-tech industries, identified according to the OECD classification, that provides a measure (although imperfect) of the intensity of production technology generated within the domestic manufacturing sector.[5]

Complete information on all these different features of a manufacturing system are retrieved for a sample of 50 countries, from all around the globe. For it is built so as to provide a general taxonomy of manufacturing behaviour, the sample also includes developed countries.

4.3 Identifying different tiers of manufacturers

4.3.1 Which countries do belong to which tier

The metrics according to which countries are classified is based upon the above-mentioned five variables and employs them as ingredients of a clustering algorithm.[6] The variables have not been re-scaled within a common range of values, as is often done before applying the clustering algorithm. This is due to the choice of not giving them the same explanatory power (the same weight), in the definition of groups. In particular, manufacturing value added per capita (here expressed in log) shows a standard deviation which is eight times larger compared to the average of the remaining four variables (see again Table 4.1). It is for this reason that it is purposely chosen without being re-scaled, for it is anyway retained as the most relevant factor in order to discriminate different degrees of industrialization.[7]

---

[5] Inter-alia, this indicator is referred to in order to measure the degree of attainment of one of the 17 sustainable development goals launched by the United Nations (2015).
   [6] Cluster analysis allows to assign each observation to a specific group on the basis on a multidimensional measure of similarity. Two applications of cluster analysis to the study of economic development can be found in Zhang and Gao (2015) and Tezanos and Sumner (2013).
   [7] This choice is consistent with the existing (almost uni-dimensional) taxonomy proposed by UNIDO (Upadhyaya 2013), while it is in contrast with the logic underlying the construction of the UNIDO Competitive Industrial Performance (CIP) index (see UNIDO, various years), which assigns to per capita manufacturing value added the same weight as to other seven structural indicators.

The number of groups is not defined a priori, but is chosen after having applied the Calinski and Harabasz (1974) optimization method to the results of a Ward's linkage cluster analysis. As to 2015, this statistical methodology leads to the identification of five different clusters. However, in order to get groups large enough to make robust statistical analysis, the fifth cluster, composed of only three countries, has been merged to the closer one (i.e. the most similar in terms of manufacturing valued added per capita), so that the final number of clusters has been set to four.[8]

The cluster analysis draws a picture of the different profiles of manufacturing countries which confirms how blurred the boundaries between the North and South have become in the course of the Globalization Age, at least when looking at industrial development (Table 4.2).

First of all, the G10 countries result assigned to both the group labelled as 'first tier manufacturers' and that labelled 'second tier manufacturers', with Germany, Japan, Sweden, and Switzerland belonging to the former, while Belgium, Canada, France, Italy, Netherlands, UK, and USA belonging to the

Table 4.2 A new taxonomy of manufacturing countries, 2015*

1st tier	2nd tier	3rd tier	4th tier
Austria	Australia	Argentina	Brazil
Denmark	Belgium	Chile	Bulgaria
Finland	Canada	China	Colombia
Germany	Czech Republic	Greece	Ecuador
Japan	France	Hungary	India
Norway	Israel	Malaysia	Indonesia
Singapore	Italy	Mexico	Iran
South Korea	Netherlands	Poland	Morocco
Sweden	New Zealand	Portugal	Pakistan
Switzerland	Slovak Republic	Romania	Philippines
	Spain	Russia	South Africa
	Taiwan	Thailand	Vietnam
	United Kingdom	Turkey	
	United States	Uruguay	
N: 10	N: 14	N: 14	N: 12

* Clusters defined according to k-means procedure, using the variables shown in Table 4.1.
Source: Sources reported in Table 4.1, own calculations.

[8] In particular, Pakistan, India, and Vietnam, with the lowest levels of manufacturing valued added per capita in the sample, have been identified by the clustering algorithm to form a separated group of manufacturers. The rationale for choosing the group in which to include these countries is provided in the next subsection.

latter. The first group comprises also other Scandinavian countries plus two Asian tigers, namely Singapore and South Korea (but it does not include Taiwan, which has been assigned to the second group).[9] Most of the remaining EU countries are classified in the second tier, but not all of them: among Eastern European members, only Czechia and Slovakia are included, while Hungary, Poland, and Romania are classified as 'third tier manufacturers', and Bulgaria as one of the 'fourth tier manufacturers'. Noticeably enough, among Westerns European members Portugal and Greece are classified in the third tier. Also BRICs appear unevenly distributed among groups, with Brazil, China, and Russia classified in the third tier, while India and South Africa in the fourth one.

4.3.2 The characterization of different tiers

But what are the specific characteristics attached to the four groups of manufacturers that have been identified by the cluster analysis? (How do they actually differ from each other?) First of all, there is a clear and strong relation between the sequence of the different tiers and the level of manufacturing value added per capita: the industrialization rates within the first tier are always higher than those within the second tier, which in turn are always higher than those within the third tier, which in turn are always higher than those within the fourth tier (Figure 4.1). This result suggests prima facie an interpretation of the different groups of manufacturers as a sequence of different degrees of industrial development, from the lowest (corresponding to the fourth tier) to the highest (first tier).

Yet such an indicator does not allow on its own to identify which thresholds have to be chosen in order to assign each country to the different groups along the continuum of the distribution. For instance, the distance in the industrialization rates existing between the United States and Norway, showing respectively the highest value within the second tier and the lowest within the first tier, is lower than that observed between South Korea and Austria or between Germany and Sweden, despite the fact that these four countries are classified as belonging to the same group. On the other hand, the four groups also differ from each other in terms of the values assumed by the other four indicators included in the clustering algorithm. In particular, each indicator seems to discriminate between different pairs of groups (Table 4.3).[10]

---

[9] The fourth Asian Tiger, Hong Kong, has been excluded because its development represents a unicum, after China's annexation in 1997.

[10] The cross-cluster analysis that follows is not driven by the presence of outliers, as similar conclusions can be drawn by comparing median instead of the mean values for each variable in the different groups.

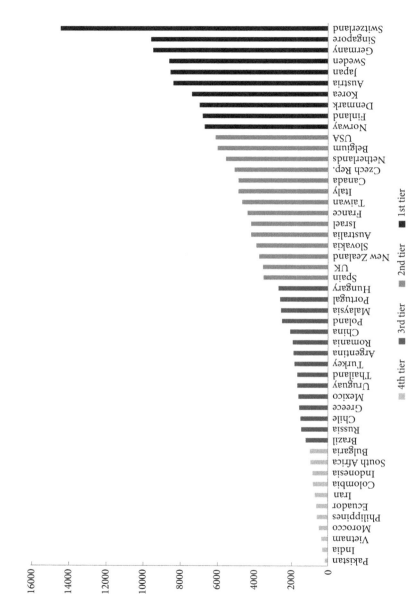

Figure 4.1 Groups of manufacturing countries by manufacturing value added per capita in 2015, current dollars

Source: Sources reported in Table 4.1, own calculations.

Table 4.3 Characterization of the different groups of manufacturing countries (2015 mean values)*

Variables used in the clustering alghoritm:	4th tier	3rd tier	2nd tier	1st tier
Manufacturing VA per capita (log)	6,29	7,52	8,41	9,04
Gini index of manufacturing VA	0,71	0,61	0,58	0,58
Share of Medium, High-Tech manufacturing VA	0,31	0,33	0,43	0,56
Normalized manufacturing trade balance	−0,22	−0,06	−0,05	0,06
Share of manufacturing VA on GDP	0,15	0,17	0,13	0,17
		Difference 4th-3rd	*Difference 3rd-2nd*	*Difference 2nd-1st*
Manufacturing VA per capita (log)		−1,23***	−0,89***	−0,62***
Gini index of manufacturing VA		0,10**	0,04	−0,01
Share of Medium, High-Tech manufacturing VA		−0,02	−0,11**	−0,13**
Normalized manufacturing trade balance		−0,18**	0,01	−0,11**
Share of manufacturing VA on GDP		−0,01	0,04	−0.04*

* Countries grouped according to the clustering procedure described in Section 4.2; *p-value < 0.10,
**p-value < 0.005, ***p-value < 0.001
Source: Sources reported in Table 4.1, own calculations.

First, as compared to third tier ones, countries classified in the fourth tier show on average a significantly lower degree of diversification (higher Gini index) of manufacturing activities, and a worse positioning in international markets, as reflected by a trade deficit that on average is five times larger. No systematic differences emerge instead between the two groups in terms of the relative contribution of manufacturing to GDP and their technological intensity. In conceptual terms, this means that the widening of the supply matrix and the contemporary improvement of the trade balance are the two conditions that go along with the transition from a low to a medium-low degree of industrialization rate.

Second, third tier countries are in turn significantly less specialized in medium and high-tech industries as compared to second tier ones, while no systematic differences between the two groups emerge in terms of either the sectoral concentration of manufacturing value added (both relative to GDP and within manufacturing) or the trade balance. Put in other words, the foremost indicator which characterizes the transition from a medium-low to a medium-high degree of industrialization rate seems to be a higher capacity to generate production technology domestically.

Third, in comparison to first tier countries, second tier ones show a systematically lower degree of specialization in medium and high-tech industries, a worse positioning in international markets (the first tier is the only cluster with a positive manufacturing trade balance on average), and also a lower share of GDP accounted for by domestic manufacturing. This means that the moving from a medium-high to a high degree of industrialization rate results in a further increase of the capacity to generate production technology domestically, a significantly better trade balance, and a higher specialization in manufacturing of the domestic economy.

4.3.3 New and old taxonomies in comparison

It is worthwhile to compare the results of the cluster analysis carried out on the basis of the above-mentioned indicators with those provided by the UNIDO classification of these same countries. Data reveal in this connection some important differences (Table 4.4). According to the UNIDO classification the entire group of first tier and of second tier, as well as a bunch of third tier countries, namely Malaysia, Portugal, and Russia, are assumed to belong to the same stage of development—and are coherently classified as 'Industrialized Economies'. The rest of the third tier and half of the countries classified within the fourth tier are instead grouped together as 'Emerging Industrial Economies', while the remaining 'fourth tier manufacturers' are classified as 'Other Developing Countries'.[11]

On the whole, the UNIDO classification, with some important exceptions (mainly within the group of the less industrialized economies), in contrast with the taxonomy proposed in this work tends to replicate the well-established dichotomy between the North and the South. Moreover, the UNIDO classification draws a picture in which the majority of manufacturing countries (52% of the sample) is assumed to be at the latest stage of industrial development, while, according to the results of the analysis carried out in these pages, the most advanced manufacturing powerhouses represent only a minority (20%) of the sample.

---

[11] As noted above, the UNIDO classification, retrieved from Upadhyaya (2013), would also include a fourth group, labelled 'Least Developed Countries'. However, none of the countries included in this group (among the poorest in terms of GDP) enters the sample considered in this work, for they all fall outside the boundaries of the industrialized world.

Table 4.4 Comparing with the UNIDO taxonomy of industrial development*

Industrialized economies			Emerging industrial economies	Other developing economies	
1st tier	Austria	3rd tier (follows)	Argentina	4th tier (follows)	Iran
"	Denmark	"	Brazil	"	Morocco
"	Finland	"	Chile	"	Pakistan
"	Germany	"	China	"	Philippines
"	Japan	"	Colombia	"	Vietnam
"	Norway	"	Greece		
"	Singapore	"	Hungary		
"	South Korea	"	Mexico		
"	Sweden	"	Poland		
"	Switzerland	"	Romania		
2nd tier	Australia	"	Thailand		
"	Belgium	"	Turkey		
"	Canada	"	Uruguay		
"	Czech Republic	4th tier	Bulgaria		
"	France	"	Ecuador		
"	Israel	"	India		
"	Italy	"	Indonesia		
"	Netherlands	"	South Africa		
"	New Zealand				
"	Slovak Republic				
"	United Kingdom				
"	Spain				
"	Taiwan				
"	United States				
3rd tier	Malaysia				
"	Portugal				
"	Russia				
	N:27		N:18		N:5

* UNIDO classification as from Upadhyaya (2013).
Source: Sources reported in Table 4.1, own calculations.

4.3.4 Evolution of the taxonomy over time

One of the benefits of approaching the definition of a new taxonomy of manufacturing countries relying on observed data is that, by construction, the attribution of each country to a specific cluster, as well as the number of clusters, are not defined a priori, but can and do change in response to the different paths of industrial development observed over time.

In fact, by applying to 2001 the same methodology described in the previous section, it is possible to appreciate how the impressive acceleration of the globalization process in the last decades, as well as the tremendous and asymmetric effects of the global financial crisis, have reshaped the geography of world manufacturing. An important point in this connection is that—as we have repeatedly said—in 2001 the economic landscape was affected by major changes at the global level, mostly due to the 'unfreezing' of large economic systems that still in the early 1990s were sealed within a parallel world, outside of the area of market exchanges. In this sense, the 2001 picture reflects the explosion of the previous 'static' North–South framework *before* it started to reorganize according to the changes brought about by the globalization process.

The analysis reveals that at the beginning of the millennium *five* different groups of manufacturers could be detected, i.e. one more as compared to nowadays (Table 4.5). In particular, a mix of the least developed Western European economies (Greece and Portugal), of the most developed Eastern European ones (Czechia and Hungary), together with Malaysia and Mexico formed a relatively homogeneous group in the middle of the distribution of manufacturing per capita value added.[12] All these countries, as already shown in Table 4.2, were then absorbed in the current group of third tier manufactures, with the exception of Czechia that was able to join the second tier. A significant reshuffling has also occurred within the group of the most advanced manufacturing countries: Belgium, Canada, Italy, Netherlands, and the United States have exited the first tier, joining the remaining old industrialized economies in the second one. South Korea, on the opposite, has become one of the leading manufacturing countries in the world, joining the first tier. Within the groups of the least developed manufacturing countries, changes have characterized especially the relative position of BRICs: while Brazil and South Africa have moved towards the bottom, joining the current fourth tier, China, on the opposite, has been able to climb from the bottom, joining the current third tier.

Of course, there is also significant heterogeneity in the underlying dynamic performance of the different manufacturing systems, even for countries that have experienced the same transition from one tier to another. For instance, the shift of Italy and Canada into the current second tier is associated with a significant reduction in their per capita manufacturing value added in real terms (−15.0% and −21.3% respectively along the 2001–15 period), while the same movement for Belgium, Netherlands, and the United States is associated

---

[12] As for the 2015 taxonomy, also in this case there is an unambiguous relation between the sequence of the different tiers and the level of manufacturing per capita value added. And also in this case a further (sixth) cluster including the three least developed manufacturing countries (Pakistan, India, and Vietnam) has been isolated by the hierarchical clustering algorithm. As for 2015, this group has then been merged with the adjacent one.

Table 4.5 The taxonomy of manufacturing countries in 2001 (data in constant dollars 2015)*

1st tier	2nd tier	3rd tier	4th tier	5th tier
Austria	Australia	2nd tier ↔ Czech Republic	3rd tier ↔ Argentina	4th tier ↔ Bulgaria
Belgium → 2nd tier	France	Greece	Brazil	3rd tier ↔ China
Canada → 2nd tier	Israel	Hungary	3rd tier ↔ Chile	4th tier ↔ Colombia
Denmark	New Zealand	Malaysia	3rd tier ↔ Poland	4th tier ↔ Ecuador
Finland	1st tier ↔ South Korea	Mexico	3rd tier ↔ Romania	India**
Germany	Spain	Portugal	3rd tier ↔ Russia	4th tier ↔ Indonesia
Italy → 2nd tier	Taiwan		South Africa	4th tier ↔ Iran
Japan	United Kingdom		3rd tier ↔ Thailand	4th tier ↔ Morocco
Netherlands → 2nd tier			3rd tier ↔ Turkey	Pakistan**
Norway			2nd tier ↔ Slovak Republic	4th tier ↔ Philippines
Singapore			3rd tier ↔ Uruguay	Vietnam**
Sweden				
Switzerland				
United States → 2nd tier				
N: 14	N: 8	N: 6	N: 11	N: 11

* Clusters defined according to Ward's linkage procedure, using the variables shown in Table 4.1. Arrows define cross-tier movements occurred between 2001 and 2015.

** See note 8.

Source: sources reported in Table 4.1, own calculations.

with a positive growth of the same indicator (4.1%, 4.4%, and 10.8% respectively), although at a slower pace as compared to the remaining first tier countries (16.7%). At the same time, although both China and Russia are currently classified in the same tier, their growth in the last 15 years has been remarkably different: the former has more than doubled its industrialization rate (+134.5%) while the latter has expanded at a speed (+36.1%) which has been below the average of the remaining countries currently belonging to the third tier (+41.6%). A negative record has also affected Greece and Portugal, which are the only two countries currently belonging to the third tier with negative manufacturing value added growth between 2001 and 2015 (−38.7% and −8.9%, respectively).

Overall, we can expect new movements across tiers to occur also in the future and new groups to possibly emerge in response to such changes. The methodology here proposed is flexible enough to accommodate for such changes, as well as for the inclusion of new explanatory variables able to capture additional (and new) dimensions of industrialization.

4.4 Institutional features

Institutions matter for development. They define the rules of the game according to which economic actors interact with each other and the scope and width of policy intervention in the economy (North 1990; Acemoglu and Robinson 2008), influencing investment decisions, the accumulation of knowledge, and the whole organization of production. As shown in Chapter 3, the different role interpreted by public institutions in order to support industrial development in the course of the twentieth century has been at the heart of the divergence in fortune observed among emerging economies. On the other hand, significant institutional and policy heterogeneity has also characterized the evolution of Western economies, despite the relatively higher degree of similarity (and harmonization) of their legal and regulatory frameworks.[13]

But institutions are not chosen once for all: they respond in the course of development to new societal and economic challenges which gradually do emerge, implying that also policies tend to (and should) be contingent on each phase of development (Hausmann et al. 2005).[14] Given this premise, one

---

[13] See, for instance, Mazzucato (2011) with reference to public policies oriented towards technological innovation.

[14] This is also in line with Lee and Kim (2009), showing how different institutional arrangements and policies have mattered for economic growth in the last decades, but with varying intensity depending on the degree of development of individual countries.

may ask whether—and to what extent—the different phases of industrialization described in the previous section also mirror cross-country differences as to the institutional side. Even if cross-country analysis does not allow to make any causal inference about the relation between the changes in the institutional sphere and industrial development, it can nevertheless be useful to look at the differences among the different tiers with reference to the specific institutional features by which they are characterized.[15]

To this end, the analysis has been enriched by looking at the Institutional Profile Database built jointly by the Agence Française de Développement (AFD), the French Direction Générale du Trésor (DG Trésor), and CEPII (2016). In particular, information about 47 institutional indicators for the 50 countries under consideration has been retrieved from the original database and compared across groups of manufacturers, to see which of them show systematic differences when moving from a tier to the next. Such indicators, measured in ordinal (Likert) scale (from 0 to 4), are classified in the original dataset according to the following six functions: Functioning of public system, Free operation of markets, Security of transactions, Market regulations, Openness (to foreign exchanges), and Coordination of stakeholders, strategic vision, and innovation (Table 4.6).[16]

The first five functions basically overlap the 'classical' good governance indicators used by the World Bank,[17] which in turn reflect the old-fashioned idea behind the Washington Consensus of a desirable State intervention mainly (if not exclusively) limited to making domestic markets work better (Stiglitz 1999). The sixth group, instead, echoes the novel approach to industrial policy, where the State is supposed to 'perform a strategic and coordinating role in the productive sphere beyond simply ensuring property rights, contract enforcement, and macroeconomic stability' (Rodrik 2004), affecting the sectoral composition of the economy and the transition towards new technological paradigms (Stiglitz 2015).

The cross-tier comparison of the indicators appears informative in different respects. First, it shows that important institutional differences do characterize each transition. This involves the fact that challenges and priorities for industrial policy *need* to vary in intensity along the different

---

[15] Within the above-mentioned limits, this may help identifying something like an 'institutional progression' (as suggested by Meisel and Ould Aoudia 2008) when moving from one level of development to the next.

[16] The original dataset comprised more than 120 indicators, covering institutional functions beyond the six considered in this work. The rationale for choosing which indicators to include in the analysis has been their direct relatedness to industrial development. So, for instance, all indicators related to security, control of violence, as well as to social cohesion and social mobility have been excluded.

[17] See Kaufmann et al. (2010) for details.

Table 4.6 Institutional differences across different tiers of manufacturing countries (2015)*

Functioning of public system	Free operation of markets	Security of transactions	Market regulations	Openness	Coordination of strategic vision innovation
Moving from 4th to 3rd tier					
+capacity of sectoral reforms -tax exemptions to economic sectors		-security of private contracts	+importance of large-scale distribution		+public support for innovation
Moving from 3rd to 2nd tier					
+capacity of sectoral reforms +transparency +efficiency of tax system and justice +freedom to establish and operate organisations	-share of state-owned companies +efficiency of state owned companies -state owned banks +mobility of workers +ease of starting a business	+security of private contracts +trade justice +insolvency law -termination of contracts by state +information on firms +respect for intellectual property	-barriers to competition +competition regulation	-obstacles to trade liberalisation -obstacles to capital liberalisation	+coordination in the public sphere +priority to development and growth +long-term sectoral strategies +technological environment for firms +adaptation of training and schooling to business needs
Moving from 2nd to 1st tier					
+efficiency of tax system +quality of the public policy making		+respect for intellectual property			+state long-term vision +public support for innovation +adaptation of the training supply to business needs

* The table reports only variables for which the difference between groups is statistically significant with a p-value <0.05.
Source: Agence Française de Développement (AFD), French Direction Générale du Trésor (DG Trésor), and CEPII (2016), own calculations.

phases of industrialization. In particular, the most important discontinuity can be observed in the advancement from the third to the second tier. This is true considering both the number of indicators for which (statistically significant) differences have been detected and the range of institutional functions involved. Therefore, results are consistent with the view according to which the institutional progression across the different phases of industrialization needs to be paralleled by the evolution of the public system, as far as it concerns the legal and regulatory framework surrounding market transactions, the openness to international markets and the degree of strategic collaboration and coordination with the private sector.

Moreover, the analysis shows that a significant portion of the institutional differences refer to the active role played by the state in curbing structural change through active support to technological innovation and coordination of public–private initiatives. This is true in all transitions, but it is particularly relevant within the group of the most advanced economies, where such institutional differences account for half of the total. In particular, first tier countries are, on average, on a higher rank as compared to second tier ones in terms of state long-term vision, public support for innovation and adaptation of training supply to business needs. Conversely, the large majority of standard market-friendly institutional arrangements, including those related to labour market rigidity or competition barriers, are systematically different only between the third and the second tier.

4.5 Conclusions

The analysis proposed in these pages has shown that industrial development is not only a matter of simply expanding the scale of manufacturing production. Changes in the degree of industrialization go along with important differences in the manufacturing output share, in the sectoral composition of the production system (both as to the range of manufacturing activities and their technological content), as well as in its external competitiveness.

Having identified different groups (tiers) of countries, corresponding to different degrees of industrial development, however, does not imply that countries are bound to follow, when developing, a mechanical path leading from one tier to another. Countries do not follow a pattern of development which is given once and for all, and the same characteristics that nowadays discriminate between different tiers of manufacturers could lose significance, change sign, or be replaced by new ones tomorrow, should changes in the prevailing technological and institutional paradigms occur, as happened in the past.

Does this imply that nothing can be said in order to suggest policy-making how to sustain industrial development? Giving precise policy prescriptions or recommendations goes well beyond the scope of this chapter, because this would require an in-depth analysis of the temporal evolution of both the institutional setting and the manufacturing system in each country. However, two general lessons for policy can be learned from the previous results.

First, the institutional progression that characterizes the transition from one tier of manufacturers to the next confirms the idea that enforcing the same development strategy with reference to different phases of development is unlikely to prove effective in reaching the policy objective. Growth strategies require a sense of priority in order to be effective, inasmuch, as observed by Hausmann et al. (2005: 2), '[g]overnments face administrative and political limitations, and their policy-making capital is better deployed in alleviating binding constraints than in going after too many targets all at once'. In this respect, the emphasis on reforming market-oriented institutions could be misguided for countries that are either very low in terms of industrialization or which have already reached relatively high standards of quality of such institutions, while it is appropriate for countries being in the middle range of industrialization.

Second, results suggest that for a correct understanding of the policy challenges that go along with industrial development, a more comprehensive look at institutions is needed, going beyond the mere support to the well-functioning of market mechanisms, as far as the functions and the scope of a direct state involvement in the economy are not the same in all phases of development.

5

The Role of External Demand in Manufacturing Development

5.1 Some theoretical premises

This chapter addresses the relationship between the timing of manufacturing take-off and the speed and shape of structural change. It is showed that the economic systems which have entered the road to industrialization as laggards (and specifically in the course of globalization) have followed a different pattern of structural change with respect to early comers. In particular, their intra- and inter-sectoral structural adjustment have been significantly faster as compared to what happened both in Old Industrialized Economies (OIEs) and in those nations that built their manufacturing base more recently, but anyway before the advent of globalization.[1]

Overall, the analysis casts a bridge between the study of the *intra*-sectoral changes as they are approached in the Imbs and Wacziarg (2003, 2012) perspective and that of the *inter*-sectoral structural change as has been debated in the Fisher-Clark-Kuznets tradition, setting them within a unique framework and providing a common explanation for both phenomena on endogenous (structural) bases. In fact, inter and intra-sectoral output shifts can be viewed as the two sides of a single coin, as they are but the consequences of what happens in the manufacturing sector as far as countries develop.

The point made here is that in late industrialized countries globalization has pushed towards an early increasing sectoral concentration of manufacturing activities relative to those economies in which industrialization occurred previously. Constrained by relatively narrow supply matrices such countries have also experienced a much earlier decline in the manufacturing share on the total economy along their process of industrial development.

These facts have strong implications on the more general pattern of growth of the whole economy, as they highlight that the timing of

---

[1] The chapter is based on the analysis proposed in Romano and Traù (2017). Some qualifications that can be found in the original work (such as the robustness checks of the econometrical analysis and two appendixes) have been here omitted.

The New Industrial World. Livio Romano and Fabrizio Traù, Oxford University Press.
© Livio Romano and Fabrizio Traù (2023). DOI: 10.1093/oso/9780192873736.003.0006

de-industrialization in different countries—meant as the progressive special-ization of the economy away from manufacturing as far as GDP grows—depends on the timing of the manufacturing take-off: the more lagged the latter, the earlier the former. From this point of view this analysis sheds new light on the very nature of structural change, underscoring the necessity to reconsider the 'one size fits all' approach followed in most contributions. Neither do countries progress in a linear fashion along their own path of development, nor they all follow the same path. The knowledge of a coun-try's economic history and institutional settings is a fundamental aspect in order to understand—and possibly predict—its pattern of growth.

As argued in previous chapters, lower trade barriers and the fading away of several institutional boundaries have exogenously increased the scale of (global) demand, and therefore the opportunities to expand domestic production to reach new customers worldwide. At the same time, the fall in telecommunication and transportation costs has paved the way to the exploitation of huge cross-country wage differentials, allowing advanced countries to abandon selected manufacturing activities via offshoring.[2] Off-shored activities have encouraged many countries that had been left behind to specialize in a series of (initially narrow) industrial activities through what has been called 'unbundling' and 'trade in tasks' (see above Chapter 1), bringing about a higher degree of competition, as far as a higher number of countries have had the possibility to enter international markets for the first time as manufacturers. As stressed in the works of Rodrik (2006), Matsuyama (2009), and Uya et al. (2013), this has pushed towards a rising importance of competitive advantages in each country, therefore calling for increasing manufacturing specialization.

Following the work by Hausmann et al. (2011), specialization can be viewed as the way to industrial development. The basic principle harks back to Smith (1776, book 1, Ch. 1), and hinges upon knowledge: as the division of labour takes place, knowledge divides itself among different actors, allowing them to develop 'local' (mostly tacit) capabilities which give rise to (dynamic) increasing returns in the sense suggested by Young (1928).[3] In the long run the whole system gets this way an increasing amount of overall knowledge, so that developed countries will be characterized by a high degree of diversity in the range of goods they are able to produce, whereas the less developed ones

---

[2] On the timing of globalization see for example Sturgeon and Memedovic (2010) and Amatori and Colli (2011).
[3] Specialization allows individuals to focus on a specific set of activities, therefore enhancing their personal knowledge about it and favouring the creation of new skills (see on this point Loasby 2000).

will be bound to a more limited set of production possibilities.[4] The division of labour leads in this sense to the diversification of the domestic production structure.

In such a mechanism, which is conceptually demand-driven, the set of production possibilities is intrinsically path-dependent, but nonetheless can be widened through conscious efforts. At the microeconomic level diversification can be envisaged in a Penrosean perspective (Penrose 1959), i.e. in terms of the enlargement of the endowment of proprietary resources enabling an extension in the range of products. The point can be looked at from the so-called 'Dynamic Capabilities' view (see for instance Helfat et al. 2007), which, starting from Penrosean premises, stresses the relevance of the capacity of firms to create and purposefully modify their resource base through a process of search and selection—so as to achieve congruence with changing environment.

Yet efforts are subject to a whole series of constraints. As a first issue, a most relevant role in limiting diversification is played by the degree of exposure to competition from abroad. In the context of a closed economy the expansion of the supply matrix can go on indefinitely as far as the structure of demand becomes more complex, whilst competitive pressure from abroad asks for stronger competitive advantages, hampering the development of non-competitive activities. On the other hand, countries joining the road to industrialization later must face global market structures (and entry barriers) that have been already established, and market shares that have been already allocated among incumbents.

A further issue lies in the length of the period along which industrialization can take place; from this point of view the longer the time span available to reach a given level of industrial development, the wider the possibility to exploit the learning curves (the dynamic increasing returns) associated to any given industrial activity—i.e. the lower the level which learning curves can get. From the point of view of the present analysis this may involve a different behaviour of newly industrialized countries with respect to older ones, insofar as they have been compelled to develop their technologies within tighter time constraints.

Other potential constraints come from the 'localized' character of technical progress (in the sense suggested by Atkinson and Stiglitz 1969 and Stiglitz

---

[4] In this view product diversity—as a measure of the range of capabilities of any given country—is as much important as their 'ubiquity', i.e. the extent to which goods can be (and actually are) produced in *other* countries.

1987) affecting the speed at which technical change can spread to other activities far from the initial core. An analogous point can be raised looking at the problems affecting later developed countries as a specific group, in the sense suggested by Fuà (1978). The point here is that by their very nature laggards *cannot* be able to get competitive advantages along the whole spectrum of manufacturing activities, due to the existence of a structural shortage in their endowments of organizational capabilities. This is very much exacerbated by globalization as well, insofar as it raises the amount of capabilities required for setting up and managing internationally competitive organizations. In this sense, 'lagged development is a different development' (Fuà 1978: 132).

Overall, in light of such premises it can be said that early industrialized countries could largely develop their manufacturing activities in the face of lower international integration and competitive pressure from abroad and had at disposal a longer time span to enlarge their supply matrix before the globalization process took place. In contrast, laggards did join industrialization in the face of a much more competitive environment, therefore having to deal with more complex problems when trying to diversify their manufacturing activities.

Moreover, laggard themselves are not an undifferentiated entity. As stressed in Chapter 1, before the advent of globalization the stock of manufacturing experience differed dramatically—not only between advanced and developing countries, but also among backward economies themselves. Whereas some of the latecomers—especially in East Asia—had already attained enough productive knowledge and technical capabilities to be able to set up (pieces of) a competitive industry, many other countries had to wait for the above-mentioned process of fragmentation of value chains at the international level in order to start powering up a modern manufacturing base—through the offshoring processes triggered by advanced countries.

From an institutional standpoint, it has to be recalled the role played by state intervention, when aimed at building 'national' industrial systems through active industrial policies (Developmental State). As highlighted in Chapter 3, such policies have been oriented to the development of proprietary competences (even in quite new activities), according to a dynamic view of the market process grounded on learning rather than on allocative efficiency, pursuing the establishing of long-run comparative advantages. But this has happened only in a limited number of countries, therefore implying further divergence in the cross-country distribution of such advantages.

So, we can say that, in principle, at any given point in time the extent to which individual countries succeed in enlarging the range of what they are able to produce can be conceived as a function of their stock of industrial competences and their ability to develop new capabilities, acting against path-dependence and institutional inertia. This means that different countries have been facing the shock represented by the advent of globalization starting from both different levels of industrial development and different production structures, as reflected by the fundamental heterogeneity of their industrial development process and institutional settings.

5.2 Research hypotheses

In a widely quoted contribution, Imbs and Wacziarg (2003) have provided a description of the transformations occurring within the manufacturing sector in the course of development. The phenomenon is represented in terms of the degree of sectoral concentration of industrial output, which is found to follow a U-shaped pattern as the economy expands—that is, sectoral concentration appears to be higher in countries characterized by relatively low or relatively high levels of economic development.[5]

According to Cadot et al. (2011), the low concentration in the middle stage of structural change can be viewed, in terms of industrial specialization, essentially as a transitory phenomenon between two steady states, as new sectors—grown endogenously or established through flows of foreign investments—become competitive in the international markets while old ones gradually die off. In a later contribution Imbs et al. (2012) argue instead that the sectoral concentration of output—which is accompanied by regional convergence in productivity and factor endowments within the country—stems endogenously from the transition from closeness to an open-economy regime, i.e. from a situation in which an increasing demand for diversified products is satisfied domestically to another in which only industries that succeed in becoming internationally competitive do thrive and grow.

The point here is that economic literature neglects the impact that the initial differences in the production structure can actually exert on the process of diversification induced by deeper economic integration. The analysis presented in the following pages is aimed at filling this gap, showing how the differences accumulated by each country *before* the rise of globalization, as

---

[5] The changes occurring at the intra-sectoral level can also be considered from the point of view of the specific nature of the industries which gradually come into existence in the course of manufacturing development. In such perspective Haraguchi and Rezonja (2013) show some differences between small and large countries in the take-off of individual manufacturing sectors by stage of development.

a result of their specific path of industrialization, have affected the intensity and the speed with which structural change has occurred along the Globalization Age (GA). In particular, the hypothesis lying at the core of this analysis can be formulated as follows: to the extent that the intensity of international competition has asked late industrializing countries to search for comparative advantages since the very beginning of their industrialization process, the narrow range of manufacturing know-how held by these countries at the time of globalization—involving a low potential for product diversification—should have strongly bound them in the search for competitiveness, therefore determining an early sectoral concentration.

This hypothesis brings about in turn a further implication, for it involves the fact that industrialization in the course of the GA has to be intended as a process which by its very nature is unbalanced at the sectoral level. This happens just because the growth potential represented by higher (global) demand manifests itself before the long-run growth of internal demand can endogenously drive the development of a fairly complete supply structure (see above). It follows that the higher the gap between the size of the domestic economy and that of the global market at the time in which globalization takes place, the more rapid the rise in the manufacturing share (i.e. the growth of manufacturing as compared to other sectors), and the faster its reach of an upper bound, due to the limited extension of the manufacturing supply matrix.

5.3 Data and sample construction

The empirical analysis is based on the information collected by IHS Markit, a leading provider of comprehensive economic and financial information about countries and industries. In particular, the World Industry Service (WIS) database combines information from numerous sources into a single and coherent platform, allowing comparisons and rankings by sectors and countries[6].

Data include, over the 1980–2011 period and with reference to 75 countries, gross domestic product, manufacturing value added, manufacturing

---

[6] In particular, WIS database is built like a pyramid with three layers. The bottom layer is the UNSNA and UNIDO data, providing the default basis for output and value added for all countries and all sectors; the data from these organizations have the desirable attributes of fine detail, consistency, and comparability. The next layer up is provided by OECD data, which replace UN statistics in those countries/industries where there is overlap; finally, both the UN- and OECD-supplied data are supplemented, when necessary, by individual country sources, and other specific data sources (including Eurostat). Export data are compiled from custom declarations.

exports, and population. Figures for manufacturing can be further broken down, on the basis of the ISIC Rev. 3 classification, into 62 sectors at the four-digit level. This is the level of disaggregation used to study the pattern of change in the sectoral concentration of manufacturing value added.

From the original sample, the city-state of Hong Kong has been omitted as well as those economies where the degree of oil-dependence is supposed to make the process of structural change strongly country-specific.[7]

Finally, as far as the focus of this chapter is on industrial development and its heterogeneity across different production systems, the analysis has been restricted to those countries that have actually experienced a process of growth in their industrial base during the last decades. In particular, the analysis looks at the countries with positive real growth of per capita manufacturing value added between (the average values in) 1990–93 and 2008–11, measuring growth in constant prices (2005 US dollars).[8] Per capita manufacturing value added is meant to provide a synthetic measure of the level of industrial development in each country, in the same way as per capita GDP is intended as a measure of economic development (as discussed in Chapter 2). As a result, the final dataset includes 44 countries.

5.4 Definition and characterization of the groups of countries

In order to test whether the globalization shock has driven industrialization in different countries along the same path of structural change, or whether initial conditions mattered in shaping the process, the analysis starts by sorting countries according to their level of per capita manufacturing value added at the beginning of the 1980s. The assumption is that countries with very large differences in their (initial) level of per capita value added in manufacturing are at different stages of their industrialization process.

Countries are then sorted according to the 1980–83 average, measured at current prices.[9] Top ranking countries are the Western economies concentrated in Europe and the United States, while countries still nowadays

---

[7] In particular, based on World Bank statistics about oil rents, Bahrain, Kuwait, Nigeria, Qatar, Saudi Arabia, Venezuela, and United Arab Emirates, whose oil rents exceeded 30% of domestic GDP in the period 1980–85, were not included in the sample. Iran was omitted because of the war against Iraq, which started in 1980 and ended in 1988.

[8] Four-year averages have been calculated so as to offset potential differences among countries in terms of their behaviour along the business cycle.

[9] The use of current instead of constant price values is preferable in this case because rankings calculated by starting from real values could not be kept constant when changing the base year used to deflate the time series.

classified as developing economies by the World Bank appear at the bottom.[10] Accordingly, we define as the most industrialized countries those that joined the OECD before the 1980s (OIEs),[11] and as the least industrialized those in which the 1980–83 average of per capita manufacturing value added was lower than that of Zimbabwe, i.e. the least industrialized country at the end of the period. Hereafter, we refer to these countries as to the group of Late Industrialized Economies—LIEs.

In the middle there is a group of 14 countries in which the degree of industrialization ranges from the 1,540 dollars per capita of Singapore to the 389 dollars of Chile. These economies, despite their heterogeneity as to the historical accumulation of manufacturing experience, are all character-ized by an intermediate level of industrial development. This, as discussed in Chapter 3, is either the result of inward-looking import-substitution strate-gies, as in the case of Latin American countries and Turkey (Baer 1972, 2002, and Celasum and Rodrik 1989), or of strong export-oriented industrial poli-cies, as in the case of the Asian Tigers including Malaysia (Bradford 1987), or the consequence of centrally-planned industrialization, as for East Euro-pean Republics formerly incorporated in the Communist bloc (see Turnock 2006). Hereafter, we refer to these countries as to the group of Intermediate Industrialized Economies—IIEs.

The list of all countries considered in the analysis is reported in Table 5.1, together with a series of further indicators (calculated as 1980–83 averages): per capita value added in manufacturing, export propensity (degree of open-ness), the Gini coefficient of intra-manufacturing value added, and the share of manufacturing value added on the total economy.

The descriptive statistics return two interesting insights about the state of industrialization that prevailed before the advent of globalization. First, in each of the three groups of countries the degree of openness of the manu-facturing sector was relatively low, and this is especially true for LIEs and IIEs, including those Asian economies that had embraced export-led indus-trialization strategies (with the notable exception of Singapore). Taking as a measure of international economic integration the sum of exports and imports on gross output in manufacturing, data show that the (unweighted) average of the ratio for the 1980–83 period is estimated equal to 0.44 for LIEs, 0.59 for IIEs and 0.75 for OIEs. As a basis for comparison, the corre-sponding values for the 2006–07 period—just before the collapse of global trade—were 1.03 for LIEs, around 1.37 for IIEs and 1.39 for OIEs. Thus,

---

[10] See: http://data.worldbank.org/about/country-classifications.
[11] The group includes Israel that joined the OECD only in 2000.

Table 5.1 Selected indicators for individual countries, average 1980–83, current prices

Countries	Manufacturing VA per capita (.000 dollars)	Openness	Gini of manuf. VA	Manuf. share	Countries	Manufacturing VA per capita (.000 dollars)	Openness	Gini of manuf. VA	Manuf. share
Austria	3.08	0.70	0.54	0.15	Bangladesh	0.04	0.16	0.83	0.13
Belgium	3.43	1.34	0.53	0.17	Bolivia	0.16	0.28	0.86	0.09
Denmark	3.07	0.91	0.58	0.13	Cameroon	0.19	0.40	0.79	0.16
Finland	3.75	0.53	0.60	0.17	China	0.14	0.10	0.63	0.23
Germany	6.34	0.45	0.46	0.29	Egypt	0.12	0.67	0.71	0.12
Ireland	1.63	1.17	0.60	0.09	Honduras	0.24	0.27	0.72	0.17
Israel	2.32	1.17	0.55	0.23	India	0.06	0.13	0.60	0.12
Netherlands	2.87	1.12	0.55	0.14	Indonesia	0.07	0.74	0.80	0.12
Portugal	0.93	0.33	0.61	0.12	Jordan	0.32	1.28	0.78	0.12
Sweden	3.83	0.67	0.53	0.16	Kenya	0.08	0.47	0.72	0.04
Switzerland	6.07	0.82	0.55	0.14	Morocco	0.24	0.25	0.71	0.16
United States	3.93	0.18	0.49	0.12	Pakistan	0.05	0.42	0.79	0.08
OIEs average	*3.44*	*0.75*	*0.56*	*0.16*	Peru	0.22	0.26	0.69	0.15
					Philippines	0.28	0.32	0.68	0.26
Argentina	1.36	0.12	0.68	0.23	Sri Lanka	0.08	0.84	0.83	0.20
Chile	0.52	0.42	0.73	0.12	Thailand	0.19	0.43	0.80	0.07
Costa Rica	0.54	0.41	0.73	0.16	Tunisia	0.26	0.60	0.69	0.20
Czech Republic	0.98	0.64	0.57	0.12	Vietnam	0.03	0.20	0.71	0.12
Hungary	0.96	0.41	0.64	0.19	*LIEs average*	*0.15*	*0.44*	*0.74*	*0.14*
Malaysia	0.53	0.98	0.68	0.15					
Mexico	1.08	0.10	0.58	0.21					
Poland	0.87	0.19	0.60	0.20					
Romania	1.01	0.12	0.65	0.24					
Singapore	2.76	3.27	0.63	0.33					
Slovakia	0.88	0.46	0.51	0.09					
South Korea	0.65	0.41	0.56	0.14					
Taiwan	1.40	0.53	0.57	0.32					
Turkey	0.65	0.13	0.72	0.18					
IIEs average	*1.01*	*0.59*	*0.63*	*0.19*					

OIEs: Old industrialized economies; IIEs: Intermediate industrialized economies; LIEs: Late industrialized economies. Openness is defined as the export plus import to output ratio in manufacturing. Manufacturing share refers to value added. Unweighted averages in italics.

in the 30 years under consideration the degree of openness has more than doubled for the groups of developing countries and almost doubled for the advanced economies. This is a clear indication of the fact that globalization has substantially increased everywhere the competitive pressure faced by the national manufacturing systems.

Second, when confronting the averages of the Gini coefficient for intra-manufacturing value added it appears that, across countries, the degree of sectoral concentration was decreasing with the level of industrial develop-ment. At the beginning of the 1980s, the production structure of OIEs was characterized by a higher degree of diversification as compared to IIEs, which in turn had a higher degree of diversification as compared to the group of LIEs. This is even more clear when the individual observations are plotted against the level of manufacturing value added per capita (Figure 5.1).

The convex cross-country path of diversification depicted in Figure 5.1 might imply the existence of a 'natural' way to industrial development: that is, it might be expected that—thanks to the growth opportunities offered by their integration in the global economy—countries that lagged behind at the beginning of the 1980s could, in the subsequent decades, follow in the foot-steps of those who preceded them.[12] However, as the theoretical discussion

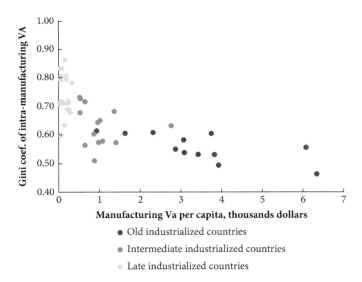

Figure 5.1 Sectoral concentration and industrial development before the globalization's take-off, country averages 1980–83

---

[12] The differences in the levels of (export) specialization observed for similar levels of development have been explained as cross-country differences in the size of accessible markets (Parteka and Tamberi

in Section 5.2 has anticipated and as the empirical analysis in the next section will demonstrate, this hypothesis does not hold true.

5.5 Structural change and industrial development: an econometric analysis

5.5.1 Intra-sectoral structural change

To test the relation between structural change and industrial development, the empirical analysis starts with estimating, for each of the three groups of countries, the following equation, using country fixed effects:

$$\text{Gini}_{itg} = \beta_0 + \beta_1 \text{ManVA}_{itg} + \beta_2 \text{ManVA}^2_{itg} + f_i + \varepsilon_{itg} \tag{5.1}$$

where Gini_{itg} is the Gini coefficient of manufacturing sectoral concentration of country i at time t belonging to group g; ManVA_{itg} is the corresponding manufacturing value added per capita, and f_i is the country fixed effect. Thus, by estimating Equation (5.1) we can test whether a convex relation between sectoral concentration and industrial development, similar to the one shown in Figure 5.1, is found within each of the three groups of countries in the course of the GA. In order to control for serial correlation in the error term, which is related to the panel structure of the data, we estimate robust standard errors clustered at the country level. For we run a fixed-effects regression with country-specific effects, in each group the intercept captures the relationship between sectoral concentration and per capita manufacturing value added for the average country.

Data are measured in constant prices (2005 US dollars). Real values are required in order to increase the comparability of trends across countries, as they are less sensitive to fluctuations in the exchange rate, a primary concern especially for the analysis of emerging economies. 'Real' adjustments of value added are based on sector-specific output indexes provided by IHS.

Then, to test for structural differences in the above relationship between groups of countries, the following equation is also estimated:

$$\text{Gini}_{itg} = \beta_0 + \beta_{11} \text{ManVA}_{itg} + \sum_g \beta_{1g} \text{ManVA}_{itg} G_{ig}$$
$$+ \sum_g \beta_{2g} \text{ManVA}^2_{itg} G_{ig} + f_i + \varepsilon_{itg} \tag{5.2}$$

2013), in the position within the product space (Minondo 2011), and in the institutional efforts to contrast rent-seeking activities (Starosta de Waldemar 2010).

where G_{ig} are two dummies that identify the groups of LIES and OIES. Estimates of β_{1g} and β_{2g} different from zero will indicate the existence of group-specific trends in the patterns of intra-manufacturing structural change, consistently with our research hypothesis.

Figure 5.2 plots the observed Gini coefficient—per capita value added pairs, together with the fitted values obtained from Equation (5.1) which

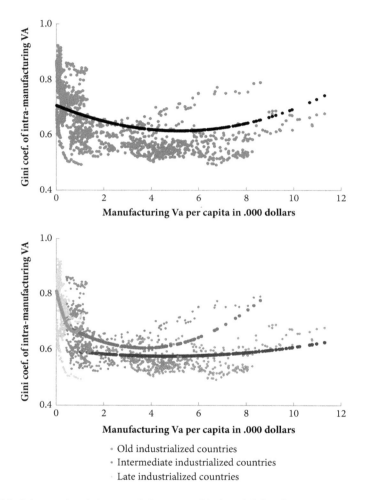

Old industrialized countries
Intermediate industrialized countries
Late industrialized countries

Figure 5.2 Intra-sectoral structural change and industrial development, 1980–2011, constant dollars*

*In the upper part of the figure all countries are pooled together and a single quadratic relation is estimated. In the lower part, instead, the different groups are analysed separately. Darker dots are obtained by estimating the quadratic within-country relation between the Gini and the manufacturing value added per capita.

are marked with darker dots. Different groups are associated with different colours and different fitted lines. Results show, for the entire sample, a clear convex pattern of intra-manufacturing specialization along the process of industrial development, with a decline in concentration as industrial development is at an early stage and a turning point in the Gini coefficient occurring at around 5,000 dollars of per capita manufacturing value added. Yet, the same figure also documents, in sharp contrast with the homogeneity assumption, that the shape of the relation varies significantly with the timing in the advent of the industrialization process.

In particular, it emerges that the later the industrialization process started, the faster the sectoral concentration of manufacturing value added was. In other words, relative to OIEs, whose industrial development involved a relatively large number of activities (the Gini coefficient is relatively stable and low along the entire period), for the other groups the sectoral distribution started concentrating (again) much earlier: for IIEs this occurred at around 4,000 dollars at constant prices, for LIEs at around 1,000 dollars. The differences in the patterns of structural change are consistent with the hypothesis set forth in Section 5.2, according to which the more lagged the process of industrialization, the narrower the opportunities to expand manufacturing know-how in the course of the GA.

Table 5.2 reports the estimates of the corresponding regression analysis. Columns (1) to (3) refer to each group of countries individually (Equation 5.1), while columns (4) to (5) refer to the entire sample (Equation 5.2).

Results show that the U-shaped relation is confirmed by the statistical analysis for each group of countries (in the case of OIEs the relation is weakly statistically significant). Moreover, relative to IIEs the relation is again statistically different for the remaining groups: concentration occurs earlier than that observed in OIEs, but later compared to LIEs. Moreover, insofar as the globalization of production has been the main driver of industrialization in the last decades (in the sense suggested above), then we should also find in the data a positive relation between the sectoral concentration of manufacturing exports and that of total manufacturing output, especially for those laggard economies where industrial development occurred largely because of the globalization itself.

To this end, Table 5.3 reports, for each group of countries, the estimates of the correlation between the Gini coefficient of manufacturing production and the Gini coefficient of manufacturing export, together with their

Table 5.2 Regression analysis of intra-sectoral structural change, 1980–2011, constant prices*

	LIEs (1)	IIEs (2)	OIEs (3)	(4)	(5)
Man VA_{igt}	−0.403***	−0.053**	−0.011	−0.053**	−0.050**
	(0.066)	(0.015)	(0.008)	(0.015)	(0.016)
Man VA^2_{igt}	0.261***	0.007***	0.001*	0.007***	0.007***
	(0.053)	(0.001)	(0.001)	(0.001)	(0.001)
Man VA_{igt} * (OIEs)				0.042**	0.045**
				(0.017)	(0.018)
Man VA^2_{igt} (OIEs)				−0.006***	−0.006***
				(0.002)	(0.002)
Man VA_{igt} * (LIEs)				(0.350)	−0.310***
				(0.067)	(0.074)
Man VA^2_{igt} * (LIEs)				0.254***	0.214***
				(0.052)	(0.056)
Constant				0.719***	0.714***
Constant				(0.009)	(0.011)
Year dummies	No	No	No	No	Yes
Observations	576	448	384	1408	1408
Within-R^2	0.43	0.30	0.08	0.34	0.38

* Robust standard errors in parentheses, clustered at the country level. The dependent variable is the Gini coefficient of intra-manufacturing value added. * $p < 0.10$, ** $p < 0.05$, *** $p < 0.01$. OIEs and LIEs are group dummies referred to old and late industrialized countries respectively. Regressions include country fixed effects. Manufacturing value added per capita in thousand dollars. OIEs: Old industrialized countries; IIEs: Intermediate industrialized countries; LIEs: Late industrialized countries.

statistical significance.[13] Export data are deflated using export price indexes provided by IHS.

In general, the sectoral concentration of manufacturing value added appears positively correlated to the sectoral concentration of manufacturing exports: a change in the relative specialization of a country's export basket is reflected in a change in the relative specialization of the domestic production structure. The only exception to this rule is the behaviour of the group of OIEs, where the correlation between the two variables is not statistically different from zero. Moreover, compared to the group of IIEs the elasticity of the Gini of manufacturing production is estimated to be significantly higher (twice as large) for the group of LIEs.

[13] As for the previous econometric specifications, estimates only rely on the within-country variation of both Gini coefficients.

Table 5.3 The effect of trade on the intra-manufacturing structural change, 1980–2011, constant dollars*

	LIEs (1)	IIEs (2)	OIEs (3)
Gini of exports	0.421***	0.195*	0.120
	(0.064)	(0.101)	(0.092)
Constant	0.392***	0.508***	0.494***
	(0.054)	(0.073)	(0.061)
Observations	576	448	384
Within-R^2	0.41	0.06	0.04
Difference w.r.to (2)	0.2*		−0.076
	(0.117)		(0.134)

* Robust standard errors in parentheses, clustered at the country level. The dependent variable is the Gini coefficient of intra-manufacturing value added. * $p < 0.10$, ** $p < 0.05$, *** $p < 0.01$. Regressions include country fixed effects. OIEs: Old industrialized countries; IIEs: Intermediate industrialized countries; LIEs: Late industrialized countries.

5.5.2 Inter-sectoral structural change

Globalization is also expected to affect the inter-sectoral allocation of resources of a country, because it directly hits, as an exogenous shock, the manufacturing base significantly more intensively than agriculture and services. In order to test the relation between the inter-sectoral structural change and the level of industrial development, the same econometric approach defined by Equations (5.1) and (5.2) is followed, replacing the Gini coefficient with the share of manufacturing value added in GDP. Thus, Figure 5.3 plots the relation between the manufacturing share and per capita manufacturing value added, together with the fitted values obtained from the econometric estimation (marked with darker dots). As before, the upper part of the figure refers to the entire sample of countries, while in the lower part different groups are associated with different colours and different fitted lines.

The figure shows that the hypothesis of a hump-shaped relation between the manufacturing value added share and the degree of industrial development cannot be rejected by the data. In the early stages of industrial development, the manufacturing system grows at a faster rate than the rest of the economy, which also implies that an increasing share of inputs is employed in this sector. However, as industrialization continues the growth rate of manufacturing relative to the other sectors decreases, up to the point where further growth of the industrial base occurs together with a decline of the manufacturing share in the economy. In other words, after a certain level

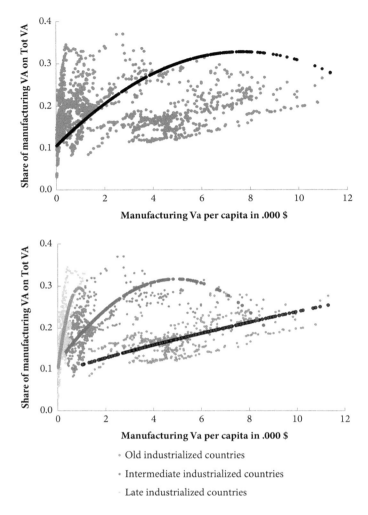

Figure 5.3 Inter-sectoral structural change and industrial development, 1980–2011, constant dollars*

* In the upper part of the figure all countries are pooled together and a single quadratic relation is estimated. In the lower part, instead, the different groups are analysed separately. Darker dots are obtained by estimating the quadratic within-country relation between the manufacturing value added share and the manufacturing value added per capita.

of industrial development, the expansion of the manufacturing base does not dominate anymore the rest of the economy.

Yet, the same figure also reveals, consistent with our second hypothesis, that the larger was the pre-globalization gap in the industrialization process, the more unbalanced has been the inter-sectoral output shift towards manufacturing along the process of industrial development. This implies that the inter-sectoral output shift towards manufacturing for the group of LIEs has been significantly larger than that experienced by IIEs, that in turn has been larger than that experienced in OIEs. Moreover, the manufacturing share is estimated to have reached a maximum at around 1,200 dollars (at constant prices) for LIEs, and at around 4,800 dollars for IIEs, whereas for OIES the turning point is not yet observed, and the relation looks linear instead.

Hence, while for OIEs industrialization took place over a long period of time, largely as an endogenous process occurring in a world of segmented markets where the opportunities for trade and specialization were limited, at the other extreme LIEs have experienced an export-led growth that, in the few decades under our scrutiny, has increased the scale of the market for manufacturing productions of a different order of magnitude as compared to the other sectors of the economy. IIEs represent an intermediate case between these two extremes, because their industrialization process is rooted, for different historical reasons, in a pre-globalized world; consistently, the slope of the relation between structural change and industrial development is steeper than that observed for OIEs but flatter than the one characterizing LIEs.

The graphical inspection is confirmed by the regression analysis reported in Table 5.4, where the estimates of the coefficients are showed together with their statistical significance. Columns (1) to (3) refer to each group of countries individually while columns (4) to (5) refer to the entire sample. The hump-shaped relation between structural change and industrial development is found for LIEs and IIEs, while for OIEs the relation is estimated linear. Moreover, compared to IIEs the relation is flatter than that estimated for LIEs countries, but steeper than that referred to OIEs.

5.6 Industrial development and economic development

So far, the empirical investigation has revealed that the process of industrial development in the last 30 years has followed heterogeneous paths of intra- and inter-sectoral structural change in different groups of countries (LIEs, IIEs, and OIEs), consistently with the research hypotheses set in Section 5.3. Such results bring about important consequences as to the process of economic development undertaken by these same countries.

In this analysis both intra- and inter-sectoral changes have been related to the level of manufacturing value added, for the reasons explained above. However, as long as the enlargement of the manufacturing base goes hand

Table 5.4 Regression analysis of inter-sectoral structural change, 1980–2011, constant prices*

	LIEs (1)	IIEs (2)	OIEs (3)	(4)	(5)
Man VA_{igt}	0.441***	0.080***	0.018**	0.080***	0.093**
	(0.078)	(0.016)	(0.007)	(0.016)	(0.017)
Man VA^2_{igt}	−0.244**	−0.008***	−0.000	−0.008***	−0.008***
	(0.095)	(0.002)	(0.001)	(0.002)	(0.002)
Man VA_{igt} * (OIEs)				−0.062**	−0.067**
				(0.017)	(0.019)
Man VA^2_{igt} (OIEs)				0.008***	0.008***
				(0.002)	(0.002)
Man VA_{igt} * (LIEs)				0.361***	0.458***
				(0.078)	(0.100)
Man VA^2_{igt} (LIEs)				−0.236**	−0.305***
				(0.093)	(0.116)
Constant	0.096***	0.114***	0.089***	0.099***	0.089***
	(0.011)	(0.020)	(0.020)	(0.009)	(0.011)
Year dummies	No	No	No	No	Yes
Observations	576	448	384	1408	1408
Within-R^2	0.59	0.54	0.68	0.58	0.62

* Robust standard errors in parentheses, clustered at the country level. The dependent variable is the manufacturing share of value added on the total economy. * $p < 0.10$, ** $p < 0.05$, *** $p < 0.01$. OIEs and LIEs are group dummies referred to old and late industrialized countries respectively. Regressions include country fixed effects. Manufacturing value added per capita in thousand dollars. OIEs: Old industrialized countries; IIEs: Intermediate industrialized countries; LIEs: Late industrialized countries.

in hand with the expansion of the whole economy, then similar relationships to those shown in Section 5.5.2 are to be expected if manufacturing value added per capita is replaced by income per capita, as usually happens in the literature about structural change, following the works of Fisher (1939), Clark (1940), Fuchs (1968), and Kuznets (1973).

This is confirmed by the results of the econometric analysis, graphically shown in Figure 5.4.

In particular, for LIEs and IIEs the estimates show the existence of a hump-shaped relationship between the level of economic development and the rate of industrialization of the economy, which is consistent with the typical stylized fact assumed in literature. At the same time, these same estimates document for the first time that the larger was the pre-globalization gap in the industrialization process, the more unbalanced has been the sectoral output shift towards manufacturing along the process of economic development.

More specifically, as to the group of LIEs, both the quadratic and the non-parametric fits estimate a decline in the share of manufacturing value added at a level of GDP per capita which is below 5,000 dollars at constant prices,

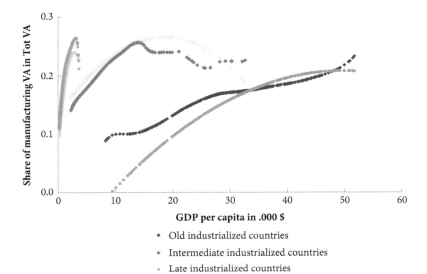

* Old industrialized countries
* Intermediate industrialized countries
* Late industrialized countries

Figure 5.4 Inter-sectoral structural change and economic development, 1980–2011, constant dollars, quadratic and non-parametric fits*

* For each group of countries lighter dots refer to the estimates of the quadratic within-country relation between the manufacturing value added share and the GDP per capita; darker dots refer to the corresponding non-parametric fit using the Epanechnikov kernel function.

less than half of the level estimated for the group of IIEs (between 10,000 and 20,000 dollars depending on the specification of the model).

As to the group of OIEs, instead, the estimated relationship between the two variables looks flatter. Indeed, both the non-parametric and the (unreported) semi-parametric fractional polynomial fit point to a monotonically increasing relationship. This trend, which is consistent with the theoretical framework outlined above, appears at odds with the general view according to which advanced economies should be 'post-industrialized' (see Rodrik 2016 for a recent reappraisal).

Yet this apparent contradiction can be easily solved by recalling that the sample of economies considered in the analysis—including the advanced ones—is represented only by those countries that have *actually* experienced a process of growth of their industrial basis (in per capita terms) during the last decades. Therefore, countries like Italy, France, or Japan, as well as developing ones like Argentina or Brazil, in which manufacturing valued added at the end of the 2010s was below the level of early 1990s, have been excluded by construction.

Moreover, it has to be highlighted that the observed pattern of structural change is not independent of the measure used to define the phenomenon

under investigation. The fact that—as set forth by Kaldor (1966) and Baumol (1967)—the manufacturing sector is characterized by relatively higher
growth rates of productivity as compared to the rest of the economy involves
that a decline in the manufacturing share of both employment and of value
added measured at current prices can well be paralleled by a constant trend—
or even an increase—in the manufacturing share of value added measured
at constant prices. And, indeed, this has already been quite clearly documented in literature, especially for some advanced economies (Rowthorn
and Ramaswamy 1997).

On the whole, the view set forth in this chapter, which represents an
original development of the traditional view about structural change, is consistent with late development being a story of 'compressed development', as
suggested by Whittaker et al. (2020). In this sense some countries have experienced, within a short time span, a stage of (late) industrialization followed
by an early halt, at a level of both industrial and economic development that
is significantly lower than that reached by earlier industrializing countries.
More generally, this shows remarkable analogies with the evidence set forth
in the 'early de-industrialization' literature, according to which in developing
countries the decline of the manufacturing share (in terms of employment or
output) has occurred at lower levels of income per capita than was the case
in advanced economies (see in particular Palma 2005, 2019a and Tregenna
2013). A similar point has been raised by Rodrik (2016), also arguing that
some 'globalization effect' is at work—due to a sudden uprise in imports for
developing countries opening up to trade, enhanced by the lower relative
prices of goods exported by advanced countries.[14]

5.7 Conclusions

Industrial development is accompanied by shifts in economic activities both
across and within sectors, which determine the overall specialization of
the economy and ultimately its relative competitiveness. Globalization has
played a crucial role in shaping this process. Sectors with a comparative
advantage could expand at an unprecedented pace while joining international markets, attracting labour and capital from the rest of the economy.

The intensity and the speed of this change differs dramatically across countries, depending on to what extent they have become part of the global

[14] Rodrik's analysis highlights the role that in this context has been played by Latin American countries;
on more descriptive grounds premature de-industrialization in such countries is also paid attention by
Castillo and Neto (2016).

economy and in particular on the timing of the industrialization process. The effect was moderate for those economies where the advent of the industrialization process predated international integration. In contrast, the effect was maximum for those developing countries that industrialized at the same time as globalization took place, in many cases by joining international value chains and becoming prominent destinations for offshoring from advanced countries. In a few years (and at a still very low level of industrial development) they became industrial economies and acquired competences and technologies in new manufacturing activities. Yet, these same countries have been facing constraints in their industrialization process due to their limited set of manufacturing capabilities, which have triggered a process of early de-industrialization.

In perspective, it can be said that, if manufacturing industries are 'escalator industries' for economic development (Rodrik 2013; Szirsmay and Verspagen 2015; Foster-McGregor and Verspagen 2016; Marconi et al. 2016) and the acquisition of production capabilities in an increasing range of goods—i.e. the opposite of the sectoral concentration here documented—is crucial for a sustainable growth to be achieved (Hausmann et al. 2011), then the catching-up process observed in Emerging economies might slow down in the near future, well before what standard economic theory would suggest.

6
The Fall of the Globalization Age

6.1 Changing conditions

The Globalization Age (GA) has been hinging on a unique combination of economic and institutional conditions (here described in Chapter 1) that have gradually faded away, eventually leading to an overall change of the global economic context. This chapter provides an account of such changes, which have been ripening as endogenous consequences of the very foundations of the GA and—in later years—have been fostered by exogenous shocks.

A preliminary image which can help appreciate their intensity can be drawn from the long-run dynamics of the degree of openness of the global economy, here expressed in terms of the ratio of world imports to value added relative to manufacturing (Figure 6.1).[1] The graph shows that, after decades during which international transactions grew significantly faster than the output value, fuelled by the process of global fragmentation of supply chains (which implied an increasing number of cross-border exchanges), concurrently with the outburst of the global financial crisis such expansion came to a halt, and subsequently left the room to a gradual but significant retreat. At the end of 2019, the world trade to output ratio was 12 percentage points lower than the peak in 2008 (from 123.9% to 111.6%).[2] This implies that for every additional unit of manufacturing value added produced globally, the amount of manufacturing trade which is activated has been in later years significantly lower than it was in the 1990s, as well as in the early 2000s. The elasticity of manufacturing trade to value added sharply decreased accordingly: from 4.2 in the 1990s to 1.6 in the 2000–08 period to less than 1 between 2010 and 2019.

---

[1] International economic integration is usually analysed by looking at the total merchandise trade; referring to manufacturing only—apart from focusing the attention on the main subject of this analysis—allows to net out the price effect of the commodity cycle registered in the first decade of 2000s.

[2] An almost identical image (see Manzocchi et al. 2020) can be obtained by calculating a participation index to global value chains, showing that the maximum degree of expansion of GVCs has been reached before the last global crisis, and in the following years it has been constantly falling: between its peak in 2008 and 2017 the GVC participation index of the main world manufacturing countries fell by 5 percentage points.

The New Industrial World. Livio Romano and Fabrizio Traù, Oxford University Press.
© Livio Romano and Fabrizio Traù (2023). DOI: 10.1093/oso/9780192873736.003.0007

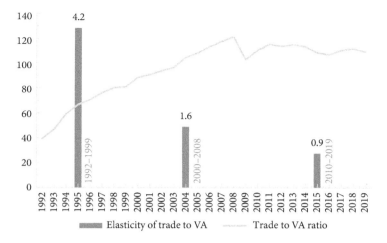

Figure 6.1 Relationship between global trade and value added in manufacturing*
*Elasticity in constant dollars, trade to VA in current dollars.
Source: UNCTAD and ComTrade, own calculations.

The slowdown of international trade has given way to a debate since the early years following the financial crisis in 2008.[3] Whereas the degree of international economic integration is anyway likely to remain sustained for long (see below), evidence (including the empirical findings gathered in this chapter) seems to dismiss the perspective of an endless process of cross-country fragmentation of global value chains. As will be argued in the following, we are facing the exhaustion of the offshoring flows which, since the final years of past century, had thrown into international markets a massive amount of intermediate and final goods previously produced in advanced countries, determining a structural increase in the amount of international market exchanges per unit of output.

The point here is that such a change runs opposite to the GA logic, according to which economic development could be basically attained through the single lever of international trade (taken as the intermediate target of a policy almost exclusively grounded on market liberalization as an instrument). This sets the conditions for a 'new normal' to come to the fore. In this perspective it has still to be added that the de-globalization has been furtherly

---

[3] See in particular the various contributions in Hoekman (2015), Auboin and Borino (2017) and Costantinescu et al. (2020), according to whom the slowdown has to be attributed to structural factors, such as a halt in the process of fragmentation of value chains at the international level. A different point of view is expressed by Borin et al. (2017), arguing that the driver of the slowdown have instead to be found in cyclical factors (so that the phenomenon should be expected to exhaust).

enhanced by the consequences of two major exogenous shocks such as the pandemic and the war in Ukraine, so that an even more radical re-thinking of the current shape of global value chains should be expected to occur in the next future also as a result of active policies, leading to an outright shortening of international supply networks.

Overall, the basic features of the new normal that seems to emerge in the aftermath of the global financial crisis can be found in a general slowdown in the rhythm of growth of manufacturing output, affecting almost all economic systems after a long phase characterized by exceptionally high growth rates in several emerging economies; and in the comeback of space (in geopolitical terms) as a key variable affecting economic behaviour, upsetting the idea according to which the very success of globalization had led to the 'death of distance' (Cairncross 1997).[4]

In this chapter these two phenomena are analysed from various intertwined perspectives, by looking at their long-run determinants. Next sections pay attention in particular to the following issues: (1) the structural reasons behind the worldwide slowdown of manufacturing growth; (2) the fall of external demand as a driver of manufacturing development; (3) the decoupling of Chinese productions from global sourcing (as well as some evidence of supply-side disengagement coming from advanced economies in terms of back-shoring); (4) the resurgence of regionalism in international trade; (5) the economic consequences of the advancements of the digital and green transitions.

6.2 The slowdown of manufacturing growth

The mechanism of the global expansion along the GA has vanished, and manufacturing growth seems to have settled down on a lower growth path. This trend is the result of changes occurred in the economic structure of both advanced and emerging economies and seems to have come to stay.[5]

As a first issue, it has to be recalled that the transfer of (a portion of) world production to the emerging world—paralleled by an unlimited liquidity supply—for many years has turned out into an outright fall in the prices of intermediate and consumption goods in advanced countries. This

---

[4] In Cairncross' view the death of distance is primarily attributed to the spreading all over the world of information and communication technologies (ICTs), deemed to be the basic force driving to a global world.

[5] See among others UNCTAD (2018), OECD (2019), World Bank (2019b).

has been the way through which, starting with the 1990s, in such countries an out-of-scale ('aberrant') boom in the demand for imports has taken place. When the financial crisis broke out, this trend turned into a sharp fall in demand, weakening the role played by external demand in sustaining the growth of emerging economies (see next section).

A second factor affecting the global path of manufacturing expansion is the simple fact that exceptionally high growth rates such those recorded in some East Asian countries, and in particular in China, cannot be maintained throughout all the stages of the development process (as had already happened in Japan or South Korea). Following Kindleberger (1958: 315), the intertemporal profile of growth can be likened to a Gompertz's curve, so that the general principle holds according to which 'the higher rate of growth has the prospect of slowing down', for 'on only a small portion of [the Gompertz curve] can geometric rates of growth be extrapolated, and then not for long'.[6] Looking ahead, even if other emerging countries are expected to find their way in the foreseeable future, the impact of a giant like China on global growth is likely to be lower.

A third factor is represented in these same countries by the shift of aggregate demand from investments to consumption brought about by the development process itself, which reflects the exhaustion of the most intense phase of capital accumulation in a context characterized by an active economic policy—in which the channelling of savings towards productive domestic investment tends to imply a relative compression of consumption—and therefore involves a reduction in the aggregate spending multiplier.

Fourth, the effects of structural change in emerging economies, in terms of the growth of a wide service sector, also have led to a gradual dwindling of the relative weight of manufacturing activities on the total economy—which can even take the form, as argued in previous chapters, of early de-industrialization. Insofar as manufacturing is the sector in which increasing returns are relatively higher (following Kaldor 1966), this translates into a slowdown of aggregate growth as well.

On the side of advanced economies, growth has been negatively affected by the fall in demand brought about by the financial crisis (see next section). But it may also be worth mentioning in this connection the consequences of the policy strategies of individual European countries, which—in the wake of the German export-led model—by constantly looking for lower input costs (i.e. relatively low wages) in order to gain external competitiveness, paid

---

[6] On this point see also Cameron (1993).

almost exclusively attention to supply conditions, therefore inducing an internal deflation. Yet for most such countries the European market is also *magna pars* of the overall market for exports, so that the compression of internal demand within each country has eventually turned out into a compression of their external demand as well, bringing about a vicious cycle of low demand—low output—low income—low demand. More generally, it may be recalled here what has already been argued in Chapter 1 with reference to the 're-entry' of advanced economies into a pathway of secular stagnation. From this point of view falling demand can be viewed as a major long-run determinant of the output slowdown, especially as to the US (Storm 2017).

Overall, the whole world seems to have turned back to a situation where the rhythm of long-run growth is far lower than that experienced along the GA, and this has happened well before the impact of the pandemic could manifest itself (Chandrasekhar and Ghosh 2021). A measure of the intensity of these changes can be drawn from Figure 6.2, showing the annual average growth rates of gross manufacturing output for some large countries, EU, and the whole world, with reference to six sub-periods over a time span ranging from 1996 to 2018.

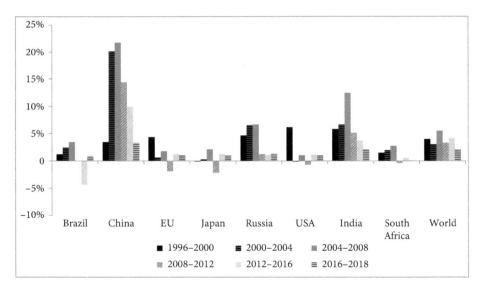

Figure 6.2 Annual average growth rates of manufacturing gross output (constant dollars)

Source: IHS, own calculations.

In the graph the dynamics of growth rates appears broadly hump-shaped: corresponding, especially for emerging economies, to the rise and fall of a rhythm of growth which appears clearly unsustainable in the long-run. From this point of view the whole world seems to have gone out of a context which has to be considered as exceptional (and unrepeatable in the foreseeable future).

It can be added that such dynamics is also characterized by a rising degree of cross-country homogeneity, as shown by the variance of annual growth rates (Figure 6.3). By excluding the peak in 2009 (simply reflecting a different degree of resilience of the different economic systems in the aftermath of the crisis), the variability in individual countries' behaviour decreases regularly (more markedly in the post-crisis years), putting into evidence a gradual convergence towards the slowdown shown in the previous graph.[7]

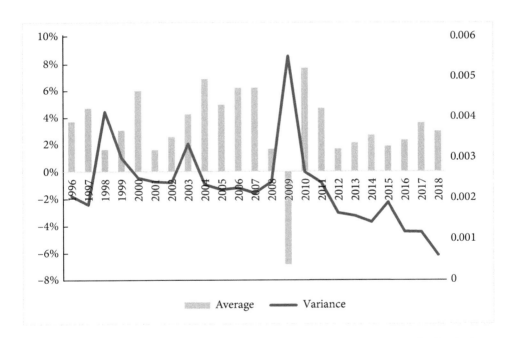

Figure 6.3 Average (left scale) and variance in gross output growth rates of individual countries at the world level (constant dollars)*

*Excluding oil producers and Ireland.
Source: IHS, own calculations.

[7] This has been underscored in particular with reference to the 'synchronized slowdown' of emerging economies, by attributing it to the fall in the external component of demand coming from advanced ones (Fayad and Perrelli 2014).

6.3 From external to internal demand

The burst of the global financial crisis in 2008 represented a huge and long-lasting negative shock to the domestic demand in advanced economies, which did not spare manufacturing. In the United States the internal demand of industrial goods, expressed as apparent consumption (sum of gross output and imports minus export) dropped by 19 percentage points between 2007 and 2009 in real terms, and it took a decade to get closer to the pre-crisis level. Similar dynamics characterize the Eurozone and Japan in the same years (Figure 6.4).

The high degree of economic integration between the North and South reached during the early 2000s was such that the drop in demand of the former had a direct impact on the supply of the latter, undermining its main source of growth till then. Hence, world trade has been declining since those years independently of the rise of protectionism: in a few words, falling demand from the North has determined a fall in exports from the South, and the latter has been compelled to do away with the former.

Indeed, the issue was quite evident as early as in the immediate post-financial crisis years:

> [I]n the large deficit economies … rebalancing … will occur through a reduction in consumption, and hence in imports. This should not be viewed as a historical aberration. Rather, it was the post-1990s boom in consumption in the large deficit economies that was aberrant.
>
> **(Kaplinski and Farooki 2010)**

This has forced a change in perspective for emerging economies, pushing them to re-orient their production either to new foreign markets outside the North and/or to internal demand, in order to escape from an otherwise strong compression of output.

Achieving a balance between domestic and international demand is a key element for development policies. In particular, the economic literature stresses the limits of a strictly export-led development strategy and the critical role played by internal demand in ensuring the possibility for output to expand in the long run.[8] From this point of view, a major point lies in the still limited size of the domestic market in a great many emerging countries, asking for a different orientation of economic policy as compared to the past.

---

[8] See the arguments suggested, among others, by Chenery et al. (1986), Razmi and Blecker (2008), Kaplinski and Farooki (2010), Palley (2011).

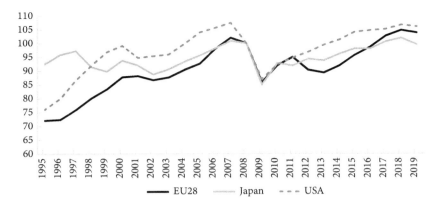

Figure 6.4 Internal demand (apparent consumption)* for manufacturing goods, 2007=100, constant prices

* Sum of gross output and imports less exports.
Source: IHS-Markit, own calculations.

The point has been raised quite explicitly since the years following the crisis:

> The policy stance of developing countries needs to adapt to an external economic environment characterized by slow recovery and weak growth in developed economies. Such adaptation implies the need for a gradual shift in the relative importance of external sources of growth towards a greater emphasis on domestic sources.
>
> **(UNCTAD 2013: 49)**

This has pushed in particular (some) emerging East Asian economies—where the dependence on exports was especially strong—towards a new centrality of their domestic demand, with the deployment of explicit strategies of Domestic Demand Led Growth (DDLG).[9] In light of this, the first priority for East Asian countries was to find alternative markets to compensate for the drop in demand in Western markets (Mizuno 2017).

The switch from external to internal demand as the engine of manufacturing growth was quite spectacular in the case of China (Figure 6.5): its export to value added ratio for manufacturing goods dropped from 106.1% in 2006 (at the peak) to 73.2% in 2009 and then, a decade after, to 64.0% in 2019. In the case of India, the second-largest Asian emerging economy but a laggard

---

[9] See in particular UNCTAD (2013, 2018), Nixson (2016), Leng (2017), Mizuno (2017), UNIDO (2018). Similar attention is paid by Mohanty (2012) to India.

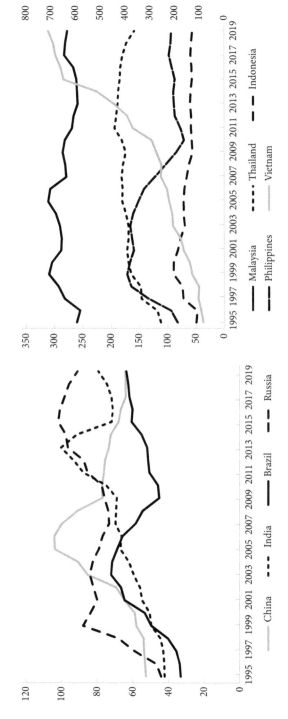

Figure 6.5 Manufacturing export to value added ratio, current dollars.

Source: UNCTAD, ComTrade, HIS-Markit, own calculations.

relative to China in terms of industrial development, the maximum contribution of export to output was attained in 2013, and since then it dropped by more than 20 percentage points. In the Philippines, Indonesia and Malaysia a lower export-to-value added ratio is also observed at the end of 2019 as compared to the early 2000s, notwithstanding the fact that the manufacturing systems of these countries have expanded their size in the meanwhile.

A notable exception in the Asian landscape is Vietnam, as its spectacular manufacturing growth rate during the GA (see Chapter 2) has been largely driven by an increasing participation in international value chains: export in 2019 was 7 times the value of output, as against 1.5 times in 2000. Yet it has to be noted that in the last few years Vietnamese exports have been increasingly oriented towards China, which has become the third trade partner after the US and the EU, with a share of 15.1% in 2019, against 4.0% in 2000.

The Vietnamese case highlights a more general trend observed in East Asia, that is the (partial) substitution of the advanced economies with China as the final destination for regional exports. In fact, the increase of the Chinese internal demand for both consumption and intermediate goods has already triggered a process of re-orientation of trade flows in the other Asian economies, making the region on the whole economically more independent from shocks originated outside. As a consequence, it can be said that East Asia has already become its most important final market. Whereas previously East Asian production—even if integrated—was primarily oriented towards Western markets, nowadays the region has become able to fuel its own demand. Behind this development there is obviously the huge expansion of Chinese demand, which has replaced the United States as the leading source of final demand for the rest of the sub-continent (Rajah 2019).

In this perspective, China's involvement in regional economic activities has shifted from the simple role of a regional assembler on behalf of Western multinationals to being a leading market also for consumer goods produced in the region (Ding and Li 2017). Therefore, in the 'new normal' a block of East Asian economies has learned to be more self-sufficient from the North on the demand side, relying both on their internal consumption and on the opportunity to serve the expanding Chinese market.[10]

For those economies, as Russia and Brazil, which failed to develop an internationally competitive industrial system during the expansionary phase of the GA, but are still abundant in natural resources, the manufacturing export-to-value added ratio has been primarily driven instead by the commodity price boom which took place at the beginning of 2000s and lasted

---

[10] See more widely below, Section 6.5.

for around a decade (see Chapter 3). In particular, the upswing of the cycle drove the relative importance of manufacturing exports down as the increase in national income positively affected the domestic demand (also) of local productions. The opposite occurred with the following downswing, which depressed domestic demand and local output, increasing the relative importance of exports.

6.4 The comeback of distance

6.4.1 Decoupling

The new role played by China in the East Asian context is at the root of a more profound change leading to a process of decoupling of the whole area from the Western world. A less integrated world as to international trade can also be associated to a partial substitution of imports with local output. When approached from the perspective of the emerging economies, the shortening of international value chains implies the possibility to become more self-reliant in terms of supply, by replacing imported productions (and related embedded technologies) with local manufacturing goods.[11]

As highlighted in Chapter 3, we cannot expect to find strong evidence of production decoupling in Latin America or Eastern Europe (and even less so in Africa), where industrial policies were largely dismantled at the beginning of the GA and never reinstated in the following decades. On the contrary, the building of national champions was an explicit target of China's development strategy already at the beginning of 2000s, following the previous successful examples of other East Asian tigers, and this strategy has been progressively expanded to cover not only traditional industries but also to shape nascent ones, related to energy, mobility, electronics, and so on.

By computing, at the country level, the evolution of the weight of imported intermediates on total purchases used in the domestic production processes such divergence among emerging economies can be easily observed (Figure 6.6). Looking at the group of BRICs (i.e. at largest emerging economies), it can be noted that whereas the Chinese trajectory clearly appears hump shaped, with import dependence sharply falling since 2005, in the case of Brazil, Russia and also India no replacement of foreign

---

[11] An evaluation of the intensity of the 'de-globalization' process that has hit international exchanges since the very early years following the crisis, leading to a shortening of the GVCs, can be found in UNCTAD (2013) and Miroudot and Nordström (2019).

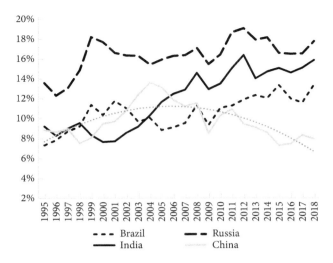

Figure 6.6 Share of intermediate imports* used by BRICs' domestic manufacturing (monetary values at current prices)

* Excluding coke and refined petroleum.
Source: OECD data, own calculations.

with domestic productions has shown up. Rather, the value of intermediate imports has grown substantially.

It is worth noting that the Chinese decoupling predates not only the neo-protectionist strategy launched by the United States in 2018, but also the global financial crisis. It looks consistent instead with the explicit target of the 10th Five-years plan approved in 2001, aimed at 'Energetically Optimizing and Improving Industrial Structure', that is at stimulating the expansion and the upgrading of the national manufacturing system. This has been done by increasing product variety, quality, and production efficiency in traditional industries, and by developing the ability to manufacture all components of integrated systems, enhancing the capability for independent development of information technology products (NPC 2010).

6.4.2 Back-shoring

From the perspective of advanced economies, switching to decoupling means both a lower dependence on imports from emerging countries (in particular East Asian ones), which is specular to what has been discussed above, and the coming back from previous offshoring processes (be they driven by FDIs or by the substitution of national suppliers with foreign ones, currently taking the name of back-shoring, or re-shoring.[12]

The second issue, dealt with since the early 2010s even in the periodical press (The Economist 2013), has been rapidly gaining ground in the literature (among others, Kinkel and Maloca 2009; Ellram et al. 2013; Gray et al. 2103; Tavassoli 2013; UNCTAD 2013; Fratocchi et al. 2014; Di Mauro et al. 2018; Elia et al. 2021; Baldwin 2022). A variety of reasons have been put forward at the theoretical level to explain the existence of back-shoring, all having to do on conceptual grounds with changes in the business strategies of offshoring firms (which makes crucial even in a de-globalization phase the role played by the productive determinants of trade flows). Basically, back-shoring may be due to either getting back from a previous strategic error, or to changes in the economic context;[13] but it may more broadly depend on a wider array of business strategies.

Data about these aspects are still rather fragmented (also due to the fact that the measurement unit itself is often difficult to identify, as the phenomenon mostly relates to *parts* of companies or of supply chains), and the results of various empirical studies differ depending on the countries, the data sets, and the time periods considered. On the whole, at the micro-level current survey data (see the above-mentioned references) highlight that the most frequently evoked problems justifying back-shoring initiatives relate to quality management, flexibility, and efficiency of the local supply chains.

A key issue in this perspective is that—as far as a key determinant of off-shoring policies has been the possibility to take advantage of huge (labour) cost differentials,—bringing back home some activities involves as such some negative shock in terms of production costs (which in turn may entail heavy consequences in terms of inflation, especially in light of the current exogenous inflationary pressures due to the consequences of the war in Ukraine, see below). Hence, the possibility to efficiently reconstitute (pieces of) supply chains at home in a reasonable time lapse is not obvious at all (Thun et al. 2021). This may be partially offset by (labour saving) technological advances, which can limit the costs burden of back-shoring, but asks anyway for some

---

[12] 'The term is agnostic as to whether the manufacturing being brought home occurred in a wholly owned facility in an offshore location or in the factory of an offshore supplier. (...) Reshoring, as such, is fundamentally concerned with *where* manufacturing activities are to be performed, independent of *who* is performing the manufacturing activities in question' (Gray et al. 2013: 28, emphasis added). This means that in-house manufacturing abroad could be replaced either by domestic in-house manufacturing (hierarchy-hierarchy) or by a domestic supplier (hierarchy-market); and a supplier abroad could be replaced either by domestic national manufacturing (market-hierarchy) or by a domestic supplier (market-market).

[13] Indeed, in many cases divestiture linked to the exhaustion of the relative advantage of offshoring may also turn into new investments abroad in *other* geographic areas deemed to be still convenient (UNCTAD 2013).

active economic policy, which can help to force relocation 'close to home' for reasons other than the mere maximization of static efficiency.

And, indeed, it is at the 'political' level that the back-shoring issue has been mainly dealt with to date, so that in perspective—also owing to the outbreak of the above-mentioned exogenous shocks in later years—the intensity of the phenomenon, still limited, is likely to increase. From this point of view it can be observed that the United States is the country where the issue has taken on the highest relevance (or in any case greatest visibility) in the political agenda since the 2008 financial crisis, as a result of the breadth and duration of the previous offshoring activity and of the emphasis given to the issue of re-industrialization in the country.[14] And it is just in the American context that the idea has been first evoked that the offshoring of manufacturing activities by large companies has ended up eroding the economies of specialization that have accumulated in the so-called 'industrial commons'.[15] According to Pisano and Shih (2012: 15–16),

> [t]he industrial commons perspective suggests that a decline of competitiveness of firms in one sector can have implications for the competitiveness of firms in another. Industries and the suppliers of capabilities to the industries need each other. (…) Even worse, the loss of a commons may cut off future opportunities for the emergence of new innovative sectors if they require close access to the same capabilities.

Put in other words, the offshoring mechanism runs opposite to the logic of Hirschman linkages, widely referred to in this book. The point is that the spatial separation of manufacturing activities from the 'brain' of the firm (R&D, innovation, commercial strategies)—even if rather boldly asserted for many years both in the economic literature and by many business consultants—is intrinsically unsustainable.[16] As far as an efficient interaction between the different segments of a company requires a certain degree of physical proximity, the relocation of previously outsourced activities becomes a relevant issue. It has anyway to be stressed that—in general—re-location typically happens through growth differentials between the different areas, that is it does not necessarily involve the *physical* re-location

---

[14] It has also to be mentioned in this connection at least the enacting of the 'Inflation Reduction Act' and the 'Chips and Science Act' in August 2022 by the US Administration, aimed at structurally lowering the dependence on foreign production.

[15] 'Today's industrial commons consist of a web of technological know-how, operational capabilities, and specialized skills that are embedded in the workforce, competitors, suppliers, customers, cooperative R&D ventures, and universities and often support multiple industrial sectors' (Pisano and Shih 2012: 13).

[16] A very similar point of view—explicitly grounded at the theoretical level on the centrality of production in determining the degree of competitiveness of a given area—is expressed by Best (2018).

of previously offshored manufacturing activities—in itself quite problematic, also due to the gradual thickening over time of forward and backward linkages in the host country.

A specific point which is worth stressing in this connection is that, anyway, the development of supply chains in the 'emerging' world, and in particular in the East Asian area, beyond the claim according to which China had become 'the factory of the world', has never come to entail the *dismantling* of manufacturing in offshoring countries. Despite the above-mentioned idea that developed countries had to concentrate their efforts only in R&D, engineering, and design, leaving the task to produce almost everything to low-cost manufacturers, as a matter of fact the actual extent of offshoring has never come to be a predominant share of their production.

This can be appreciated by looking at the US, i.e. at the country where offshoring has been theorized and exploited the most (Figure 6.7), and in which

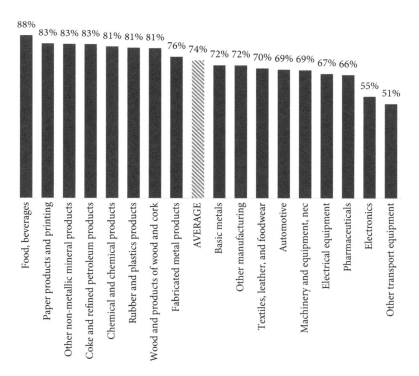

Figure 6.7 Domestic manufacturing inputs on total manufacturing inputs (%) by US industry, 2018, current dollars

Source: OECD, own calculations.

the share of manufacturing inputs produced domestically has remained close or higher than 70% in almost every industrial supply chains, with the only notable exceptions of electronics and the aggregate of 'other transport equipment' (remaining anyway over 50%).

The point here is that the absolute size of the activities that have been offshored has been large enough to trigger the industrialization process of laggards, in which the size of manufacturing—even in China—was initially quite small. Still in 2000, the 10% of US manufacturing in terms of value added was equal to the 51% of manufacturing in China, 1.1 times the Mexican one, 4.5 times the manufacturing of Thailand, and 27 times that of Vietnam. As to Europe, in the same year the 10% of German manufacturing was 2.7 times that of the Czech Republic and about 10 times that of Slovakia. This means that even minimal transfers of manufacturing activities can have been able to activate a visible output increase in developing economies.

6.5 From regionalism to multilateralism and back

The 'return of (geopolitical) distance' is most apparent in the evolution of the logic of international trade, and in particular in the 'resurgence' of regionalism. Indeed, it can be said that multilateralism and regionalism have been crossing the whole post-war period jointly, often overlapping to each other, and never really appearing as alternative. So that their close relatedness makes it difficult to explain the actual differences between them even in point of theory (De Melo and Panagariya 1993).

In the aftermath of World War II, the emergence of a network of international exchanges based on a multilateral approach (i.e. according to the principles of non-discrimination and reciprocity) produced the launch of the GATT (General Agreement on Trade and Tariffs).[17] This has to be considered as a second-best solution, for the United States did not accept the institution of the then International Trade Organization (ITO) which was supposed to join the IMF and the World Bank as a third pillar of the edifice of post-war economic reconstruction contemplated by the Bretton Woods Agreements in 1944. Whilst the ITO—as it later happened for the WTO—should have acted as an authority of peers, which could not be blocked by any single member (defaulters could be 'punished' by the Organization), the GATT was simply a multilateral agreement, produced by a process of negotiation among

---

[17] The GATT was born on 1 January 1948, after the Havana Conference in 1947; the countries originally involved were 23, but the final text was signed (on 15 April 1994!) by 117 countries.

its members (Sassoon 1997). The birth of this institution, under the name of WTO (World Trade Organization) had to wait up to 1995, after the end of the Uruguay Round (1986–94), under the growing pressure of the globalization process.

In the meanwhile, and notwithstanding the institution of the GATT itself (or possibly due to its very limits), regionalism kept on expanding all over the world.[18] Along these same years the notable exception is represented by Asia, where large countries were still strongly inward-looking (India and China) or, on the contrary, Japan played the whole field by exporting on a global scale.[19] But even the US were still alone, owing to the sheer size of their economy, which allowed them to largely rely, in these years, on their internal demand. A fundamental trait of this form of regionalism is that it almost exclusively followed a North–North or South–South path. Apart from the EC, the orientation was towards preferential agreements lowering the level of tariffs.

This first phase ran out—at least outside Europe—at the beginning of the 1970s (following the extinction of the Golden Age). But during all these years regionalism was paralleled by multilateralism, which was promoted by the GATT and accompanied the most intense period of post-war development through seven rounds of negotiations, from 1947 to 1979. The last one (Tokyo Round) involved 99 countries, and determined an abatement of tariff barriers among the nine most industrialized countries from 7 to 4.7 per cent (Sassoon 1997). The overall result of this dual track was a general fall of tariffs, due to both regional and multilateral agreements. Yet the GATT agreements always took into account the protection of less developed economies—by non-imposing reciprocity clauses.[20]

---

[18] Regional agreements spread rapidly towards different areas: to Western Europe with the institution of the European Community (EC) in 1957 (the birth of the EC was, indeed, first of all an attempt to foster the degree of cohesion among the European countries at the political level in order to reduce potential conflicts, and only gradually evolved towards economic integration), and then with the creation of the EFTA in 1960; to the American continent, with the Latin American Free Trade Area (LAFTA) in 1960 (and afterwards with the Central American Common Market (CACM) in 1961; to Africa with the Arab Common Market (ACM) in 1964, the Union Douanière et Économique del l'Afrique Centrale (UDEAC) starting in 1964, the Southern Africa Customs Union (SACU) in 1969, and two distinct areas in Western Africa, the Communautè Économique de l'Afrique de l'Ouest (CEAO) in 1972 and the Economic Community of West African States (ECOWAS) in 1975 (Grilli 1997). In these same years also a sprawl of *bilateral* (or anyway selective) trade agreements took place, even between non-neighbouring countries (De Melo and Panagariya 1993; Grilli 1997; Carpenter 2008).

[19] The ASEAN, also set up in 1967, came into existence for security reasons, and up to 1992 did not translated into any trade liberalization at the local level.

[20] On the other hand, the very same period witnessed a constant increase in non-tariff barrier (Sassoon 1997).

The history of such a long phase of world trade provides in itself an answer to the issue addressed at the beginning of this section: in fact, it can be said that

[o]n the one hand, RTAs [Regional Trade Agreements] weaken the GATT to the extent that they imply a preferential treatment of members' import flows and thereby they violate the most basic principle of non-discrimination enshrined in the GATT system. On the other hand, RTAs often imply a substantial liberalization of trade within a region and can be seen as a move towards a freer system. This is the main reason that led trade negotiators early on not to forbid RTAs despite their incompatibility with the non-discrimination principle.

(Faini 1997: 144–145)

A second wave of regionalism took place in the second half of the 1980s. In particular in the United States it happened that the rising deficit in the current accounts of the balance of payments (even if compensated by the capital inflows fuelled by high interest rates) nurtured a strong protectionist sentiment, activating in turn the request for the defence of national producers. The US, therefore, rapidly changed their mind, moving from a multilateral view to a much more inward-looking stance (also due to a persistent tightness of the Japanese market). There followed the creation in 1988 of a new free-trade area between United States and Canada, which ended in 1992 in the North American Free Trade Agreement, including Mexico (1992).[21] Meanwhile, in Latin America the existence of various free-trade areas translated into the institution of the MERCOSUR (1991). In the same years it was born the Arab Maghreb (1989), later associated to the CE through the Mediterranean Agreements, and in 1992 a free trade area was set up within the ASEAN (Asia Free Trade Area—AFTA). In Europe, the ties within the continent gradually became stronger, leading to the inclusion of Spain and Portugal within the EC and to the building of the single market.

In a few years, a new wave of continental agreements did take off; this time, however, the agreements also involved North–South relationships. Above all, they were not so much related to the reduction of tariffs (which by then had been generally lowered by the very same liberalization rounds implemented within the GATT framework): rather, they reflected a 'defensive' logic (so as to hedge the risk of a failure of the Uruguay Round, started in 1986, by maintaining a dual track) and the idea of a 'strategic regionalism' (even on a

[21] Since November 2018, the NAFTA has been substituted by the United States Mexico and Canada Agreement (USMCA).

bilateral basis), so as to add to the advantages of multilateralism those deriv-
ing from a greater market power, as a consequence of acting as a group.
Moreover, belonging to a regional agreement helped smaller countries to get
an easier access to wider markets.[22]

Overall, this orientation led to the consolidation of a system of exchanges at
the regional level that the subsequent developments of the Uruguay Round—
aimed at restoring instead the multilateral view about international trade—
could not entirely upset: as early as at the beginning of the 1980s the authors
of a series of collected papers on the subject could ask themselves:

> [i]s the world evolving towards trading blocs: one around the United States encom-
> passing the Americas, another around the European Community encompassing
> most of Europe, and a third around Japan including most of Asia? To many
> observers, this is indeed the case and the issue is whether such a move should be
> welcomed.
>
> **(De Melo and Panagariya 1993: 4)**

As will be shown below, this is just the pattern of international trade that
can still be observed nowadays.

Be that as it may, the Uruguay Round turned in the end towards a multilateral approach, and its conclusion (1994) and the following institution
of the WTO (1995), even if still burdened by a further series of regional
agreements (Carpenter 2008), led back the system to the post-war view. Multilateralism was the basic feature of the most intense phase of globalization;
but when—in the early years of the new century, after the substantial failure
of the Doha Round (the last round acted under the aegis of WTO)—the multilateral approach was challenged by the pay-back effects of the globalization
process itself and more widely by the emergence of new global players, a new
reversal of trade policy took place.

The new trend appeared most pronounced in the United States, where
it represented an attempt to answer several questions: a huge trade deficit
(indeed, still rising); the need to face the crowding out of internal supply
by emerging economies, due to their price competitiveness, on the one side,
and to the transfer of manufacturing activities to those areas via FDIs on the

---

[22] On such premises 'regionalism appeared to be the key movement in international trade relations
during the late 1980s and early 1990s, acting either as a substitute for the faltering multilateral system
or as the building block of a new and vastly simplified international trade framework in which country
groups would be the main actors' (Grilli 1997: 200).

other; the increase in economic inequality ascribed to globalization, feeding a parallel increase in social conflict.[23]

Starting with the 2008 financial crisis, trade policies became more selective: either by excluding some partners, or by choosing them through bilateral agreements (Gaudiosi 2018; Amiti et al. 2019; Fajgelbaum et al. 2019; IMF 2019). The multilateral logic survived for some years despite the impasse of the Doha Round, even under the 'selective' variant of the very much emphasized transoceanic agreements (TTIP—Transatlantic Trade and Investment Partnership, and TPP—Trans Pacific Partnership), but in the end it began to collapse. It may be added that it fell down also due to the weight, for long underscored, of its very complexity, that is the growing complexity of the production process and the length of the value chains, the growing relevance of services and the complexity of their tradeability, the problems tied to the industrial property in a context of fragmented productive chains.

On empirical grounds, the outcome of these overall trends can be synthetically highlighted by calculating a measure of the degree of regionalism of international trade over the long run. Figure 6.8 shows the behaviour of a 'regionalization' index (RI). The index has been built first with reference to the most important trade areas, and then aggregated, through a weighted average, at the world level.[24]

The graph is straightforward: in a first phase, broadly following the birth of the great regional agreements (NAFTA, MERCOSUR, Single European Market, and the subsequent enlargement to Eastern Europe), the index shows an uprise, corresponding to an increase in the share of regional trade; after 2004, the IR registers a reversal of this trend and falls regularly along almost a decade, as a consequence of the unfolding of the globalization process, connecting to each other many countries belonging to different areas, in spite of their distance, through the development of GVCs. In later years, the globalization effect loses grounds, and after 2012 the index seems to

---

[23] It has to be stressed in this connection the high degree of similarity between the logic of the current phase of regionalism and what already happened in the mid 1980s, especially as to the reasons lying behind the reversal in the policy stance.

[24] The literature on the subject provides several types of solutions (among others, Faini 1997; Iapadre 2006; Iapadre and Tironi 2009). In the present case the index is calculated, for each area, as the ratio of two ratios: (1) the amount of the internal trade (exports plus imports) of the area divided by the amount of its external trade (export plus imports towards the rest of the world); and (2) the trade of the rest of the world with the same area divided by the trade of the rest of the world with itself. Data are net of fuel. The logic of the index is the same as that of the Balassa index of revealed comparative advantages (Balassa 1965). In symbols: $[_{Ai} (X+M)_{Ai} / _{Ai} (X+M)_{RoW}] / [_{RoW} (X+M)_{Ai} / _{RoW} (X+M)_{RoW}]$; where X and M have the usual meaning, A_i is the i-th Area and RoW means 'Rest of the World' (i.e. World$-A_i$). When values are higher than 1 the share of intra-area exchanges is higher than that of the exchanges of the rest of the world with the area. The areas are Europe, North America, Latin America, Asia, Africa, Oceania.

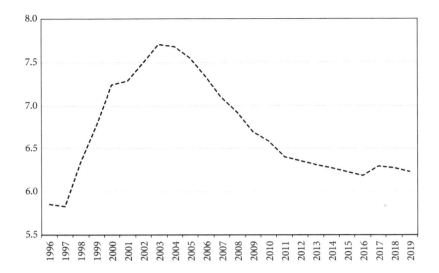

Figure 6.8 Degree of regionalism (see note 24) in world trade, three-term moving average

Source: UN-Comtrade, own calculations.

stabilize.[25] On the whole, the degree of regional integration appears remarkable (always much higher than 1) even in the years of rampant globalization. In fact, a relevant share of regional trade seems to be a fundamental feature of global exchanges over the long run.

This said, which sorts of linkages among different countries at the world level do come out of the above-mentioned shifts in the logic of international trade? (What is the present shape of international trade flows?). The point here is that not even globalization, despite the push towards a more widespread diffusion of trade all across the world, has succeeded in making exchanges really independent of distance. This can be appreciated through the graph reported in Figure 6.9. The graph has been built on the basis of a clustering algorithm, in order to identify groups of countries characterized by a relatively high intensity of trade exchanges.[26]

[25] As shown in Pensa and Pignatti (2022), the observed trend is strongly influenced by the behaviour of Asia, where in the course of GA the fall in the degree of regionalization appears most pronounced due to the growing involvement of (East) Asian countries in world trade exchanges.

[26] The algorithm is taken from the GEPHI software. Calculations refer to exports flows above the 0.01% threshold of global exchanges. The diameter of the nodes measures the market share of each country in 2017, that is the amount of its trade flows in both directions (export and imports), corresponding to the weighted average degree, where the sum of trade exchanges is weighted by their monetary value. The higher the degree to which a country is linked to the rest of the world, the more central its position within the graph. The degree of intensity of the grey colour is to distinguish different clusters. Oil products are excluded from calculations.

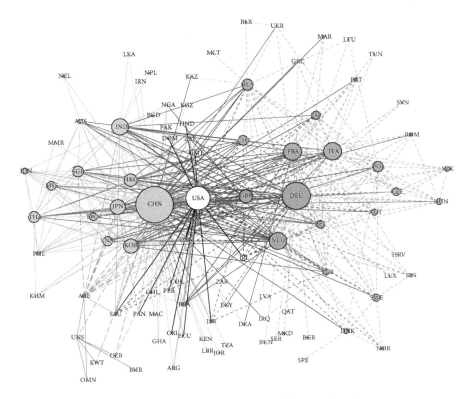

Figure 6.9 World network of trade exchanges, manufactured goods, 2019

Source: UN-Comtrade, own calculations.

The image that comes out of calculations can be easily divided into three parts: Europe on the right side, with Germany at the centre; the USMCA area in the middle, linked to Latin America; and on the left side the Asian area, with China at the centre, large enough to include some Central Asian countries and Africa. This means that the unquestionably high intensity of globalization, that is the most striking feature of the last phase of industrial development in the world, *has left basically unchanged the linkages among the economic systems characterized by spatial proximity*, as they had been modelled over time (with China replacing Japan at the centre of the stage in Eastern Asia). This is not simply a matter of distance: what has happened is that hinging on spatial proximity a series of trade agreements has been set up over the years, which have determined in the long run the emergence of three distinct trade centres of gravity in the world. And the breaking down of trade barriers, driven by the role that international institutions (mostly the WTO) have played in encouraging the liberalization of trade and capital movements, has not radically altered this legacy.

It can be recalled here that the appearance of such a pattern does not merely reflect the logic of market exchanges as it is stated in the theory of international trade, for the fragmentation of value chains on a global scale has shaped the structure of trade also according to *industrial* reasons, so that it entails a high degree of inertia (also as a consequence of the weight of intra-firm cross-country exchanges). This same structure can also be viewed as an image of the selective emergence, during the GA, of previously under-developed economies. As we have seen in previous chapters, successfully entering into the international trade system—and, more than this, using this as a lever for manufacturing development—has been possible only for some economies, and it has not happened by chance.

At the same time, the very existence of productive linkages among manu-facturing traders has involved in the medium term—especially in intermedi-ate markets—a thickening of the exchanges at the local level: whereas initially the fragmentation of production may well link together different areas of the world (enhancing this way the globalization of trade), once a new loca-tion has been chosen, the creation of forward and backward linkages in the sense suggested by Hirschman (1958) tends to bind the development of the supply chain to that specific area. A great many local supply chains in emerg-ing countries have just been triggered by the offshoring mechanism. In this framework a reorganization of Asian production networks is currently taking place: countries that were previously included in North–South global value chains as assemblers are now shifting to the production of upstream inputs, as a part of regional production networks oriented towards domestic consumers (Escaith et al. 2010).

This means that the East Asian region—also due to the very size of its largest country, that is China—has gradually become a self-contained eco-nomic entity, which can follow an autonomous growth path independent of the global business cycle (Kimura and Obashi 2011). It is interesting to note in this connection that the strong linkages tying together East Asian economies, as a result of both a process of institution creation and bottom-up societally driven processes (mostly coming from corporate trade and invest-ment flows) have been stressed as a striking feature of world development since the very early 2000s.[27]

The structure of GVCs has itself undergone, in recent years, significant changes which, in some emerging countries, have resulted in upgrading

---

[27] See in particular on this point (Pempel 2005), stressing the relevance of the phenomenon in spite of the many (generally overlooked) and wide-ranging diversities in terms of cultural, linguistical and reli-gious traditions, not to say of historical conflicts, among the various countries belonging to the area. An account of what this process has come to involve in terms of the development of supply chains at the sectoral level is provided by Nathan et al. (2018).

processes that have often modified the relations among firms in terms of market power, transforming some suppliers into evolved partners and driving towards a greater concentration in intermediate markets (Gereffi 2014; Neilson et al. 2014). Among the consequences of such a process there is the gradual loss of competitiveness, in relative terms, of the developed world—i.e. of its ability to extract value from productive activities. But these trends are also dividing the emerging economies themselves, between those that are capable of upgrading and those that are not.

6.6 The effects of the digital and the green transition

6.6.1 Digitalization

As already stressed in Chapter 1, the widespread adoption of Information and Communication Technologies (ICTs) by Western multinationals which occurred in the 1990s (the so-called ICT revolution), by dramatically reducing the costs of long-distance communications, made the coordination of production at the international level cheap and reliable, thus enabling the 'second great unbundling' which spread value chains on a global scale. The subsequent developments of those technologies, and the advent of digitalization in the production process in particular, has long been interpreted as an enabler of industrialization for emerging economies, which could benefit from imported digital technology infrastructures in order to exploit their comparative advantages in the (labour-intensive) stages of productions in which they were involved.

Recent advancements in digital platforms for business e-commerce (such as Alibaba), as well as improvements in the technologies for securing online firm-to-firm data transmission (i.e. blockchains), push in the direction of furtherly reducing the costs of managing global value chains, therefore allowing the number of cross-border transactions to increase. This could also eliminate entry barriers to suppliers from peripheral areas of the trade network, favouring the development of industrial activities in countries hitherto excluded from the globalization process (Antràs 2021). Moreover, advances in teleconferencing, cloud storage and communication speed are lowering the barriers to trade in intermediate services, opening up new opportunities for furtherly spreading value chains on a global scale (Baldwin 2019).

However, such optimism about the positive impact of digital technologies on the future of global value chains is contrasted by at least two counterarguments. First, advanced digitalization applied to production technologies is also expanding the number of activities which can be profitably automated, therefore eroding the cost-advantage of low-wage manufacturing hubs in developing countries (Rodrik 2022). Coupled with the increasing demand for fast-delivery productions (which pushes firms to stay physically closer to the point of consumption), such labour-saving technologies could make (some) back-shoring a profitable solution for Western multinationals in order to intercept new needs in these markets. On the other hand, automation is not confined to manufacturing activities anymore, as artificial intelligence is expanding the possibilities to make use of software for carrying out relatively simple cognitive tasks previously performed by low-qualified workers. Hence, some of the potential for service offshoring could be destroyed by service automation.

Second, the introduction of advanced digital technologies into manufacturing is also increasing the quality standards suppliers are required to meet along the value chains, which may be incompatible with the intensive use of unskilled labour force. Already in the course of the GA some skill-biased technological change has been detected in many middle and low-income economies (Reijnders and Timmer 2021), contributing to a weak industrialization process in many of them, as sustained endogenous growth in output was constrained by the low endowment of qualified human capital (Rodrik 2018). The further development of digital technologies, requiring complementary human capital investments, can make such problem even tougher, therefore inducing multinationals to reduce the number of supplying partners (and countries).

The overall effect of such forces is difficult to predict (Sturgeon 2017). However, it seems plausible to say that, despite an ongoing process of advanced digitalization, the net positive contribution of the new technologies on the length of global value chains in the last years of the GA has been, if any, of a lower order as compared to what occurred at the start of the process three decades ago, and that this trend should not be expected to change in the years to come.

6.6.2 Going green

The impact of the green transition seems far less ambiguous. The current geography of global manufacturing largely reflects the search, made in previous decades by Western multinationals, of wage differentials across countries, without an explicit recognition of the environmental costs associated with these decisions (UNCTAD 2020a). Such costs arise from pollution, beginning with CO_2 emissions which are the principal cause of the global warming, and from the over-exploitation of natural resources, which is causing a decrease in the stock of non-renewables available for future generations. They originate both as a by-product of physical extraction and transformation of inputs into output, and because of fossil-fueled transport and energy services.

Inasmuch as a relevant share of the negative environmental externalities generated along the global value chains translates into higher operational expenditures for multinational firms, then their activities in developing countries are at risk of downsizing, for at least two reasons. First, due to their lower economic, institutional, and technical capacity to cope with higher environmental standards, manufacturing activities performed in these countries tend to be less sustainable for the planet as compared to those performed by firms belonging to advanced economies. This is found to be true even controlling for the fact that emerging economies are more specialized in industries which, at the current state of the technologies, generate structurally higher levels of pollution (see Figure 6.10, referring to the carbon footprint of major industrial economies relative to the EU28 average).

Second, the process of slicing up global value chains into elementary stages allocated to different countries is not neutral from an environmental point of

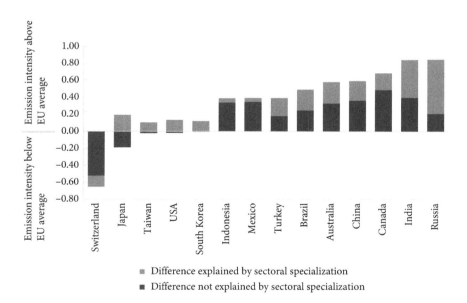

Figure 6.10 CO_2 emissions for dollar of manufacturing value added relative to EU (2018, EU average =1), current prices*

* The net difference from EU is given by the sum of the two components shown in the graph.
Source: Adapted from Romano (2021).

view, as pollution associated with international transport services increases with the number of physically distant firms involved into the production. International aviation and shipping accounts nowadays for around 4% of global greenhouse gas emissions, as transports have the highest reliance of fossil fuels compared to any other sector (IEA 2022a, 2022b). Therefore, an environmentally compliant cost/benefit analysis of the different nodes of the global trade network may end up excluding those which are more peripheral, both geographically and economically, from the manufacturing hubs in Europe, North America, and East Asia.

Overall, such issues imply that the shortening of supply chains, and in particular back-shoring and regional consolidation of (some of) the stages of production, could be an optimal response to more stringent environmental regulations adopted by national governments—which include carbon border adjustment tariffs—and to the increasing pressure, from both financial markets and final consumers, for reporting the degree of coherence of investment and production choices to ESG (Environmental, Social and Governance) standards.

6.7 The twin shocks of the pandemic and the war

The arrival of the pandemic and the outburst of the war at the very boundaries of Europe have brought about further reasons for the world to become less flat than before, and for uncertainty to come to the fore.[28]

As to the pandemic, a first push towards a radical change of the economic policy stance at the global level has been called for by the dramatic fall in income following the 2020 lockdown,[29] asking for an interventionist approach in order to provide countervailing measures.[30] But, above all, when shortages of surgery masks, lung ventilators, and vaccines hit the world in 2020 as a result of unilateral political decisions, taken by producing countries to contrast individually the effects of the Covid-19 pandemic, it became clear all over the world that free trade could not be the solution to the new threat.

In fact, the logic according to which the international division of labour was pursued during the GA brought about a substantial lack of control by

---

[28] On this point see also Manzocchi and Traù (2022).
[29] According to UNCTAD (2020a, p. II): 'between 90 million and 120 million people [have been] pushed into extreme poverty in the developing world, with hunger and malnutrition certain to follow, while income gaps [have widened] everywhere. These developments point toward a massive uptick in sickness and death.' On the same point see also ILO (2021).
[30] This has happened even in the European context, where the 'expansive austerity' has been substituted by a new instrument like the Next Generation EU.

national governments about the availability of goods that are deemed to be strategic (for healthcare, economic, or security reasons). The problem, exacerbated in 2021 by the scarcity of micro-chips (almost entirely produced in a bunch of Asian countries) and by an outright default, in some cases, of the transports system (especially as to maritime transports), undermined the confidence not only in the efficiency of the GVCs, but also in the ability of multilateral institutions to preside over the well-functioning of international trade. The result was a general claim for the return of State interventionism in the economy, with the goal of re-establishing national strategic autonomy, due to an increase in the option value of relying on autonomous resources and inputs as an alternative to their purchases from abroad. This was true even for the European Union, which had become, during the last decades, the staunchest defender of the liberal order designed around the GA.

This change in perspective involves a modification in the 'make or buy' trade-off, for it raises the cost one can be willing to sustain for a given item, simply to be sure to get it. In this light 'industrial policies are increasingly targeting industries considered strategic not only for job creation and long-term economic growth, but also for (broadly interpreted) national security reasons' (UNCTAD 2020b).

In the early months of 2022, the need for active policies has been even more enhanced by the arrival of the war in Ukraine. This time the push has come from the insurgence of new geo-political problems and the threat of an escalation of the conflict. As a first consequence, the new context has led to the explosion of global inflationary pressures caused by unprecedented shortages of natural gas supply, which may potentially involve important effects also in terms of the possible curbing of greening ambitions in the medium term.[31] The dissipation of the confidence in the existence of an economic regime, agreed by all major global economies, centred around multilateralism and market-driven capitalism is vividly represented by the words of the US President, when saying that 'the post-Cold War era is definitively over and a competition is underway between the major powers to shape what comes next' (White House 2022: 6).

A key point in this context lies in the perspective from which all this is looked at. As a matter of fact, the persistence (and the overlapping) of the aforementioned shocks goes against the idea that economic systems are but

---

[31] Concerns about short-term energy supply security may force, at least in the short term, the use of coal as an alternative for natural gas, pushing towards a more inward-looking and reductive thinking on the matter and discouraging the investments on renewable sources. This would contribute in turn to make it more difficult meeting the goals set forth by the International Panel on Climate Change (IPCC). See on this point for example Kuzemco et al. (2022).

homeostatic mechanisms, characterized as to themselves by the capability to get back on their own to the position they held before the shock (i.e. by the prevailing of negative feedbacks). Indeed, in such respect things seem to run opposite, and the restoring of the previous situation appears simply inconceivable: in the words of UNCTAD (2020a: I), '[t]he *status quo ante* is a goal not worth the name'. In terms of the usual metaphor of the tunnel, it is worth remembering that escaping from a tunnel always involves getting out into a different hillside, where the landscape itself is likely to be quite different.

Conclusion

The industrial world is facing the economic consequences of the exhaustion of what in this book has been called the Globalization Age (GA). That is the period (roughly going from the beginning of the 1980s to the financial crisis that broke out at the end of the first decade of the twenty-first century) in the course of which a new paradigm emerged, gained ground, and finally foundered: leaving behind a substantial integration of production systems at the global level, an important change in the relative economic power between old and new manufacturing systems, but also wider inequalities as to the persistence of underdevelopment in many areas of the world.

The appearance of the GA marked the transition from a world characterized by strong regulation and policy intervention to an era dominated by the constant search for 'flexibility' and market liberalization at international level. Its unfolding was driven by the advent of the so-called Washington Consensus (WC), the building blocks of which were the pursuit of tight macroeconomic policies aimed at controlling inflation and deficit spending; the liberalization of trade so as to exploit static comparative advantages (paralleled by the liberalization of capital flows); the widening of market boundaries through privatization and deregulation processes. In historical terms, the GA has coincided with an enlargement of the industrial world, that is with the industrialization of several economies that in the final decades of past century were still lagging behind. On the real side of the economy, this has been the most relevant change occurring since World War II.

Such industrialization process, however, has been limited to a group of countries characterized by both previous knowledge accumulation in the industrial field and by an active role of industrial policy, mainly located in South East Asia, where the so-called 'Developmental State' purposefully pursued manufacturing development. Building on such premises, and in particular on conditional economic policies, these countries have succeeded in developing endogenous manufacturing capabilities and in getting new comparative advantages via dynamic increasing returns in selected industries—stemming from the creation of 'forward and backward linkages'. In this sense, it can be said that the countries that have actually succeeded in emerging as

The New Industrial World. Livio Romano and Fabrizio Traù, Oxford University Press.
© Livio Romano and Fabrizio Traù (2023). DOI: 10.1093/oso/9780192873736.003.0008

manufacturing producers have followed a strategy that runs opposite to that indicated by the WC.

In general, the key to industrialization in underdeveloped countries has been the establishing of the so-called trade in tasks, that has allowed them to enter *some* manufacturing activities by specializing in specific tasks, most suited to their skills. This has been made possible by the previous fragmentation (vertical dis-integration) of manufacturing activities in old industrialized countries, that had occurred in the last quarter of past century and had already fed the expansion of markets for intermediates within national boundaries, through the outsourcing of several production phases and the fragmentation of the value chains at national level. As soon as the 'great doubling of the labour market' due to the entrance in world exchanges of large underdeveloped economies created after the 1980s an 'industrial reserve army', this paved the way to the exploitation of huge cost differentials, transforming outsourcing into offshoring and setting the conditions for the 'unbundling' of value chains on a global scale. Outsourcers and recipients have been tied together since then into cross-country networks, making international exchanges more and more dependent on production strategies, and linking the North and South as never before.

On the one side the North (partially) transferred its production flows into the emerging South with the aim of reimporting cheaper intermediates (as well as final goods); on the other the South loaded on its shoulders the task to produce and export such goods to the North, so as to enter the path to industrialization. This linkage—paralleled by an unlimited liquidity supply—was the way through which the out-of-scale consumer boom starting from the 1990s in advanced countries was managed.

International trade has therefore become the 'fuel' for manufacturing development, acting as a lever for those developing countries which succeeded in establishing new competitive industries through adequate industrial policies. This way to globalization—grounded on the liberalization of internal and external markets—has been led by the idea according to which the whole world could be pushed towards economic development by relying upon a single—and indirect—instrument such as free trade, by transforming the 'production problem' in the North into a trade problem.

From this point of view it has to be stressed that a major role in this process has been played by the very scale of the countries involved, differently from what had already happened in the course of the 1970s, when only small countries such as the so-called NICs did also emerge as new manufacturers. The process was also speeded up, this time, by the 'unfreezing' of many economic systems that still in early 1990s were sealed within a parallel world, outside of the area of market exchanges: within an extremely narrow period of time (little over a decade, from Deng's launch of the 'four modernizations' in 1978 to the re-entry of the main South American economies into the area of representative democracy in the mid-1980s to the 'fall of the Wall' in Eastern Europe) new economic areas and populations came at the very same time to be part of the global world.

Yet, the trade in tasks did not end up into widespread industrial growth all over the underdeveloped world. The main reason is that, in general, those economic systems which have entered the road to industrialization as laggards (i.e. in the course of globalization), have been compelled to follow a different pattern of structural change as compared to early comers. For late industrializers domestic demand was so small that the way out from underdevelopment had necessarily to come from external demand. But in order to get comparative advantages in a world characterized by global competition they have been pushed to concentrate their (scarce) resources within a few activities (generally by joining international value chains as global suppliers of specific goods or even natural commodities), therefore moving towards an early increasing sectoral concentration. By constraining their activities within relatively narrow supply matrices, they underwent an earlier decline in the output manufacturing share (that is to say early de-industrialization). More broadly, the need to face raised competition from abroad has also harmed those emerging economies which had already experienced an industrialization process *before* the advent of the GA, but without opening up to international trade, leading some of them to a decay of their manufacturing endowments.

At the same time, internal demand in the course of the GA has played a limited role even in many developed countries, where the idea according to which manufacturing development can be a function of external competitiveness has been stretched to the limit, and interpreted in a wholly acritical way. This has been especially true in the European context, where an obsessive orientation towards foreign markets (in the wake of the German model) has translated into internal deflation as a way to gain (or preserve) price competitiveness. By leading to falling internal demand, this has brought about an overall fall of external demand as well, insofar as two-thirds of the global European exports belong to the intra-area trade (i.e. they are but the sum of the internal demand of individual European countries themselves). This failure in achieving higher growth rates highlights the limits of a supply-side view according to which growth is simply driven by productivity (assuming that higher efficiency—paralleled by trade liberalization—finds always and in any case its demand on global markets).

So, at the end of the first decade of the 2000s the world globally entered the financial crisis strongly relying on external demand as the main driver of output growth; for this to keep working, it would have required multilateral exchanges and trade liberalization not to be questioned. But this has not been the case. When the financial crisis broke out, bringing about a fall in consumption, world trade started to be affected by a lower international demand on the part of the developed economies, in the face of a growing supply potential from the emerging world.

This situation asked for a rebalancing of supply in emerging countries towards internal demand, giving back to the size of individual economies a key role in determining the rhythm of their growth (a larger country enjoys potentially higher internal demand) and emphasizing the importance of economic policy (i.e. the possibility of a given country to act so as to exogenously enlarge the size of its internal demand). For two giants such as China and India, this allowed the development path to gradually move away from an export led logic, reducing at the same time the overall importance of external trade relative to output (as it structurally happens in large-sized economies). In turn, it set the premises for a decoupling between the economic systems that the globalization process had previously tied together, as well as to a potential divergence in the growth paths among emerging economies of different size.

Overall, in the aftermath of the global financial crisis a 'new normal' did emerge on fundamentally endogenous grounds, which can be stylized in two main facts. The first is a general slowdown in the rhythm of manufacturing growth, after a long phase characterized by exceptionally high growth rates in several emerging economies. The second is the comeback of geography and politics as key determinants of economic behaviour (sub specie of a resurgence of regionalism in international trade and the emergence of backshoring processes), upsetting the idea according to which the very success of globalization had led to the 'death of distance'.

This is the shape the world economic landscape had assumed before the arrival of the pandemic and the war in Ukraine, which in turn have put sand in the wheels of already worn-out global trade relationships, by challenging the mutual confidence among the various players of GVCs and by pushing the whole world into uncertainty. It could be said in this perspective that—by adding to the endogenous determinants of the fall of the GA—these shocks come as the bringing down of the curtain after the end of the play.

The 'rise and fall' of the Globalization Age closely echoes the quite analogous dynamics of another major phase in world development process such as the Golden Age. Even if hinging on opposite premises—grounded on strong regulation the latter, aimed at abolishing any sorts of regulation in all markets the former—both Ages have been characterized by the ambition to shape something like a world order, aimed at leading the development process at global level. As far as it has also been led by an exceptional set of one-off events, the Globalization Age can be defined, other than as a 'regime', also as a 'historical aberration', no less than the Golden Age has been said to be. In the same way, its dissipation sets the premises for a growing variance in single countries' behaviour to arise, as far as the very mechanism of integrated (North–South) development has been challenged. And, as it happened in the years following the fading away of the Golden Age, this may also involve in the years to come lower and more unstable growth (higher intertemporal variance in growth rates).

To imagine a future beyond the vanishing of the GA is by no means straightforward. At its onset, as far as the world was then tied up by a 'plethora of regulations and other restrictive practices in the product, capital and labour markets', hindering the possibility to manage the problems that were at stake (above all the stagflation challenge), the solution of 'making things simpler' by reducing the overall degree of regulation of the economic system could take place easily, and for the new paradigm to establish it took just a few years. But the current context is far more difficult to manage.

First, moving from a regulated world to a deregulated one is by definition easier and quicker than the opposite: if what is currently needed is a somewhat less liberalized context, in which economic (industrial) policy is required once again to play a role, then the re-building of the rules and the procedures for implementing a new regulation framework is not a snap of the fingers, and takes time for being put in place. Second, the whole world is now overloaded with big and urgent problems, asking for correspondingly urgent responses: the global warming; the uprise of unemployment as a structural issue (also linked to fast-growing technological change); the widening of income and wealth inequalities both among and within countries; the dramatic upward trend of migrations, driven by demography (the sheer dynamics of population) and by shocks of any kind. Third, the shift from a hegemonic international economic order towards a multi-polar one seems to give way to a time of global conflicts instead of cooperation: a key issue, in this regard, is that the economic systems which can play a role in determining a new international order are more than 30 years ago, and this poses new challenges at the political level.

This last issue deserves in itself some more attention, for it directly addresses a problem that has long been almost completely put in the shadow.[1] The point here is that the unfolding of the GA—culminating in the institution of the WTO in 1995—has been strongly driven by the idea that at geopolitical level the world had become fundamentally a unipolar entity. From this point of view the birth of the WTO in those years—fifty years after the US boycotted the birth of the ITO at Bretton Woods—is the outcome of the idea that after the 'fall of the wall' in Berlin in November 1989 human history had come to an end, so that for Western countries no challenge from an USSR that was going to collapse or from other economic powers (still to come to the fore like China) was to be expected *forever*. This has been quite explicitly anticipated in the famous paper by Francis Fukuyama, then embedded in the US Administration at a high level position,[2] according to whom

> [w]hat we may be witnessing is not just the end of the Cold War, or the passing of a particular period of postwar history, but the end of history as such: that is, the end point of mankind's ideological evolution and the universalization of Western liberal democracy as the final form of human government
>
> **(Fukuyama 1989: 4)**

In Fukuyama's view, the consequence is that the world has come to be

> dominated by economic concerns, in which there are no ideological grounds for major conflict between nations, and in which, consequently, the use of military force becomes less legitimate.
>
> **(Fukuyama 1989: 17)**

In this framework, therefore, even beyond what was then happening in the USSR, the possibility for a cross-country conflict at the political level to explode was to be considered as having been overcome, once and for all, by the sheer strength of market forces: so that once even 'China ... began its reform process[,] Chinese competitiveness and expansionism on the world scene have virtually disappeared' (Fukuyama 1989: 17).

Given these premises, it seems not too far-fetched to say that, in a quite few years, the US view about the logic of the international distribution of manufacturing activities sharply changed as soon as history has proved not to be ended at all. That is, as soon as the idea of a unipolar world faded away, the US de facto abandoned the logic of multilateralism and of free trade and started playing instead a strong role in fuelling the forces pushing towards

---

[1] On this point see more widely Traù (2023).

[2] It is worth noting that at the time he wrote his paper Fukuyama was Deputy Director of the Policy Planning Staff of the State Department. That is, his words—published in *The National Interest*—came from the top political level in the country.

de-globalization.[3] Up to the point that, as to China in particular, the current approach in US documents has come to be blatantly at odds with Fukuyama's view. As publicly stated,

> [g]iven the size of China's economy and the extent of its market distorting policies, China's economic aggression now threatens not only the U.S. economy but also the global economy as a whole
>
> **(White House 2018: 1).**

The roots of such sharp a reversal have to be found at the political level, as they stem from the fact that history is alive more than ever—so that the problem of contrasting other political systems has come to the fore. As a consequence, as far as policy has now taken the scene in driving global changes, the economic determinants of development have been correspondingly weakening. This is likely to be true the most in perspective, as the current tensions between world superpowers seem to call again for policies aimed at building walls, rather than at letting them fall. In the years to come, economic thinking is going to play a less important role in affecting the course of history.

---

[3] The new approach has been followed by three different presidents, beginning with the Reshoring initiative in 2013 followed by the more emphatic Make America Great Again policy, up to the launching of the Chips and Science Act and the Inflation Reduction Act in 2022.

References

Abramovitz M. (1989), *Thinking about Growth*, Cambridge, Cambridge University Press.

Acemoglu D., & Robinson J.A. (2008), The Role of Institutions in Growth and Development, *Commission on Growth and Development Working Paper* 10.

Amatori F. & Colli A. (2011), *Business History: Complexities and Comparisons*, Routledge, Abingdon and New York.

Amiti M., Redding S.J., & Weinstein D. (2019), The Impact of the 2018 Trade War on U.S. Prices and Welfare, *Centre for Economic Policy Research, Discussion Papers* 13564, March.

Amsden A. (2001), *The Rise of the Rest. Challenges to the West from Late-Industrializing Economies*, New York, Oxford University Press.

Amsden A. & Hikino T. (1994), Staying Behind, Stumbling Back, Sneaking Up, Soaring Ahead: Late Industrialization in Historical Perspective, in W.J. Baumol, R.R. Nelson, & E.N. Wolff (eds), *Convergence of Productivitiy. Cross-National Studies and Historical Evidence*, New York, Oxford University Press: 285–315.

Antràs P. (2021), *De-Globalisation? Global Value Chains in the Post-COVID-19 Age*, 2021 ECB Forum: 'Central Banks in a Shifting World' Conference Proceedings.

Anzolin G. & Pietrobelli C. (2021), Local Content Policies: Why Mining Need Consistent Policy Packages to Support Capabilities Development, *The Extractive Industries and Society*, https://doi.org/10.1016/j.exis.2020.11.013

Arestis P. & Eatwell J. (2008, eds), *Issues in Economic Development and Globalization*, Basingstoke and New York, Palgrave Macmillan.

Åslund A. (2018), What Happened to the Economic Convergence of Central and Eastern Europe after the Global Financial Crisis?, *Comparative Economic Studies*, 60: 254–270.

Atkinson A.B. & Stiglitz J.E. (1969), A New View of Technological Change, *Economic Journal*, 89 (315): 573–578.

Auboin M. & Borino F. (2017), *The Falling Elasticity of Global Trade to Economic Activity: Testing the Demand Channel, Improving Global Trade Forecasts*, VOXEU.org, 26 June.

Baer W. (1972), Import Substitution and Industrialization in Latin America, *Latin American Research Review* 7 (1): 95–122.

Baer W. (1984), Industrialization in Latin America: Successes and Failures, *Journal of Economic Education*, 15 (2): 124–135.

Baer W. (2002), Neo-Liberalism in Latin America—a Return to the Past?, *Financial Markets and Portfolio Management*, 16 (3): 309–315.

Bairoch P. (1971), *Le Tiers-Monde Dans l'Impasse. Le Démarrage Économique du XVIIIᵉ au XXᵉ Siècle*, Paris, Gallimard.

Bairoch P. & Kozul-Wright R. (1996), Globalization Myths: Some Historical Reflections on Integration, Industrialization and Growth in the World Economy, *UNCTAD Discussion Papers*, n. 113, March.

Balassa B. (1965), Trade Liberalisation and 'Revealed' Comparative Advantage, *Manchester School of Economic and Social Studies*, 33 (2): 99–123.

Baldwin R. (2006), *Globalization: The Great Unbundling(s)*, Prime Minister's Office, Economic Council of Finland, 20 September.

Baldwin R. (2013), Global Supply Chains: Why They Emerged, Why They Matter, and Where They Are Going, in D.K. Elms & P. Low (eds), *Global Value Chains in a Changing World*, Geneva, WTO Publications: 13–60.

Baldwin R. (2014), Trade and Industrialization after Globalization's 2nd Unbundling: How Building and Joining a Supply Chain Are Different and Why It Matters, in R.C. Feenstra & A.M. Taylor (eds), *Globalization in an Age of Crisis: Multilateral Economic Cooperation in the Twenty-first Century*, Chicago, Chicago University Press: 165–212.

Baldwin R. (2019), *The Globotics Upheaval. Globalization, Robotics and the Future of Work*, Oxford, Oxford University Press.

Baldwin R. (2022), The Peak Globalisation Myth: Part 3. How Global Supply Chains Are Unwinding, *CEPR/VOXEU Blog*, 2 September.

Bamber P., Daly J., Frederick S., & Gereffi G. (2018), The Philippines. A Sequential Approach to Upgrading in Global Value Chains, in D. Nathan, M. Tewary, & S. Sarkar (eds), *Development with Global Value Chains. Upgrading and Innovation in Asia*, Cambridge, Cambridge University Press: 107–131.

Basu K. & Maertens A. (2007), The Pattern and Causes of Economic Growth in India, *Oxford Review of Economic Policy*, 23 (2): 143–167.

Baumol W.J. (1967), Macroeconomics of Unbalanced Growth: The Anatomy of Urban Crisis, *American Economic Review* 57 (3): 415–426.

Berger S. (2009, ed), *The Foundations of Non-equilibrium Economics. The Principle of Circular and Cumulative Causation*, Abingdon, Routledge.

Best M.H. (1990), *The New Competition. Institutions of Industrial Restructuring*, Oxford, Polity Press.

Best M.H. (2018), *How Growth Really Happens. The Making of Economic Miracles Through Production, Governance and Skills*, Princeton and Oxford, Princeton University Press.

Borin A., Di Nino V., Mancini M., & Sbracia M. (2017), *Trade Illusion and Disillusion: A Cyclical Phenomenon*, VOXEU.org, 26 March.

Bradford C.I. Jr & Branson W.H. (1987), Trade and Structural Change in Pacific Asia, Chicago, *The University of Chicago Press*.

Bruton H.J. (1998), A Reconsideration of Import Substitution, *Journal of Economic Literature*, 36 (2): 903–936.

Cadot O., Carrère C., & Strauss-Kahn V. (2011), Export Diversification: What's Behind the Hump?, *Review of Economics and Statistics*, 93 (2): 590–605.

Cairncross F. (1997), *The Death of Distance*, Brighton (Ma.), Harvard Business School Press.

Calinski T. & Harabasz, J. (1974), A Dendrite Method for Cluster Analysis, *Communications in Statistics*, 3 (1): 1–27.

Cameron R. (1993), *A Concise Economic History of the World*, New York, Oxford University Press.

Carpenter T. (2008), A Historical Perspective on Regionalism, in R. Baldwin & P. Low (eds), *Multilateralizing Regionalism*, New York, Cambridge University Press: 13–27.

Castillo M. & Neto A.M. (2016), Premature Deindustrialization in Latin America, *ECLAC Production Development Series*, n. 205, Santiago, United Nations.

Cattaneo O., Gereffi G., & Staritz C. (2010, eds), *Global Value Chains in a Post-Crisis World. A Development Perspective*, Washington, The World Bank.

Celasum M. & Rodrik D. (1989), Turkish Economic Development: An Overview, in J.D. Sachs, & S.M. Collins (eds), *Developing Country Debt and Economic Performance, Vol. 3: Country Studies—Indonesia, Korea, Philippines, Turkey*, Chicago, The University of Chicago Press: 617–629.

CEPII (2016), http://www.cepii.fr/institutions/EN/ipd.asp

Chandler A.D., jr. (1990), *Scale and Scope. The Dynamics of Industrial Capitalism*, Cambridge (Ma) and London, Harvard University Press.

Chandrasekhar C.P. & Ghosh J. (2021), No Escape from Low Growth, *IDEAs Business Line*, 11 February.

Chang H.J. (1994), *The Political Economy of Industrial Policy*, New York, S. Martin's Press.

Chang H.J. (1995), Return to Europe? Is There Anything for Eastern Europe to Learn from East Asia? in H.J. Chang & P. Nolan (eds), *The Transformation of the Communist Economies. Against the Mainstream*, New York, St Martin's Press: 382–399.

Chang H.J. (1997), The Economics and Politics of Regulation, *Cambridge Journal of Economics*, 21 (6): 703–728.

Chang H.J. (1999), The Economic Theory of the Developmental State, in M. Woo-Cumings (ed.), *The Developmental State*, Ithaca and London, Cornell University Press: 182–199.

Chang H.J. (2002), *Kicking Away the Ladder. Development Strategy in Historical Perspective*, London, Anthem Press.

Chang H.J. (2003), Introduction, in H.J. Chang (ed.), *Rethinking Development Economics*, London and New York, Anthem Press: 1–18.

Chang H.J. (2006), *The East Asian Development Experience. The Miracle, the Crisis and the Future*, London and New York, Zed Books.

Chang H.J. (2008), The Third World Industrial Revolution in Historical Perspective, in P. Arestis & J. Eatwell (eds), *Issues in Economic Development and Globalization*, Basingstoke, Palgrave Macmillan: 8–27.

Chang H.J. (2011), Institutions and Economic Development, *Journal of Institutional Economics*, 7 (4): 473–498.

Chang H.J. & Nolan P. (1995), Europe versus Asia: Contrasting Paths to the Reform of Centrally Planned Systems of Political Economy, in H.J. Chang & P. Nolan (eds), *The Transformation of the Communist Economies. Against the Mainstream*, Basingstoke and London, Macmillan: 3–45.

Chenery H., Robinson S., & Syrquin M. (1986), *Industrialization and Growth. A Comparative Study*, New York, Oxford University Press.

Chhair S. & Ung L. (2016), Cambodia's Path to Industrial Development: Policies, Lessons, and Opportunities, in C. Newman, J. Page, J. Rand, A. Shimeles, M. Söderbom, & F. Tarp (eds), *Manufacturing Transformation. Comparative Studies of Industrial Development in Africa and Emerging Asia*, Oxford, Oxford University Press: 213–234.

Cimoli M. & Correa N. (2005), Trade Openness and Technology Gaps in Latin America: A 'Low-Growth' Trap, in J.A. Ocampo (ed.), *Beyond Reforms. Structural Dynamics and Macroeconomic Vulnerability*, Palo Alto (Ca.) and Washington, Stanford University Press and The World Bank: 45–69.

Cimoli M., Dosi G., & Stiglitz J.E. (2009), The Political Economy of Capabilities Accumulation: The Past and Future of Policies for Industrial Development, in M. Cimoli, G. Dosi, & J.E. Stiglitz (eds), *Industrial Policy and Development*, New York, Oxford University Press: 1–16.

Clark C. (1940), *The Conditions of Economic Progress*, Macmillan and Co, London.

Cohen W.M. & Levinthal D.A. (1990), Absorptive Capacity: A New Perspective on Learning and Innovation, *Administrative Science Quarterly*, 35 (1): 128–152.

Correa F. & Stumpo G. (2017), Brechas de Productividad y Cambio Estructural, in J.E. Stiglitz, G. Dosi, M. Mazzucato, M. Pianta, & W. Luktenhorst (eds), *Political Industriales y Tecnologicas en America Latina*, CEPAL Publishing, Santiago, Chile: 35–60.

Costantinescu C., Mattoo A., & Ruta M. (2020), The Global Trade Slowdown: Cyclical or Structural? *The World Bank Economic Review*, 34 (1): 121–142.

Crafts N. & Hughes A. (2013), Industrial Policy for the Medium to Long-Term, *Center for Business Research Working Paper Series*, n. 455, University of Cambridge.

Crane K. & Skoller D. (1988), Specialization Agreements in the Council for Mutual Economic Assistance, *RAND Report* R-3518.

Dahlman C.J. (2009), Growth and Development in China and India: The Role of Industrial and Innovation Policy in Rapid Catch-Up, in M. Cimoli, G. Dosi, & J.E. Stiglitz (eds), *Industrial Policy and Development*, New York, Oxford University Press: 303–335.

Damijan J., Kostevc Č., & Rojec M. (2018), Global Supply Chains at Work in Central and Eastern European Countries: Impact of Foreign Direct Investment on Export Restructuring and Productivity Growth, *Economic and Business Review*, 20 (2): 237–267.

Dasgupta S. & Singh A. (2005), Will Services Be the New Engine of Economic Growth in India?, *Centre for Business Research Working Paper Series*, n. 310, September.

De Melo J. & Panagariya A. (1993), Introduction, in J. De Melo & A. Panagariya (eds), *New Dimensions in Regional Integration*, Cambridge, Cambridge University Press: 3–21.

Devlin R. & Moguillansky G. (2013), What's New in the New Industrial Policy in Latin America?, in J.E. Stiglitz, & J.Y. Lin (2013, eds), *The Industrial Policy Revolution I, The Role of Government beyond Ideology*, Basingstoke and New York, Palgrave Macmillan: 276–317.

de Vries G., Timmer M., & de Vries K. (2015), Structural Transformation in Africa: Static Gains, Dynamic Losses, *Journal of Development Studies*, 51 (6): 674–688.

Di Mauro C., Fratocchi L., Orzes G., & Sartor M. (2018), Offshoring and Backshoring: A Multiple Case Study Analysis, *Journal of Purchasing and Supply Management*, 24 (2): 108–134.

Ding Y. & Li X. (2017), The Past and Future of China's Role in the East Asian Economy: A Trade Perspective, *Canadian Public Policy/Analyse de Politiques*, 43 (S2): 545–556.

Dingemans A. & Ross C. (2012), Free Trade Agreements in Latin America since 1990: An Evaluation of Export Diversification, *CEPAL Review*, 108: 27–48.

Easterly W. (2001), The Lost Decades: Developing Countries' Stagnation in Spite of Policy Reform 1980–1988, *Journal of Economic Growth*, 6 (1): 135–157.

Easterly W. & Fischer S. (1994), The Soviet Economic Decline: Historical and Republican Data, *NBER Working Papers*, n. 4735.

EBRD (various years), *Transition Report*, European Bank for Reconstruction and Development.

ECLAC (1990), *Changing Production Patterns with Social Equity. The Prime Task of Latin American and Caribbean Development in the 1990s*, Santiago (Chile), United Nations.

ECLAC (2000), *Equity, Development and Citizenship*, Santiago (Chile), United Nations.

The Economist (2013), *Here, There and Anywhere*, Special Report, 19 January.

The Economist (2017), *The Retreat of the Global Company*, 28 January.

Edwards S. (1995), *Crisis and Reform in Latin America: From Despair to Hope*, Oxford, Oxford University Press.

Eichengreen B. (2014), Secular Stagnation: A Review of the Issues, in C. Teulings, & R. Baldwin (eds), *Secular Stagnation: Facts, Causes and Cures*, A VoxEU.org eBook, London, CEPR Press: 41–46.

Elia S., Fratocchi L., Barbieri P., Boffelli A., & Kalchschmidt M. (2021), Post-pandemic Reconfiguration from Global to Domestic and Regional Value Chains: The Role of Industrial Policies, *Trasnational Corporations*, 28 (2): 67–96.

Ellram L.M., Tate W.L., & Petersen K.J. (2013), Offshoring and Reshoring: An Update on the Manufacturing Location Decision, *Journal of Supply Chain Management*, 49 (2): 14–22.

Ernst C. (2005), Trade Liberalization, Export Orientation and Employment in Argentina, Brazil and Mexico, *ILO Employment Strategy Papers*, n. 15.

Escaith H. (2009), *Trade Collapse, Trade Relapse and Global Production Networks: Supply Chains in the Great Recession*, paper presented at the OECD Roundtable on Impacts of Economic Crisis on Globalizations and Global Value Chains, Paris, 28 October.

Escaith H., Lindenberg N., & Miroudot S. (2010), Global Value Chains and the Crisis: Reshaping International Trade Elasticities? In O. Cattaneo, G. Gereffi, & C. Staritz (eds), *Global Value Chains in a Postcrisis World. A Development Perspective*, Washington, The World Bank: 73–123.

Eurofound (2016), *ERM Annual Report 2016: Globalisation Slowdown? Recent Evidence of Offshoring and Reshoring in Europe*, Publications Office of the European Union, Luxembourg.

European Commission (2009), Economic Crisis in Europe. Causes, Consequences and Responses, *European Economy*, 7, Directorate General for Economic and Financial Affairs, Bruxelles.

Faini R. (1997), Integration or Polarization? Regionalism in World Trade during the 1990s, in E. Grilli & E. Sassoon (eds), *Multilateralism and Regionalism after the Uruguay Round*, Basingstoke and New York, Macmillan and St Martin's Press: 144–160.

Fajgelbaum P.D., Goldberg P.K., Kennedy P.J., & Khandelwal A.K. (2019), The Return to Protectionism, *NBER Working Papers*, 25638, March.

Fayad G. & Perrelli R. (2014), Growth surprises and synchronized slowdowns in emerging markets – an empirical investigation, *IMF Working Papers*, WP/14/173, Washington.

Feenstra R.C. (1998), Integration of Trade and Disintegration of Production in the Global Economy, *Journal of Economic Perspectives*, 12 (4): 31–50.

Felipe J., Abdon A., & Kumar U. (2012), Tracking the Middle-Income Trap: What Is It, Who Is in It, and Why?, *Levy Economic Institute Working Paper Series*, n. 715, April.

Filippetti A. & Peyrache A. (2013), Is the Convergence Party Over? Labour Productivity and the Technology Gap in Europe, *Journal of Common Market Studies* 51 (6): 1006–1022.

Findlay R. (2019), Asia and the World Economy in Historical Perspective, in D. Nayyar (ed.), *Asian Transformations. An Inquiry into the Development of Nations*, Oxford, Oxford University Press: 80–105.

Fischer S., Sahay R., & Vegh C.A. (1996), Stabilization and Growth in Transition Economies: The Early Experience, *Journal of Economic Perspectives*, 10 (2): 45–66.

Fisher A. (1939), Production: Primary, Secondary and Tertiary, *Economic Record*, 15 (1): 24–38.

Foreman-Peck J. & Federico G. (1999, eds), *European Industrial Policy*, Oxford, Oxford University Press.

Foss N.J. (1997, ed.), *Resources, Firms, and Strategies*, New York, Oxford University Press.

Foss N.J. (2005), *Strategy, Economic Organization, and the Knowledge Economy*, New York, Oxford University Press.

Foster-McGregor N. & Verspagen B. (2016), The Role of Structural Change in the Economic Development of Asian Economies, *Asian Development Review*, 33 (2): 74–93.

Fratocchi L., Di Mauro C., Barbieri P., Nassimbeni G., & Zanoni A. (2014), When Manufacturing Moves Back: Concepts and Questions, *Journal of Purchasing & Supply Management*, 20 (1): 54–59.

Freeman R.B. (2007), The Great Doubling: The Challenge of the New Global Labor Market, in J. Edwards, M. Crain, A.L. Kalleberg (eds), *Ending Poverty in America. How to Restore the American Dream*, New York, The New Press: 55–65.

Fuà G. (1978), Lagged Development and Economic Dualism, *Banca Nazionale del Lavoro Quarterly Review* 31 (125): 123–134.

Fuchs V.R. (1968), *The Service Economy*, NBER General Series n. 87.

Fujita N. (2007), Myrdal's Theory of Cumulative Causation, *Evolutionary and Institutional Economics Review*, 3 (2): 275–284.

Fukuyama F. (1989), The End of History? *The National Interest*, 16: 3–18.

Gaudiosi F. (2018), Economic Nationalism and the Post-Global Future, *IAI Commentaries*, 04, January.

Geebreyesus M. (2016), Industrial Policy and Development in Ethiopia, in C. Newman, J. Page, J. Rand, A. Shimeles, M. Söderbom, & F. Tarp (eds), *Manufacturing Transformation. Comparative Studies of Industrial Development in Africa and Emerging Asia*, Oxford, Oxford University Press: 27–49.

Gereffi G. (2014), Global Value Chains in a Post-Washington Consensus World, *Review of International Political Economy*, 21 (1): 9–37.

Gereffi G., Humphrey J., & Sturgeon T. (2005), The Governance of Global Value Chains, *Review of International Political Economy*, 12 (1): 78–104.

Gerschenkron A. (1962), *Economic Backwardness in Historical Perspective*, Cambridge (Ma.), Belknap, Harvard University Press.

Giovannetti G. & Sanfilippo M. (2009), Do Chinese Exports Crowd-out African Goods? An Econometric Analysis by Country and Sector, *European Journal of Development Research*, 21: 506–530.

Glyn A., Hughes A., Lipietz A., & Singh A. (1990), The Rise and Fall of the Golden Age, in S.A. Marglin & G.B. Schor (eds), *The Golden Age of Capitalism. Interpreting the Postwar Experience*, Oxford, Clarendon Press: 39–125.

Godart O., Gorg H., & Gorlich D. (2009), Back to Normal? The Future of Global Production Networks, in H. Klodt & H. Lehment (eds), *The Crisis and Beyond*, Kiel Institute for the World Economy, Kiel: 119–126.

Gonzalez J.L., Meliciani V., & Savona M. (2019), When Linder Meets Hirschman: Inter-Industry Linkages and Global Value Chains in Business Services, *Industrial and Corporate Change*, 28 (6): 1555–1586.

Gordon R.J. (2014), The Turtle's Progress: Secular Stagnation Meets the Headwinds, in C. Teulings & R. Baldwin (eds), *Secular Stagnation: Facts, Causes and Cures*, A VoxEU.org eBook, London, CEPR Press: 47–59.

Gore C. (2000), The Rise and Fall of the Washington Consensus as a Paradigm for Developing Countries, *World Development*, 28 (5): 789–804.

Gorenstein S. & Ortiz R. (2018), Natural Resources and Primary Sector-dependent Territories in Latin America, *Area Development and Policy*, vol. 3 (1): 42–59.

Gray J.V., Skowronski K., Esenduran G., & Rungtusanatham M.J. (2013), The Reshoring Phenomenon: What Supply Chain Academics Ought to Know and Should Do, *Journal of Supply Chain Management*, 49 (2): 27–33.

Grazzi M., Pietrobelli C., & Szirmai A. (2016), Determinants of Enterprise Performance in Latin America and the Caribbean: What Does the Micro-Evidence Tell Us?, in M. Grazzi & C. Pietrobelli (eds), *Firm Innovation and Productivity in Latin America and the Caribbean*, New York, Palgrave Macmillan: 1–36.

Greenaway D. & Milner C. (1986), *The Economics of Intra-industry Trade*, Oxford and New York, Blackwell.

Grilli E. (1997), Multilateralism and Regionalism: A Still Difficult Coexistence, in E. Grilli & E. Sassoon (eds), *Multilateralism and Regionalism after the Uruguay Round*, Basingstoke and New York, Macmillan and St Martin's Press: 194–233.

Hackett J., Krueger A.O., Myint H., & Nove A. (2017), Economic Planning, entry in *Encyclopedia Britannica*.

Hansen A.H. (1939), Economic Progress and Declining Population Growth, *American Economic Review*, 29 (1): 1–15.

Haraguchi N. & Rezonja G. (2013), Emerging Patterns of Structural Change in Manufacturing, in A. Szirmai, W. Naudè, & L. Alcorta (eds), *Pathways of Industrialization in the Twenty-First Century. New Challenges and Emerging Paradigms*, Oxford, Oxford University Press: 102–128.

Haugh D., Kopoin A., Rusticelli E., Turner D., & Dutu R. (2016), *Cardiac Arrest or Dizzy Spell: Why Is World Trade So Weak and What Can Policy Do about It?*, OECD Economic Policy Paper n. 18, Paris.

Hausmann R., Hidalgo C.A., Bustos S., Coscia M., Chung S., Jimenez J., Simoes A., & Yildirim M.A. (2011), *The Atlas of Economic Complexity. Mapping Paths to Prosperity*, Harvard University, Center for International Development, Harvard Kennedy School and MIT MediaLab.

Hausmann R.D., Rodrik D., & Velasco A. (2005), *Growth Diagnostics*, John F. Kennedy School of Government, Cambridge (Ma.), Harvard University.

Helfat C., Finkelstein S., Mitchell W., Peteraf M., Singh H., Teece D.J., & Winter S.G. (2007), *Dynamic Capabilities. Understanding Strategic Change in Organizations*, Oxford, Blackwell Publishing.

Hellman J.S., Jones G., & Kaufmann D. (2000), Seize the State, Seize the Day: An Empirical Analysis of State Capture and Corruption in Transition Economies, *World Bank Research Working Papers*, n. 2444.

Herrendorf B., Rogerson R., & Valentinyi A. (2014), Growth and Structural Transformation, in: P. Aghion & S.N. Durlaufthe (eds), *Handbook of Economic Growth*. Vol. 2, Amsterdam, Elsevier: 855–941.

Hirschman A. (1958), *The Strategy of Economic Development*, New Haven, Yale University Press.

Hirschman A.O. (2013), A Generalized Linkage Approach to Development, with Special Reference to Staples, in A.O. Hirschman, *The Essential Hirschman*, Princeton, Princeton University Press [Firstly published in *Economic Development and Cultural Change*, 1977, 25 (Supplement): 67–98].

Ho P.S. (2012), Revisiting Prebisch and Singer: Beyond the Declining Terms of Trade Thesis and on to Technological Capability Development, *Cambridge Journal of Economics*, 36 (4): 869–893.

Hoekman B. (2015, ed.), *The Global Trade Slowdown: A New Normal?*, VOXEU.org, https://voxeu.org/sites/default/files/file/Global%20Trade%20Slowdown_nocover.pdf

Hoyos López M. (2017), Trade Liberalization and Premature Deindustrialization in Colombia, *Journal of Economic Structures*, doi 10.1186/s40008-017-0095-6.

Hymer S. (1976), *The International Operations of National Firms: A Study of Direct Investment*, Cambridge (Ma.), The MIT Press.

Iapadre L. (2006), Regional Integration Agreements and the Geography of World Trade: Statistical Indicators and Empirical Evidence, in P. De Lombaerde (ed.), *Assessment and Measurement of Regional Integration*, London, Routledge: 65–85.

Iapadre L. & Tironi F. (2009), Measuring Trade Regionalisation: The Case of Asia, *UNU-CRIS Working Papers*, W - 2009/9.

IEA (2022a), *Aviation*, IEA, Paris.

IEA (2022b), *International Shipping*, IEA, Paris.

ILO (2021), *World Employment and Social Outlook. Trends 2021*, Geneva, International Labour Office.

Imbs J., Montenegro C., & Wacziarg R. (2012), *Economic Integration and Structural Change*, mimeo.

Imbs J. & Wacziarg R. (2003), Stages of Diversification, *American Economic Review*, 93 (1): 63–86.

IMF (2012), *The Liberalization and Management of Capital Flows: An Institutional View*, Washington, International Monetary Fund, November.

IMF (2017), *World Economic Outlook. Gaining Momentum?*, Washington, International Monetary Fund, April.

IMF (2019), Growth slowdown, precarious recovery. The drivers of bilateral trade and the spillovers from tariffs, *World Economic Outlook*, April.

IMF, World Bank, OECD, EBRD (1991), *A Study of the Soviet Economy*, Paris, OECD Publishing.

Jenkins R. (1991), The Political Economy of Industrialization: A Comparison of Latin American and East Asian Newly Industrializing Countries, *Development and Change*, 22 (2): 197–231.

Jenkins R., Dussel Peters E., & Mesquita Moreira M. (2008), The Impact of China on Latin America and the Caribbean, *World Development*, 36 (2): 235–253.

Johnson C. (1982), *MITI and the Japanese Miracle: The Growth of Industrial Policy, 1925–1975*, Stanford, Stanford University Press.

Johnson C. (1999), The Developmental State: Odissey of a Concept, in M. Woo-Cumings (ed.), *The Developmental State*, Ithaca and London, Cornell University Press: 32–60.

Johnson R.C. & Noguera G. (2017), A Portrait of Trade in Value-Added over Four Decades, *Review of Economics and Statistics*, 99 (5): 896–91.

Johnson S., McMillan J., & Woodruff C. (2002), Property Rights and Finance, *American Economic Review*, 92 (5): 1335–1356.

Kaldor N. (1966), *Causes of the Slow Rate of Economic Growth in the United Kingdom*, Cambridge, Cambridge University Press.

Kaldor N. (1981), The Role of Increasing Returns, Technical Progress and Cumulative Causation in the Theory of International Trade and Economic Growth, *Economie Appliquée*, 34 (4): 593–617.

Kambhampati U. (2016), Industrial Development in India, in J. Weiss & M. Tribe (eds), *Routledge Handbook of Industry and Development*, Abingdon and New York, Routledge: 335–349.

Kanbur R. (2019), Gunnar Myrdal and Asian Drama in Context, in D. Nayyar (ed.), *Asian Transformations. An Inquiry into the Development of Nations*, Oxford, Oxford University Press: 29–51.

Kaplan D. (2016), Linkage Dynamics and Natural Resources: Diversification and Catch-Up, in P.G. Sanpath & B.O. Oyeyinka (eds), *Sustainable Industrialization in Africa. Toward a New Development Agenda*, Basingstoke and New York, Macmillan: 66–84.

Kaplinski R. & Farooki M. (2010), Global Value Chains, the Crisis, and the Shift of Markets from North to South, in O. Cattaneo, G. Gereffi, & C. Staritz (2010, eds), *Global Value Chains in a Post-Crisis World. A Development Perspective*, Washington, The World Bank: 125–153.

Kaser M. & Zielinski J.G. (1970), *Planning in East Europe. Industrial Management by the State*. London, The Bodley Head.

Kattel R. (2010), Financial and Economic Crisis in Eastern Europe, *Journal of Post Keynesian Economics*, 33 (1): 41–59.

Katz J.M. (2001), Structural Reforms, Productivity and Technological Change in Latin America, *Libros de la CEPAL*, n. 64, United Nations Publications, Santiago, Chile.

Kaufmann D., Kraay A., & Mastruzzi M. (2010), The Worldwide Governance Indicators: Methodology and Analytical Issues, *World Bank Policy Research Working Paper* WPS 54.

Kaulich F. (2012), *Diversification vs. Specialization as Alternative Strategies for Economic Development: Can We Settle a Debate by Looking at the Empirical Evidence?*, Working Paper 3/2012, Vienna, UNIDO.

Kharas H. & Kohli H. (2011), What Is the Middle Income Trap, Why do Countries Fall into It, and How Can It Be Avoided, *Global Journal of Emerging Market Economies* 3 (3): 281–289.

Kimura F. & Obashi A. (2011), Production Networks in East Asia: What We Know So Far, *ADBI Working Paper Series*, n. 320, Asian Development Bank Institute, Tokyo.

Kindleberger C. (1958), *Economic Development*, New York, McGraw-Hill.

Kindleberger C. (1992), Why Did the Golden Age Last So Long? In A. Cairncross and F. Cairncross (eds), *The Legacy of the Golden Age*, London and New York, Routledge: 15–44.

Kinkel S. & Maloca S. (2009), Drivers and Antecedents of Manufacturing Offshoring and Backshoring. A German Perspective, *Journal of Purchasing and Supply Management*, 15 (3): 154–165.

Klapper L.F., Sarria-Allende V., & Sulla V. (2002), Small- and Medium-Size Enterprise Financing in Eastern Europe, *World Bank Research Working Papers*, n. 2933.

Kozul-Wright R. (1995), Transnational Corporations and the Nation State, in J. Michie & J. Grieve-Smith (eds), *Managing the Global Economy*, New York, Oxford University Press: 135–171.

Kruger J.J. (2008), Productivity and Structural Change: A Review of the Literature, *Journal of Economic Surveys*, 22 (2): 330–363.

Krugman P. (2014), Four Observations on Secular Stagnation, in C. Teulings & R. Baldwin (eds), *Secular Stagnation: Facts, Causes and Cures*, A VoxEU.org eBook, London, CEPR Press: 61–68.

Kuzemco C., Blondeel M., Dupont C., & Brisbois M.C. (2022), Russia's War on Ukraine, European Energy Policy Responses and Implications for Sustainable Transformations, *Energy Research & Social Science*, 93: 102842.

Kuznets S. (1973), Modern Economic Growth: Findings and Reflections, *American Economic Review*, 63 (3): 247–258.

Kuznets S.S. (1965), *Economic Growth and Structure*, New York, W.W. Norton & Co.

Lall S. (2003), Technology and Industrial Development in an Era of Globalization, in H.J. Chang (ed.), *Rethinking Development Economics*, London and New York, Anthem Press: 277–298.

Lall S. & Pietrobelli C. (2002), *Failing to Compete: Technology Development and Technology Systems in Africa*, Cheltenham (UK) and Lyme (US), Edward Elgar.

Lall S. & Pietrobelli C. (2005), National Technology Systems in Sub-Saharan Africa, *International Journal of Technology and Globalization*, 1 (3-4): 311–342.

Landes D.S. (1969), *The Unbound Prometheus*, Cambridge, Cambridge University Press.

Lavigne M. (1979), *Les Economies Socialistes Soviétiques et Européennes*, Paris, Armand Collin Edition.

Lee K. & Kim B.Y. (2009), Both Institutions and Policies Matter But Differently for Different Income Groups of Countries: Determinants of Long-Run Economic Growth Revisited, *World Development*, 37 (3): 533–549.

Leng Y.K. (2017), Domestic Demand-driven Growth: Analytical Perspectives and Statistics Needed, *Advances in Economics and Business*, 5 (3): 109–128.

Lewis W.A. (1954), Economic Development with Unlimited Supplies of Labour, *The Manchester School*, 22 (2): 139–191.

Liang, M.Y. (2010), Confucianism and the East Asian Miracle, *American Economic Journal: Macroeconomics*, 2: 206–234.

Lin J.Y. (2009), *Economic Development and Transition. Thought, Strategy, and Viability*, New York, Cambridge University Press.

Lo D. (1995), Economic Theory and Transformation of the Soviet-Type System: The Challenge of the Late Industrialisation Perspective, in H.J. Chang & P. Nolan (eds), *The Transformation of the Communist Economies. Against the Mainstream*, New York, S. Martin's Press: 78–110.

Lo D. & Wu M. (2014), The State and Industrial Policy in Chinese Economic Development, in J.M. Salazar-Xirinachs, I. Nübler, & R. Kozul-Wright (eds), *Transforming Economies: Making Industrial Policy Work for Growth, Jobs and Development*, ILO Publishing: 307–326.

Loasby B.J. (1998), *The Concept of Capabilities*, in N.J. Foss & B.J. Loasby (eds), *Economic Organization, Capabilities and Co-ordination. Essays in Honour of G.B. Richardson*, London and New York, Routledge: 163–182.

Loasby B.J. (1999), *Knowledge, Institutions and Evolution in Economics*, London and New York, Routledge.

Loasby B.J. (2000), The Division and Organisation of Knowledge, *European Journal of Economic and Social Systems*, 14 (2): 143–155.

Lyubimov I. (2019), Russia's Diversification Prospects, *Russian Journal of Economics*, 5 (2): 177–198.

Manzocchi S. Romano L., & Traù F. (2020), The Times They Are A-Changin'. A Few Notes on Italian Industry Beyond 2020, in A. Goldstein & G. Bellettini (eds), *The Italian Economy after Covid-19. Short-term Costs and Long-term Adjustments*, Bologna, Bononia University Press: 159–169.

Manzocchi S. & Traù F. (2022), La distanza e l'incertezza. Percorsi della manifattura globale negli anni degli shock sistemici, *Rivista di Politica Economica*, 111 (1): 5–12.

Marconi N., Fròes de Borja Reis C., & de Araùjo E.C. (2016), Manufacturing and Economic Development: The Actuality of Kaldor's First and Second Laws, *Structural Change and Economic Dynamics*, 37 (2): 75–89.

Marx K. (1867), *Das Kapital. Kritik der Politischen Oekonomie*, Buch I, Hamburg, Verlag von Otto Meissner.

Matsuyama K. (2009), Structural Change in an Interdependent World: A Global View of Manufacturing Decline, *Journal of the European Economic Association*, 7 (2-3): 478–486.

Matthews R.C.O. (1982, ed.), *Slower Growth in the Western World*, London, Heinemann.

Mazzucato M. (2011), *The Entrepreneurial State*, London, Demos.

McMahon R.G.P. (1998), Stage Models of SME Growth Reconsidered, *Small Enterprise Research*, 6 (2): 20–35.

McMillan M. & Zeufack A. (2022), Labor Productivity Growth and Industrialization in Africa, *Journal of Economic Perspectives*, 36 (1): 3–32.

Meisel N. & Ould Aoudia J. (2008), Is Good Governance a Good Development Strategy? *Agence Française de Développement Working Paper* n. 58.

Mendes A.P., Bertella M.A., & Teixeira R.F.A.P. (2014), Industrialization in Sub-Saharan Africa and Import Substitution Policy, *Brazilian Journal of Political Economy*, 34 (1): 120–138.

Meyer K.E. & Pind C. (1999), The Slow Growth of Foreign Direct Investment in the Soviet Union successor states, *Economics of Transition and Institutional Change*, 7 (1): 201–214.

Michie J. & Grieve-Smith J. (1995, eds), *Managing the Global Economy*, New York, Oxford University Press.

Michie J. & Grieve-Smith J. (1996, eds), *Creating Industrial Capacity. Towards Full Employment*, Oxford, Oxford University Press.

Michie J. & Grieve-Smith J. (1997, eds), *Employment and Economic Performance*, Oxford, Oxford University Press.

Milberg W. & Winkler D. (2010), Trade, Crisis and Recovery: Restructuring Global Value Chains, in O. Cattaneo, G. Gereffi, & C. Staritz (2010, eds), *Global Value Chains in a Post-Crisis World. A Development Perspective*, Washington, The World Bank: 23–72.

Minondo A. (2011), Does Comparative Advantage Explain Countries' Diversification Level?, *Review of World Economics*, 147 (3): 507–526.

Miroudot S. & Nordström H. (2019), Made in the World Revisited, *EUI Working Papers*, European University Institute, RSCAS 20189/84.

Mizuno K. (2017), The East Asian Economy Post-rebalancing: Domestic Demand-led Growth, Social Security and Inequality, *The Indonesian Journal of Southeast Asian Studies*, 1 (1): 47–67.

Mohanty S.K. (2012), Economic Growth, Export and Domestic demand in India: In Search of a New Paradigm of Development, in Y. Zhangh, F. Kimura, & S. Oum (eds), *Moving toward a New Development Model for East Asia. The Role of Domestic Policy and Regional Cooperation*, ERIA Research Project Report 2011-10, Jakarta, ERIA: 190–222.

Morris-Suzuki T. (1994), *The Technological Transformation of Japan*, Cambridge, Cambridge University Press.

Myrdal G. (1957), *Economic Theory and Under-Developed Regions*, London, General Duckworth & Co.

Myrdal G. (1968), *Asian Drama: An Inquiry into the Poverty of Nations*, New York, Pantheon Press.

Nassif A. & Castilho M.R. (2020), Trade Patterns in a Globalised World: Brazil as a Case of Regressive Specialisation, *Cambridge Journal of Economics*, 44 (3): 671–701.

Nassif A., Feijò C., & Araùjo E. (2020), Macroeconomic Policies in Brazil Before and After the 2008 Global Financial Crisis: Brazilian Policy Makers Still Trapped in the New Macroeconomic Consensus Guidelines, *Cambridge Journal of Economics*, 44 (3): 671–701.

Nathan D., Tewary M., & Sarkar S. (2018), Introduction, in D. Nathan, M. Tewary, & S. Sarkar (eds), *Development with Global Value Chains. Upgrading and Innovation in Asia*, Cambridge, Cambridge University Press: 1–19.

Naudé W., Surdej A., & Cameron M. (2019), The Past and Future of Manufacturing in Central and Eastern Europe: Ready for Industry 4.0?, *IZA Working Paper* n. 12141.

Nayyar D. (2003), Globalization and Development, in H.J. Chang (ed.), *Rethinking Development Economics*, London and New York, Anthem Press: 61–82.

Nayyar D. (2019, ed.), *Asian Transformations. An Inquiry into the Development of Nations*, Oxford, Oxford University Press.

Neilson J., Pritchard B., & Yeung H.W. (2014), Global Value Chains and Global Production Networks in the Changing International Political Economy: An Introduction, *Review of International Political Economy*, 21 (1): 1–8.

Newfarmer R.S, Page J., & Tarp F. (2018), *Industries without Smokestacks. Industrialization in Africa Reconsidered*, Oxford, Oxford University Press.

Newman C., Page J., Rand J., Shimeles A., Söderbom M., & Tarp F. (2016, eds), *Manufacturing Transformation. Comparative Studies of Industrial Development in Africa and Emerging Asia*, Oxford, Oxford University Press.

Nielsen L. (2011), Classification of Countries Based on Their Level of Development: How it is Done and How it Could be Done, *IMF Working Paper*, 11/31, February, Strategy, Policy and Review Department, International Monetary Fund.

Nixson (2016), Import Substituting Industrialisation (ISI): Can or Should We Divorce Industrialisation and Trade Strategies? in J. Weiss & M. Tribe (eds), *Routledge Handbook of Industry and Development*, Abingdon and New York, Routledge: 151–165.

Nolan P. (1996), Large Firms and Industrial Reform in Former Planned Economies: The Case of China, *Cambridge Journal of Economics*, 20 (1): 1–29.

Nolan P., Zhang J., & Liu C. (2008), The Global Business Revolution, the Cascade Effect, and the Challenge for Firms from Developing Countries, *Cambridge Journal of Economics*, 32 (1): 29–47.

North, D. (1990), *Institutions, Institutional Change and Economic Performance*, Cambridge, Cambridge University Press.

NPC (2010), *Report on the Outline of the Tenth Five-Year Plan for National Economic and Social Development*, http://www.npc.gov.cn/zgrdw/englishnpc/Special_11_5/2010-03/03/content_1690620. htm

Ocampo J.A. (2005), The Quest for Dynamic Efficiency: Structural Dynamics and Economic Growth in Developing Countries, in J.A. Ocampo (ed.), *Beyond Reforms. Structural Dynamics and Macroeconomic Vulnerability*, Palo Alto (Ca.) and Washington, Stanford University Press and The World Bank: 3–43.

Ocampo J.A. (2014), The Latin American Debt Crisis in Historical Perspective, in: J.E. Stiglitz & D. Heymann, (eds), *Life After Debt*, International Economic Association Series, London, Palgrave Macmillan: 87–115.

Ocampo J.A. & Martin J. (eds) (2003), *A Decade of Light and Shadow. Latin America and the Caribbean in the 1990s*, CEPAL publication, Santiago, Chile.

OECD (2019), *Interim Economic Outlook*, 6 March, Paris.

Opoku E.E.O. & Kit-Ming Yan I. (2019), Industrialization as Driver of Sustainable Economic Growth in Africa, *Journal of International Trade and Economic Development*, 28 (1): 30–56.

Oqubay A. (2019), The Structure and Performance of the Ethiopian Manufacturing Sector, in F. Cheru, C. Cramer, & A. Oqubay, *The Oxford Handbook of the Ethiopian Economy*, Oxford Online, Oxford University Press. DOI: 10.1093/oxfordhb/9780198814986.013.48.

Oreiro J.L., D'Agostini L.L.M., & Gala P. (2020), Deindustrialization, Economic Complexity and Exchange Rate Overvaluation: The Case of Brazil (1998–2017), *Textos para Discussão, Ecopol*, Agosto.

Page J. (2012), Can Africa Industrialise? *Journal of African Economies*, 21: ii86–ii125.

Palley T.I. (2011), The Rise and Fall of Export-led Growth, *Investigación Económica*, 71 (280): 141–161.

Palma J.G. (2003a), The Latin American Economies during the Second Half of Twentieth Century. From the Age of 'ISI' to the Age of 'The End of History', in H.J. Chang (ed.), *Rethinking Development Economics*, London and New York, Anthem Press: 125–151.

Palma J.G. (2003b), Trade Liberalization in Mexico: Its Impact on Growth, Employment and Wages, *Employment Paper* n. 55, International Labour Office, Geneva.

Palma J.G. (2005), Seven Main Stylized Facts of the Mexican Economy, *Industrial and Corporate Change* 14 (6): 941–991.

Palma J.G. (2009), Flying Geese and Weddling Ducks: The Different Capabilities of East Asia and Latin America to 'Demand-Adapt' and 'Supply-Upgrade' Their Export Productive Capacity, in M. Cimoli, G. Dosi, & J.E. Stiglitz (eds), *Industrial Policy and Development*, New York, Oxford University Press: 203–238.

Palma J.G. (2019a), Deindustrialization, Premature Deindustrialization, and Dutch Disease, *El Trimester Economico*, vol. 86 (4): 901–966.

Palma J.G. (2019b), The Chilean Economy since the Return to Democracy in 1990. On How to Get an Emerging Economy Growing, and Then Sink Slowly into the Quicksand of a 'Middle Income Trap', *Cambridge Working Papers in Economics*, n. 1991, Faculty of Economics, University of Cambridge.

Parteka A. & Tamberi M. (2013), What Determines Export Diversification in the Development Process? Empirical Assessment, *The World Economy*, 36 (6): 807–826.

Pearson D.S. (1969), *Industrial Development in East Africa*, Nairobi, Oxford University Press.

Pekarčik M., Ďurčova J., & Glova J. (2022), Intangible ICT and Their Importance within Global Value Chains: An Empirical Analysis Based on Longitudinal Data Regression, *Mathematics*, 10, 1198. https://doi.org/10.3390/math10071198

Pempel T.J. (2005), *Remapping East Asia. The Construction of a Region*, Ithaca and London, Cornell University Press.

Penrose E.T. (1959), *The Theory of the Growth of the Firm*, Oxford, Basil Blackwell.

Pensa C. & Pignatti M. (2022), La Regionalizzazione Degli Scambi Mondiali: Lungo le Dimensioni Geografica e Mercelogica, *Rivista di Politica Economica*, 112 (1): 143–167.

Pensa C., Romano L., & Traù F. (2020), Esaurimento di un Paradigma di Sviluppo: (Neo)Regionalismo, Slowdown della Domanda Estera, Rallentamento Produttivo della Manifattura Mondiale, *Economia Italiana*, 2: 155–202.

Peres W. (2013), Industrial Policies in Latin America, in A. Szirmai, W. Naudé, & L. Alcorta (eds), *Pathways to Industrialization in the Twenty-First Century*, Oxford, Oxford University Press: 223–243.

Perkins D.H. (2012), *Industrial Policy Reform in Myanmar*, Ash Center for Democratic Governance and Innovation, Cambridge, MA, Harvard Kennedy School.

Perroux F. (1955), Note Sur la Notion de 'Pôle de Croissance', *Economie Appliquée*, 7 (1–2): 307–320.

Piore M.J. & Sabel C.F. (1984), *The Second Industrial Divide*, New York, Basic Books.

Pisano G.P. & Shih W.C. (2012), *Producing Prosperity. Why America Needs a Manufacturing Renaissance*, Boston (Ma.), Harvard Business Review Press.

Pitelis C. (1991), *Market and Non-market Hierarchies*, Oxford, Blackwell.

Polanyi K. (1944), *The Great Transformation*, New York, Holt, Rinehart & Winston.

Pomeranz K. (2000), *The Great Divergence. China, Europe and the Making of the Modern World Economy*, Princeton, Princeton University Press.

Popov V. & Jomo K.S. (2018), Are Developing Countries Catching Up? *Cambridge Journal of Economics*, 42 (1): 33–46.

Prebisch R. (1970), *Change and Development. Latin America's Great Task*, Washington, Inter-American Development Bank.

Rajah R. (2019), East Asia's Decoupling, *Lowy Institute Working Paper* n. 1, January.

Razmi A. & Blecker R.A. (2008, Developing Country Exports of Manufactures: Moving Up the Ladder to Escape the Fallacy of Composition?, *Journal of Development Studies*, 44 (1): 21–48.

Reijnders L.S.M., Timmer M.P., & Ye X. (2021), Labour Demand in Global Value Chains: Is There a Bias against Unskilled Work?, *The World Economy*, 44 (9): 2547–2571.

Reinert E.S. (1999), The Role of the State in Economic Growth, *Journal of Economic Studies*, 26 (4/5): 268–325.

Reinert E.S. (2007), *How Rich Countries Got Rich ... and Why Poor Countries Stay Poor*, London, Constable.

Reinert E.S. (2009), Emulation vs. Comparative Advantage: Competing and Complementary Principles in the History of Economic Policy, in M. Cimoli, G. Dosi, & J.E. Stiglitz (eds), *Industrial Policy and Development*, New York, Oxford University Press: 79–106.

Rekiso Z.S. (2017), Rethinking Regional Economic Integration in Africa as if Industrialization Mattered, *Structural Change and Economic Dynamics*, 43: 87–98.

Reynolds L.G. (1983), The Spread of Economic Growth to the Third World: 1850–1980, *Journal of Economic Literature*, 21 (2): 941–980.

Reynolds L.G. (1986), *Economic Growth in the Third World. An Introduction*, New Haven, Yale University Press.

Rodrik D. (1994), Foreign Trade in Eastern Europe's Transition: Early Results, in O.J. Blanchard, K.A. Froot, & J.D. Sachs (eds), *Transition in Eastern Europe*, vol. 2, Chicago, University of Chicago Press: 319–356.

Rodrik D. (2004), Industrial Policy for the Twenty-First Century, *KSG Working Paper*, RWP04-047.

Rodrik D. (2005), Policies for Economic Diversification, *CEPAL Review*, 87: 7–23.

Rodrik D. (2006), Industrial Development: Some Stylized Facts and Policy Directions, in *Industrial Development for the 21st Century: Sustainable Development Perspective*, Report of the U.N.DESA.

Rodrik D. (2013), The Past, Present, and Future of Economic Growth, *Global Citizen Foundation Working Paper*, n. 1.

Rodrik D. (2016), Premature Deindustrialization, *Journal of Economic Growth*, 21 (1): 1–33.

Rodrik D. (2018), *New Technologies, Global Value Chains, and the Developing Economies*, Background Paper, Pathways for Prosperity Commission.

Rodrik D. (2022), *Prospects for Global Economic Convergence under New Technologies*, Brookings Report.

Romano L. (2021), Il ruolo della manifattura nella transizione ecologica e il contributo dell'Italia, *Rivista di Politica Economica*, 111(1): 199–224.

Romano L. & Traù F. (2014), Il Ruolo delle Istituzioni nello Sviluppo Manifatturiero del Mondo Emergente. Tre 'Modelli' di Intervento Pubblico negli Anni Successivi al Secondo Dopoguerra, *Rivista di Storia Economica*, 30 (2): 121–159.

Romano L. & Traù F. (2017), The Nature of Industrial Development and the Speed of Structural Change, *Structural Change and Economic Dynamics*, 42: 26–37.

Romano L., Traù F. (2022), La manifattura globale al tempo della pandemia, *Rivista di Politica Economica*, 112 (1): 13–45.

Rosa J.J. (2000), *Le Second XXᵉ Siècle. Déclin des Hiérarchies et Avenir des Nations*, Paris, Grasset & Fasquelle.

Rosenstein-Rodan P.N. (1943), Problems of Industrialisation of Eastern and South-Eastern Europe, *Economic Journal*, 53 (210/211): 202–211.

Rostow W.W. (1960), *The Stages of Economic Growth*, Cambridge, Cambridge University Press.

Rowthorn R. & Ramaswamy R. (1997), Deindustrialization: Causes and Implications, *IMF Working Papers* 42.

Saith A. (2008), Explaining Differential Performance: The Institutional Factor in Indian and Chinese Development, in P. Arestis & J. Eatwell (eds), *Issues in Economic Development and Globalization*, Basingstoke, Palgrave Macmillan: 28–48.

Sampaolo G., Di Tommaso M., & Liakh O. (2021), Structural Changes and Policies in China: From the New Dream to COVID-19 Era, in F. Spigarelli & J. McIntyre (eds), *The New Chinese Dream. Industrial Transition in the Post-Pandemic Era*, Cham (Switzerland), Palgrave Macmillan: 1–20.

Sandrey R. & Edinger H. (2011), China's Manufacturing and Industrialization in Africa, *African Development Bank Working Paper Series*, n. 128, May.

Sanpath P.G. & Ayitey D. (2016), External Opportunities, Innovation and Industrial Growth: The Case of GVCs in Africa, in P.G. Sanpath and B.O. Oyeyinka (eds), *Sustainable Industrialization in Africa. Toward a New Development Agenda*, Basingstoke and New York, Macmillan.

Sassoon (1997), Objectives and Results of the Uruguay Round, in E. Grilli & E. Sassoon (eds), *Multilateralism and Regionalism After the Uruguay Round*, Basingstoke and New York, Macmillan and St. Martin's Press: 1–60.

Schoenberger E. (1988), Multinational Corporations and the New International Division of Labor: A Critical Appraisal, *International Regional Science Review*, 11 (2): 105–119.

Schroter H.G. (1997), Small European Nations: Cooperative Capitalism in the Twentieth Century, in A.D. Chandler, F. Amatori, & T. Hikino (eds), *Big Business and the Wealth of Nations*, New York, Cambridge University Press: 176–204.

Sengenberger W., Loveman G.W., & Piore M.J. (1990, eds), *The Re-emergence of Small Enterprises. Industrial Restructuring in Industrialised Countries*, Geneva, International Institute for Labour Studies.

Shafaeddin S.M. (2005), Trade Liberalization and Economic Reform in Developing Countries: Structural Change or De-Industrialization?, *UNCTAD Discussion Papers*, n. 179, April.

Signé L. (2018), *The Potential of Manufacturing and Industrialization in Africa. Trends, Opportunities, and Strategies*, Africa Growth Initiative, Brookings Institution.

Singer H.W. (1964), *International Development: Growth and Change*, New York, Mc Graw Hill.

Singh A. (1977), UK Industry and the World Economy: A Case of De-Industrialisation?, *Cambridge Journal of Economics*, 1 (2): 113–136.

Singh A. (1987), Manufacturing and De-Industrialisation, in J. Eatwell, M. Milgate, & P. Newman (eds), *The New Palgrave*, London and Basingstoke, Macmillan, Vol. 3: 301–308.

Singh A. (1994a), 'Openness' and the 'Market Friendly' Approach to Development: Learning the Right Lessons from Development Experience, *World Development*, 22 (12): 1811–1823.

Singh A. (1994b), Industrial Policy in Europe and Industrial Development in the Third World, in Bianchi P. Cowling K, & Sugden R., *Europe's Economic Challenge*, London, Routledge: 40–51.

Singh A. (1995), Institutional Requirements for Full Employment in Advanced Economies, *International Labour Review*, 134 (4-5): 471–495.

Singh A. (1997), Liberalization and Globalization: an Unhealthy Euphoria, in: J. Michie & J. Grieve-Smith (eds), *Employment and Economic Performance*, Oxford, Oxford University Press: 11–35.

Singh A. (2009), The Past, Present and Future of Industrial Policy in India: Adapting to the Changing Domestic and International Environment, in M. Cimoli, G. Dosi, & J.E. Stiglitz (eds), *Industrial Policy and Development*, New York, Oxford University Press: 277–302.

Singh A., Belaisch A., Collyns C., De Masi P., Krieger R., Meredith G., & Rennhack R. (2005), Stabilization and Reform in Latin America: A Macroeconomic Perspective on the Experience Since the Early 1990s, *IMF Occasional Papers*, n. 238.

Singh A. & Zammit A. (2010), The Global Economic and Financial Crisis. A Review and a Commentary, *Centre for Business Research Working Paper Series*, n. 415, December.

Smith A. (1976 [1776]), *An Inquiry into the Nature and Causes of the Wealth of Nations*, Oxford, Clarendon Press.

Starosta de Waldemar F. (2010), How Costly Is Rent-Seeking to Diversification: An Empirical Approach, *Proceedings of the German Development Economics Conference*, Hannover, n. 4.

Stein H. (1992), Deindustrialization, Adjustment, the World Bank and the IMF in Africa, *World Development*, 20 (1): 83–95.

Stigler G.J. (1951), The Division of Labor is Limited by the Extent of the Market, *Journal of Political Economy*, 54 (3): 185–193.

Stiglitz J.E. (1987), Learning to Learn, Localized Learning and Technological Progress, in Dasgupta P. & Stoneman P., *Economic Progress and Technological Change*, Cambridge, Cambridge University Press: 125–153.

Stiglitz J.E. (1999), More Instruments and Broader Goals: Moving toward the PostWashington Consensus, in G. Kochendorfer-Lucius and B. Pleskovic (eds), *Development Issues in the 21st Century*, Berlin, German Foundation for International Development: 11–39.

Stiglitz J.E. (2002), *Globalization and Its Discontents*, New York and London, Norton.

Stiglitz J.E. (2015), Industrial Policy, Learning, and Development, *WIDER Working Paper* 2015/149.

Stiglitz J.E. & Lin J.Y. (2013, eds), *The Industrial Policy Revolution I, The Role of Government Beyond Ideology*, Basingstoke and New York, Palgrave Macmillan.

Storm S. (2017), The New Normal: Demand, Secular Stagnation, and the Vanishing Middle Class, *International Journal of Political Economy*, 46 (4): 169–210.

Sturgeon T.J. (2008), From Commodity Chains to Value Chains: Interdisciplinary Theory Building in an Age of Globalization, *Industry Studies Association Working Papers*, WP 2008-02.

Sturgeon T.J. (2017), The 'New' Digital Economy and Development, *UNCTAD Technical Notes on ICT for Development*, n. 8, Geneva, UNCTAD.

Sturgeon T.J. & Memedovic O. (2010), Mapping Global Value Chains: Intermediate Goods Trade and Structural Change in the World Economy, *UNIDO Working Paper*, n. 5.

Summers L.H. (2014), Reflections on the 'New Secular Stagnation Hypothesis', in C. Teulings & R. Baldwin (eds), *Secular Stagnation: Facts, Causes and Cures*, A VoxEU.org eBook, London, CEPR Press: 27–38.

Summers L.H. (2015), Demand Side Secular Stagnation, *American Economic Review*, Papers & Proceedings, 105 (5): 60–65.

Szirmai A., Naudé W., & Alcorta L. (2013), Introduction and Overview: The Past, Present, and Future of Industrialization, in A. Szirmai, W. Naudé, & L. Alcorta (eds), *Pathways to Industrialization in the Twenty-First Century*, Oxford, Oxford University Press: 3–50.

Szirmai A. & Verspagen B. (2015), Manufacturing and Economic Growth in Developing Countries, 1950–2005, *Structural Change and Economic Dynamics*, 34: 46–59.

Tavassoli S. (2013), Manufacturing Renaissance: Return of Manufacturing to Western Countries, Center for Strategic Innovation Research, *Electronic Working Paper Series* n. 2013/4, September.

Teulings C. & Baldwin R. (2014, eds), *Secular Stagnation: Facts, Causes and Cures*, A VoxEU.org eBook, London, CEPR Press.

Tezanos V.S. & Sumner A. (2013), Revisiting the meaning of development: A multidimensional taxonomy of developing countries, *Journal of Development Studies*, 49 (12): 1728–1745.

Thun E., Taglioli D., Sturgeon T.J., & Dallas M.P. (2021), Massive modularity: Why reshoring supply chains will be harder than you may think, *World Bank Blogs*, 17 June.

Toye J. (2003), Changing Perspectives in Development Economics, in H.J. Chang (ed.), *Rethinking Development Economics*, London and New York, Anthem Press: 21–40.

Traù F. (2003), *Structural Macroeconomic Change and the Size Pattern of Manufacturing Firms*, Basingstocke and New York, Palgrave Macmillan.

Traù F. (2016), La Globalizzazione e lo Sviluppo Industriale Mondiale, *Rivista di Politica Economica*, 105 (10-12): 353–408 (English version 'Twenty-Five Years of Industrial Development. Rise, Decline and Legacy of Globalization', *CSC Working Paper Series*, n. 4, 2018, Centro Studi Confindustria, Rome).

Traù F. (2023), Globalization and History, *Luiss Institute for European Analysis and Policy*, Working Paper n. 6/2023, Roma. https://leap.luiss.it/publication-research/publications/f-trau-globalization-and-history/

Tregenna F. (2013), Deindustrialization and Reindustrialization, in A. Szirmai, W. Naudé, & L. Alcorta (eds), *Pathways to Industrialization in the Twenty-First Century*, Oxford, Oxford University Press: 76–101.

Turnock D. (2006), *The Economy of East Central Europe, 1815–1989. Stages of Transformation in a Pheriferal Region*, Abingdon, Routledge.

UNCTAD (2013), *World Investment Report. Global Value Chains: Investment and Trade for Development*, New York and Geneva, United Nations.

UNCTAD (2016), *Trade and Development Report 2016. Structural Transformation for Inclusive Growth*, New York and Geneva, United Nations.

UNCTAD (2018), *Trade and Development Report 2018. Power, Platforms and the Free Trade Delusion*, New York and Geneva, United Nations.

UNCTAD (2020a), *Trade and Development Report 2020. From Global Pandemic to Prosperity for All: Avoiding Another Lost Decade*, New York and Geneva, United Nations.

UNCTAD (2020b), *World Investment Report 2020. International Production beyond the Pandemic*, New York and Geneva, United Nations.

UN-DESA (2010), *World Economic and Social Survey 2010. Retooling Global Development*, New York, United Nations.

UNIDO (2009), *Industrial Development Report. Breaking In and Moving Up: New Industrial Challenges for the Bottom Billion and the Middle-Income Countries*, Vienna, United Nations.

UNIDO (2013), *Industrial Development Report. Sustaining Employment Growth: The Role of Manufacturing and Structural Change*, Vienna, United Nations.

UNIDO (2016), *Industrial Development Report. The Role of Technology and Innovation in Inclusive and Sustainable Industrial Development*, Vienna, United Nations.

UNIDO (2018), *Industrial Development Report. Demand for Manufacturing: Driving Inclusive and Sustainable Industrial Development*, Vienna, United Nations.

United Nations (1992), *World Economic Survey*, New York, United Nations.

United Nations (2000), *United Nations Millennium Declaration*, Resolution Adopted by the General Assembly, 55th Session, Agenda Item 60 (b), 18 September.

United Nations (2015), http://stats.unctad.org/Dgff2016/prosperity/goal9/target_9_b.html

United Nations (2017), *World Economic and Social Survey. Reflecting on Seventy Years of Development Policy Analysis*, Washington.

Upadhyaya S. (2013), Country Grouping in UNIDO Statistics, Working Paper 01/2013, Vienna, UNIDO.

Uya T., Yi K., & Zhang J. (2013), Structural Change in an Open Economy, *Journal of Monetary Economics*, 60 (6): 667–682.

Verdoorn P.J. (1949), Fattori che regolano lo sviluppo della produttività del lavoro, *L'Industria*, (1): 45–53.

Wade R. (1990), *Governing the Market. Economic Theory and the Role of Government in East Asian Industrialization*, Princeton, Princeton University Press.

Watanabe M. (2014), *The Disintegration of Production. Firm Strategy and Industrial Development in China*, Cheltenham, Edward Elgar.

Weber M. (1968 [1922]), *Economy and Society*, New York, Bedminster Press Inc.

Weisbrot M., Baker D., & Rosnik D. (2006), *The Scorecard on Development: 25 Years of Diminished Progress*, DESA Working Paper n. 31, September, United Nations, Department of Economic and Social Affairs.

Westney D.E. (1987), *Imitation and Innovation. The Transfer of Western Organizational Patterns to Meji Japan*, Cambridge (Ma.) and London, Cambridge University Press.

White House (2018), *How China's Economic Aggression Threatens the Technologies and Intellectual Property of the United States and the World*, White House Office of Trade and Manufacturing Policy Report.

White House (2022), *National Security Strategy*, Washington (DC).

Whittaker D.H. (1997), *Small Firms in the Japanese Economy*, Cambridge, Cambridge University Press.

Whittaker D.H., Sturgeon T.J., Okita T., & Zhu T. (2020), *Compressed Development. Time and Timing in Economic and Social Development*, Oxford, Oxford University Press.

Williamson J. (2009), Short History of the Washington Consensus, *Law and Business Review of the Americas*, 15 (1): 7–26.

Winters L.A., Yusuf S. (2007, eds), *Dancing with Giants. China, India, and the Global Economy*, Washington and Singapore, The World Bank and The Institute for Policy Studies.

Woo-Cumings M. (1999, ed.), *The Developmental State*, Ithaca and London, Cornell University Press.

World Bank (1996), *World Development Report. From Plan to Market*, Washington, The World Bank.

World Bank (2009), *World Development Report. Reshaping Economic Geography*, Washington, The World Bank.

World Bank (2019a), *Global Value Chain Development Report 2019: Technological Innovation, Supply Chain Trade, and Workers in a Globalized World*, Washington, The World Bank.

World Bank (2019b), *Global Economic Prospects. Darkening Skies*, Washington, The World Bank.

WTO – IDE-JETRO (2011), *Trade Patterns and Global Value Chains in East Asia: From Trade in Goods to Trade in Tasks*, http://www.wto.org/english/res_e/publications_e/stat_tradepat_globalchains_e.htm

Yang M. & Yu H. (2011, eds), *China's Industrial Development in the 21ˢᵗ Century*, Singapore, World Scientific Publishing.

Young A. (1928), Increasing Returns and Economic Progress, *Economic Journal*, 38 (152): 528–542.

Yusuf S. & Nabeshima K. (2010), *Changing the industrial geography in Asia*, Washington, The World Bank.

Zhang Z. & Gao Y. (2015), Emerging Market Heterogeneity: Insights from Cluster and Taxonomy Analysis, *IMF Working Paper* 15/155.

Index

For the benefit of digital users, indexed terms that span two pages (e.g., 52–53) may, on occasion, appear on only one of those pages.

A

Africa, 88
  competitive pressure on underdeveloped
    areas, 59–60
  manufacturing goods, degree of trade openness,
    and normalized trade balance for, 58
  per capita GDP and sectoral concentration
    in manufacturing in terms of value
    added, 23
  percentage annual GDP growth rates, 14
  production coupling, 146
  regional agreements, 152 n.18
  reversal in trade openness with OIEs, 57–59
  world network of market exchanges, 157
  yearly average growth rate of per capita
    value, 49
  yearly average growth rates of manufacturing
    per capita value added, 48
  see also South Africa
ASEAN (Association of Southeast Asian
  Nations), 152 n.19, 153
Asia
  bursting onto global scene, 17
  Central, 23, 157
  comparison with Latin American industrial
    policies, 79–80, 82
  degree of openness of manufacturing
    sector, 122–124
  growth rates, 14, 42–43, 48, 49
  increasing competitive pressure on world's
    production systems, 59–60
  production of micro-chips, 162–163
  regionalism, 152, 155–156 n.25
  reorganization of production networks, 158
  'the Rest' countries, 27
  Southeastern, 48–49, 51, 58, 165–166
  stronger driver of change in trade openness
    towards OIEs coming from, 57–59
  world network of market exchanges, 157
  see also East Asia
Asian Developmental State, 2, 27–28, 65–67,
  71–72, 79, 82–83, 165–166
Asian model
  China, 75
  overview, 68

  South Korea, 72
Asian Tigers, 42–43, 52 n.19, 69, 97, 102–103,
  122, 146

B

back-shoring, 147, 159–160, 162
Berlin Wall, fall of, 34, 85, 166–167, 169–170
BRIC (Brazil, Russia, India, China), 38, 42,
  87–88, 97, 102–103, 108, 146–147

C

capitalism
  advent of, in former Soviet Union and Eastern
    Europe, 82
  'modern,' 69–70
China
  accession to WTO, 54
  bursting onto global scene, 17
  CO_2 emissions relative to EU, 161
  cumulated world manufacturing output
    shares, 40
  and decoupling, 146
  driver of change in trade openness towards
    OIEs, 57–59
  as emerging industrial country in Asian
    model, 75
  as 'factory of the world,' 150
  growth rates, 14, 40–44, 48, 49, 108–110, 139,
    140
  growth tied to widening of internal
    demand, 37–38
  impact of financial crisis, 54–55
  involvement in regional economic
    activities, 145
  manufacturing growth against degree of
    industrialization, 62
  manufacturing value added, 38, 45, 50, 104,
    123
  move away from export-led logic, 168
  in new taxonomy of manufacturing
    countries, 102–103, 108
  share of intermediate imports, 147
  as strongly inward-looking, 152
  structure and change of relative manufacturing
    output flows in long run, 39

China (*Continued*)
  switch from external to internal demand
    as engine of manufacturing
    growth, 143–145
  in UNIDO taxonomy, 107
  US manufacturing in comparison with, 151
  US *versus* Fukuyama, 169–171
  world network of market exchanges, 157
  see also East Asia
COMECON (Council for Mutual Economic
  Assistance), 83–84, 86–87
comparative advantage
  and digitalization, 159
  dynamic, 2, 12, 27–28, 67–68, 74, 79, 92, 94,
    165–166
  exploitation of current, 29
  and globalization logic, 34–35
  and globalization process, 37
  and industrial policies, 118
  for late industrializers, 119–120, 167
  recommendation for, 95
  and selective policies, 94–95
  static, 19–20, 67–68, 80, 92, 165
compressed development, 21, 134
Covid-19 pandemic, 4, 32–33, 162, 168

D
decoupling, 3, 5–6, 54–55, 146, 168
de-industrialization, 5, 20, 21, 35, 51–52, 54, 68,
  115–116, 134–135, 139, 167
demand
  aggregate, 32–33, 139
  collapse in, and financial crisis, 30–31,
    139–140
  factors exogenously increasing scale of, 116
  falling, as long-run determinant of output
    slowdown, 139–140
  and 'free choices,' 25–26
  global foreign, 20–21
  for imports, boom in, 138–139
  increasing, for fast-delivery
    productions, 159–160
  internal, in African countries, 92
  international, 1, 142, 168
  and labour, 21–22
  market, 19–20, 93
  OIEs as less self-sufficient in relation to
    manufacturing, 55–56
  shrinkage of, in advanced countries, 3
  sourced by North, export-led growth driven
    by, 61
  South as more independent from North in
    relation to, 55
  and stagnation, 32–33
  unprecedented shock, 17

  see also domestic demand; external demand;
    internal demand
digitalization, 159
distance, return of, 146–151
diversification, 21, 105, 116–117, 119–120,
  124–125
Doha Round, 13, 154–155
domestic demand
  achieving balance with international
    demand, 142
  effect of financial crisis, 142
  emerging East Asian world pushed towards
    new centrality of, 77, 143
  and growth differentials between North and
    South, 51
  in laggard countries, 16
  for late industrializers, 167
  in Latin America, 79, 145–146
  in old *versus* new industrial economies, 53–55
  in Russia, 83–84, 87–88, 145–146
Domestic Demand Led Growth (DDLG), 77, 143

E
East Asia
  'Asian approach,' 85 n.36
  comparison with Africa, 91–92
  current success of economies, 70
  and decoupling, 146–148
  development of supply chains in, 150
  export-led growth model, 28
  facing domination of North Western economies
    in manufacturing, 67
  growing involvement in world trade
    exchanges, 155–156 n.25
  growth rates, 13–14, 139, 145
  latecomers, 118
  manufacturing goods, degree of trade openness,
    and normalized trade balance for, 58
  per capita manufacturing value added, 48–50
  public intervention, 67–68
  pushed towards new centrality of domestic
    demand, 77, 143–145
  as self-contained economic entity, 158
  serving China's expanding market, 145
  strong dependence on exports, 3, 143
  successful industrialization project, 68
  see also Asia
Eastern Europe
  advent of capitalism in, 86–88
  industrialization, 50–51
  manufacturing value added, 41–42, 45, 47–48,
    50, 104
  production decoupling, 146
  rising trade openness, 57–59

in taxonomies of manufacturing
    countries, 102–103, 107, 108–109
yearly average growth rate of per capita
    value, 47–48
Economic Commission for Latin America and the
    Caribbean (ECLAC/CEPAL), 11–12
economic development
    according to GA logic, 137–138
    of advanced countries, 43–44
    and changing rules, 8
    early period of, in Africa, 92–93
    and industrial development, 131, 135
    Japanese consensus on, 70–71
    per-capita GDP as measure of, 46–47, 121
    and route to globalization, 166
    and sectoral concentration, 119
    as strongly affected by institutional
        factors, 69–70
economic growth, 13, 21, 28, 47 n.13, 82,
    110–111, 163
emerging economies (EEs)
    catching up with respect to OIEs, 36
    crowding out of internal supply by, 154–155
    decoupling, 146
    degree of extra-area trade openness, 53
    determinants of manufacturing
        development, 15–23, 35
    effects of financial crisis, 3
    external and internal demand, 142
    grouping, 47–48
    growth rates, 14
    growth tied to widening of internal
        demand, 37–38
    higher competition from abroad harming, 167
    industrialization
        Africa, 88
        among laggards, 61–62
        Asian model overview, 68
        China, 75
        digitalization as enabler of, 159
        and export-led growth, 61
        Latin America, 78
        manufacturing growth against degree of, 62
        political economy of, 63
        and public institutions, 110
        road to, 26
        South Korea, 72
        Soviet Union and Eastern Europe, 82
        and state intervention, 82–83
        study conclusions, 94
    manufacturing goods
        degree of trade openness, and normalized
            trade balance, 58
        share of extra-area imports and total import
            to output ratio, 56

manufacturing growth as export-led, 3
manufacturing value added, 45, 48
method of distinguishing for purposes of
    study, 47
and pollution levels, 161
real values as primary concern in analysis
    of, 125
relative growth and international economic
    integration
    versus advanced economies, 56, 60
    versus OIEs, 51, 59
slowdown of manufacturing growth, 138, 168
employment growth, 76–77
endogenous determinants
    of decoupling, 3
    of fall of GA, 3, 5–6, 165–168, 170–171
endogenous growth, 19, 51, 64, 88–90, 119, 160
endogenous manufacturing development, 19,
    31–32, 34–35, 165–166
endogenous process
    industrialization, 63–64, 68, 131
    taking on form of, 19
EU-15, 38
export-led growth, 3, 22, 28, 61, 77, 131, 139–140,
    142
export-led industrialization, 52, 87–88, 122–124
external demand
    fall of, 5–6, 51–52, 138–140, 141 n.7, 167
    and financial crisis, 3, 168
    move to internal demand, 142
    role in manufacturing development
        data and sample construction, 120
        definition and characterization of groups of
            countries, 121
        economic development and industrial
            development, 131
        research hypotheses, 119
        structural change and industrial
            development, 125
        study conclusions, 134
        theoretical premises, 115

F
FDI
    in China's East Asian model, 76–77
    and multilateralism, 154–155
    outflows and inflows, 24
    and trade liberalization, 92–93 n.48
    from West to Eastern Europe, 87 n.40
financial crisis
    effects of, 3, 149, 154–155, 168
    long-run trends, 32
    slowdowns following
        degree of openness of OIEs towards EEs, 53
        demand for imports, 138–139

financial crisis (*Continued*)
    demand from US, EU, and Japanese
        economies, 77
    domestic demand, 54, 142
    expansion in general, 136
    international demand, 168
    of international trade, 137
    Latin America's current accounts, 57–59
    level of trade in intermediates, 18–19
    manufacturing growth rates, 5–6, 42, 47–48,
        138, 168
    outward FDIs of advanced countries, 24
    trigger, 30. 35

G
G7, 34, 43
G10, 2, 43, 52, 102–103
GA *see* Globalization Age (GA)
GATT (General Agreement on Tariffs and
        Trade), 151–154
Globalization Age (GA)
    blurring of boundaries between North and
        South, 102
    coinciding with manufacturing expansion
        beyond G10, 97
    fall of
        changing conditions affecting, 136
        digitalization, effects of, 159
        endogenous determinants, 3, 5–6, 165–168,
            170–171
        from external to internal demand, 142
        green transition, effects of, 160
        manufacturing growth slowdown, 138
        pandemic and war, effects of, 7, 162, 168
        from regionalism to multilateralism and
            back, 151
        return of distance, 146–147
        summary, 165–171
    industrial imbalance at sectoral level, 120
    producing varying results in different
        areas, 61–63
    regime based on generalized liberalization, 1
    rise of
        diversification in, 21
        and great financial crisis, 30–32
        growth rates, 11
        levels of development, 8
        multinationals and control of value
            chains, 23
        nature of growth, 19
        new linkages, 15
        new paradigm, 8
        premise, 8
        summary, 34, 165–171
        towards industrialization, 26

    and South-to-South manufacturing
        exchanges, 59
global trade
    effect of Ukraine war, 168
    relationship with value added in
        manufacturing, 137
    sluggishness of, 31–32
global value chains (GVCs)
    changes in structure of, 158–159
    cross-country fragmentation of, 137
    and digitalization, 159–160
    effects of development of, 155–156
    and endogenous manufacturing
        development, 19
    expansion first achieved by, 18–19
    expected radical re-thinking of, 137–138
    factors challenging confidence in, 162–163,
        168
    firms taking role of 'sub-system integrators'
        in, 25
    and neo-colonial dependence, 93
    participation index to, 136 n.2
    shortening of, 146 n.11
    in sub-Saharan Africa, 91–92
    and unfolding of globalization process, 158
    unfolding of, via trade in tasks, 61
    see also supply chains; value chains
Golden Age, 1, 9, 14, 43–44, 65, 92–93, 168–169
green transition, 160, 163
growth *see* economic growth; endogenous growth;
        export-led growth; industrial growth;
        manufacturing growth; relative growth
growth differentials, 40, 51, 149–150
growth rates, 11
    exceptionally high, in emerging
        economies, 139, 168
    of gross output, 140–141
    manufacturing
        slowdown of, 4, 90–91
        Vietnam's spectacular, 145
    of manufacturing value added
        per capita, 48
        yearly average, 41
    of per capita value, 49
    percentage annual GDP, 14
    world output, 15

I
IMF (International Monetary Fund), 10, 32–33
        n.43, 98 n.3
import substitution, 27–28, 67–68, 71–72, 78, 79,
        89–91, 122
Import-Substitution Industrialization (ISI), 9–12,
        68, 78–80, 82, 90, 92, 94–95
India

in Asian Drama, 69–70
as Asian giant, 38–40, 75
bursting onto global scene, 17
CO$_2$ emissions relative to EU, 161
cumulated world manufacturing output
    shares, 40
degree of industrialization, 45–46
growth rates of gross output, 140
as large emerging economy, 12
manufacturing export to value added
    ratio, 143–145
manufacturing growth against degree of
    industrialization, 62
manufacturing output growth, 70
moving away from export-led logic, 168
in new taxonomy of manufacturing
    countries, 102–103
as part of 'the Rest,' 27
per capita GDP and sectoral concentration
    in manufacturing in terms of value
    added, 23
per capita manufacturing value added, 45, 50,
    104
population, 42–43, 48–50
selected indicators for, 123
share of intermediate exports, 147
as strongly inward-looking, 152
structure and change of relative manufacturing
    output flows in long run, 39
in UNIDO taxonomy, 107
yearly average growth rate of per capita
    value, 49
industrial development
in African countries, 89
anomalous phase, 43–44
Asian Developmental State's pursuit of, 71–72
blurring of boundaries between North and
    South, 102–103, 106–107
China's goal, 76
collapse of 'model' of, 59–60
comparison with UNIDO taxonomy of, 107
countries with intermediate level of, 122
defining, 97
dynamics during last 30 years, 59
in Eastern European countries, 41–42
Eastern Europe and USSR, divergence in
    paths, 86–87
and economic development, 131, 134–135
of fast-growing latecomers, 42–43
globalization as last phase of, 8, 157
in Global North, 43
and manufacturing value, 121
as not having occurred everywhere, 56–57
overview, 1–4
policy lessons for manufacturing countries 114

political economy of, 63
polycentric shape of, 36
public intervention for pursuit of, 94
requiring active role of economic policy, 30
and sectoral concentration, 124–125
specialization viewed as way to, 116–117
state-driven policies at root of, 63
and structural change 125–129
before take-off of globalization, 124
time span for, 117
in years following World War II, 27
industrial growth, 65–66, 129–130, 133, 167
industrialization
degree of, 5, 15–16, 44–47, 62, 96–97, 101,
    105–106, 113, 114, 122
digitalization as enabler of, 159
and endogenous growth, 20–21, 34–35
GA coinciding with, 165
and growth differentials, 41–42
heterogeneous paths to
    Africa, 88
    Asian model, 68–75
    introduction, 61
    Latin America, 78
    political economy of, 63
    Soviet Union and Eastern Europe, 82
    study conclusions, 94
international trade at root of take-off, 3
mass, 42
old industrial economies and emerging
    economies, 45
rates of, 4, 21, 34–37, 41–42, 46–47, 46–47
    n.12, 47–48, 56–57, 59, 75, 103–106,
    108–110, 132
road to
    groups of countries, 121
    North–South linkage, 166
    'the Rest' *versus* 'the Remainder,' 26, 35
    and structural change, 125–129, 134, 167
    study conclusions, 134–135
    theoretical premises and
        hypotheses, 115–119
    successful countries, 165–166
    trade in tasks as key to, 166
    see also de-industrialization
institutional change, 69–70, 80, 85
institutional factors, 15, 63, 69–70, 96–97
institutional features, 110, 113–114
institutional inertia, 78, 118–119
institutions
    African, 91–93
    creation of, in East Asia, 158
    at dawn of GA, 9
    economic, 98 n.3
    as important for development, 110

institutions (*Continued*)
  for industrialization, 15–16, 27–28, 35, 71,
    94–95
  international, 2–3, 9, 10, 12, 28, 46–47, 63, 92,
    151–152, 157
  and market system, 86
  multilateral, 162–163
  public, 12, 27–28, 69, 79, 110
  role in China, 75
  and underdevelopment problem, 66
intermediate goods, 4, 18–19, 32, 77, 83–84,
    86–87, 146–147, 166
Intermediate Industrialized Economies (IIEs)
  definition, 122
  economic development and industrial
    development, 132–133
  inter-sectoral structural change, 130–131
    and economic development, 133
    and industrial development, 130
    regression analysis, 132
  intra-sectoral structural change, 127–128
    effect of trade on, 129
    and industrial development, 126
    regression analysis, 128
  prior to globalization
    industrialization indicators, 122–124
    sectoral concentration and industrial
      development prior to globalization's
      take-off, 124
internal demand
  compression of, 139–140
  earlier expansion of, 1
  factors contributing to weakness, 92
  Golden Age driven partly by, 9 n.1
  growth in EEs tied to widening of, 37–38
  long-run growth of, 120
  for manufacturing goods, 143
  move from external demand, 142, 168
  playing limited role, 167
  US reliance on, 152
international economic integration
  factors leading to weakness, 4
  fuelling manufacturing development, 94
  measure of, 122–124
  method of analysis, 136 n.1
  old *versus* new industrial economies, 51
  'the Remainder' and South–South
    competition, 56
  and slowdown of international trade, 137
international trade
  as driver of manufacturing
    development, 34–35, 158, 166
  and economic development, 137–138
  globalization process driven by, 37
  intra-firm exchanges, 23

Latin America, 81–82
  and multilateral institutions, 162–163
  regionalism in, 151, 154, 155–156, 168
  at root of take-off of industrialization, 3
  slowdown of, 137
  unprecedented expansion of, 1–2
inter-sectoral structural change, 115, 129
  and economic development, 133
  and industrial development, 130
  regression analysis, 132
intra-sectoral structural change, 115, 125
  effect of trade on intra-manufacturing, 129
  and industrial development, 126
  regression analysis, 128

L
laggard countries
  and 'advantages of backwardness,' 64–65
  and competitive advantages, 117–118
  as cut off from imitating early
    industrializers, 17–18
  development and manufacturing
    diversification, 22–23
  development issue in, 11–12
  difficulties in achieving expansion of supply
    matrix, 34–35
  division into two groups, 27–28
  examples, 68–69, 86–87, 143–145
  exploiting possibilities of trade
    liberalization, 26
  failure to catch-up with OIEs, 66
  industrialization, 50, 56–57, 61, 62, 93–94, 115,
    118, 127, 151, 167
  as not an undifferentiated entity, 118
  and unbundling, 16, 20
latecomers, 27–28, 42–43, 60, 65, 67, 118
Late Industrialized Economies (LIEs)
  definition, 121–122
  economic development and industrial
    development, 132–133
  inter-sectoral structural change, 130–131
    and economic development, 133
    and industrial development, 130
    regression analysis, 132
  intra-sectoral structural change, 127–128
    effect of trade on, 129
    and industrial development, 126
    regression analysis, 128
  prior to globalization
    industrialization indicators, 122–124
    sectoral concentration and industrial
      development prior to globalization's
      take-off, 124
Latin America
  abandonment of Developmental State, 30

abolition of ISI policies in, 11–12, 68
eruption of debt crisis, 9–10
free-trade areas, 153
growth rates of manufacturing per capita
    value, 47–48
from import substitution to market openness
    in, 78
inward-looking import-substitution
    strategies, 122
as part of 'the Rest,' 27
per capita manufacturing value added, 50
production decoupling, 146
world network of market exchanges, 157
yearly average growth rate of per capita
    value, 49
LIEs *see* Late Industrialized Economies (LIEs)

M
manufacturing countries
    characterization of different groups of, 105,
        121
    context, 96
    groups by manufacturing value added per
        capita, 104
    institutional features, 110
    sectoral concentration and industrial
        development prior to globalization's
        take-off, 124
    selected indicators for individual, 123
    taxonomy
        2001, 109
        comparison of old and new, 106–107
        evolution over time, 107
        general policy lessons, 114
        new, 102–103
        relevance of industrial development to
            building, 97, 113
        UNIDO, 101 n.7, 106–107
    tiers
        characterization of, 103, 113–114
        countries belonging to each, 101
        institutional differences across, 112
    variables used, 100–101
manufacturing export
    Gini coefficient of, 127–129
    higher, of OIEs, 54
    replacing import productions with local, 146
    sectoral concentration of, 128
    to value added ratio, 143–146
manufacturing goods
    Asian emerging economies as net exporters
        of, 59
    for blocs of countries, 53, 56
    China's export to value added ratio
        for, 143–145

for different South regions, 58
in East Asia, 78
and European colonies, 89
internal demand for, 143
in Latin America, 78
most 1990s exchanges occurring in
    North, 53–54
satisfying increasing domestic demand
    for, 54–55
world network of market exchanges, 157
manufacturing growth
    in African countries, 88–91
    against degree of industrialization, 62
    as export-led in emerging economies, 3
    involving fairly large countries, 36–37
    slowdown, 4, 138, 168
    switch from external to internal demand as
        engine of, 142
        in China and India, 143–145
        in Vietnam, 145
manufacturing growth rates *see* growth rates:
    manufacturing
manufacturing knowledge, 11–12, 15–16, 27–28,
    34, 41–42, 119–120, 127
manufacturing output
    countries characterized by highest increase
        in, 47–48
    flows, structure and change of relative, 39
    growth, 6, 70, 138, 140
    initial backwardness, 41
    parity of per capita GDP as, 44
    and rate of industrialization, 59
    relation between backwardness and speed of
        development, 61
    total, 127
    see also output shares
manufacturing production
    context and premise, 36
    downsizing in Global North, 96
    early, 59–60, 65–66
    Gini coefficient of, 127–128
    growth differentials, 40
    industrialization, 45
    output shares, 38
    relative growth and international economic
        integration, 51–56
    in Russia and Eastern Europe, 87
    size, 42
    study conclusions, 59
manufacturing value added
    African, 90–91 n.46
    CO_2 emissions relative to EU, 161
    decline in share of for LIEs, 132–133
    intra-, Gini coefficient for, 124, 128, 129
    and manufacturing trade, 136

manufacturing value added (*Continued*)
  overall world share, 38–40
  per capita
    countries characterized by positive growth
      of, 47, 121–122
    groups of manufacturing countries by, 104,
      108–110
    inter-sectoral structural change, 129–132
    intra-sectoral structural change, 125–128,
      131–132
    as measure of manufacturing
      development, 46–47
    sectoral concentration, 124, 128
    selected countries sorted by rank, 48–50
    as variable used to build
      taxonomy, 100–101, 103
  ratio, manufacturing export to, 144
  relationship with global trade, 137
  yearly average growth rates, 41
market exchanges
  fall in growth of, post-financial crisis, 3
  and offshoring flows, 137
  world network of, 157–158
market openness, 21–22, 75, 78
multilateralism, 3, 16, 151, 170–171
multinationals, 23
  arrival of, impact on emerging
    economies, 18–19, 23
  and digitalization, 159–160
  and endogenous growth, 19–20
  foreign
    and China, 76–77, 145
    and Latin America, 81–82
    and Russia, 88
  and green transition, 161
  and manufacturing knowledge, 27
  profile of activities in GA, 24

N
NAFTA (North American Free Trade
      Agreement), 79 n.24, 153, 155–156
New Development Economics (NDE), 11–12
new industrialized economies (NIEs), 36–37, 67,
      68–69
  see also emerging economies (EEs)

O
OECD (Organization for Economic Cooperation
      and Development), 98 n.3, 100–101,
      121–122
OIEs *see* Old Industrialized Economies (OIEs)
Old Industrialized Economies (OIEs)
  catching up process of EEs, 36–37, 66
  definition, 122
  and technological discontinuity, 64

economic development and industrial
    development, 133
  exploitation of third-world commodities
    by, 1–2
  in Global South, 57–59
  growth differentials, 40–41
  industrialization, 45–47
  inter-sectoral structural change, 130–131
    and economic development, 133
    and industrial development, 130
    regression analysis, 132
  intra-sectoral structural change, 127–128
    effect of trade on, 129
    and industrial development, 126
    regression analysis, 128
  and laggards, 66, 115
  prior to globalization
    industrialization indicators, 122–124
    sectoral concentration and industrial
      development prior to globalization's
      take-off, 124
  and public intervention, 66, 76
  relative growth and international economic
    integration, 51, 59
  and state-driven policies, 63
  yearly average growth rates of manufacturing
    value added, 41
output shares, 38
  correlation to degree of industrialization, 113
  cumulated world manufacturing, in top 20
    non-advanced countries, 40
  and de-industrialization, 65
  EEs *versus* OIEs, 59
  as first rising, then falling, in any
    country, 46–47
  increasing in EEs for physiological reasons, 51
  India's ranking, 45–46
  ranking, in small economies, 43
  reflecting absolute size of output flows, 44–45
  in shipbuilding industry, 74
  turning point, and industrialization rate, 21,
    46–47 n.12

P
political economy
  approach in Latin America, 80
  of industrial development, 63
productivity growth, 33, 46–47 n.12, 167

R
regionalism, 151, 156, 168
relative growth
  old *versus* new industrial economies, 51
  'the Remainder' and South–South
    competition, 56

'the Remainder'
    definition, 27–28, 56–57
    relative growth and international economic
        integration, 56
    road to industrialization, 26, 60
'the Rest'
    countries defined as, 27
    as economies lagging behind in mid-twentieth
        century, 26–27, 64
    no solution to economic predicament, 65–66
    road to industrialization, 26, 60, 65
Russia
    annual average growth rates of gross
        output, 140
    CO_2 emissions relative to EU, 161
    early industrialization process, 61
    industrialization in, 83 n.32, 86–88
    manufacturing export to value added
        ratio, 144–146
    manufacturing growth against degree of
        industrialization, 62
    in new taxonomy of manufacturing
        countries, 102–103, 108–110
    output shares, 38–40
    per capita GDP and sectoral concentration
        in manufacturing in terms of value
        added, 23
    per capita value added in manufacturing, 45,
        104
    share of intermediate imports, 146–147
    structure and change of relative manufacturing
        output flows in long run, 39
    as struggling to diversify away from extraction
        industries, 82
    in UNIDO taxonomy, 106–107
    and Washington Consensus, 2–3, 29

S
sectoral concentration
    acquisition of production capabilities in
        increasing range of goods as opposite
        of, 135
    as changing in course of industrial
        development, 5
    decreasing with level of industrial
        development, 124
    Gini coefficient of, 125
    of late industrializers, 5, 115, 167
    level of disaggregation used to study change
        in, 120–121
    in manufacturing in terms of value added, 23
    of manufacturing value added and
        manufacturing exports, 128
    measure of, over time, 100–101

no systematic differences between second and
        third tier countries, 105–106
    positive relation with total manufacturing
        output, 127
    research hypotheses, 119–120
    speed of, in relation to timing of
        industrialization, 127
    before take-off of globalization, 124
size of country, 42
South Africa
    annual average growth rates of gross
        output, 140
    cumulated world manufacturing output
        shares, 40
    as exception to general African pattern, 89
    exhibiting stagnant complexity of economy, 88
    manufacturing growth against degree of
        industrialization, 62
    manufacturing value added per capita, 104
    in new taxonomy of manufacturing
        countries, 102–103, 108
    peculiar features exhibited by, 88–89 n.43
    in UNIDO taxonomy, 107
South Korea
    CO_2 emissions relative to EU, 161
    and Developmental State, 67
    and FDI flows from abroad, 76–77
    industrialization, 72, 77
    manufacturing growth against degree of
        industrialization, 62
    manufacturing value added per capita, 45, 104
    as new industrialized economy, 68–69
    in new taxonomy of manufacturing
        countries, 102–103
    as part of 'the Rest,' 27
    population, 42–43
    selective allocation of credit flows, 76
    success as manufacturer, 44 n.10, 45–46, 108
    in UNIDO taxonomy, 107–108
South–South competition, 56
Soviet Union, former
    advent of capitalism in, 82
    and Washington Consensus, 29
structural change
    in Africa, 92–93
    analysis shedding new light on, 115–116
    effects of, in emerging economies, 41 n.4, 139
    institutions and state, 113
    and laggard economic systems, 115, 167
    in Latin America, 82
    lower intensity of trade flows prior to financial
        crisis, 31–32
    and output shares, 46–47, 74
    overview, 5
    research hypotheses, 119–120

structural change (*Continued*)
  research results, 133–134
  sample construction, 121
  testing globalization shock, 121
  and trade openness, 55
  variables commonly referred to in literature
    on, 100–101
  see also inter-sectoral structural change;
    intra-sectoral structural change
supply chains
  development of, 150–151, 158
  efficiency of local, 148
  fragmentation of, 17, 136
  global, 31
  international, 19 n.1
  reconstituting pieces of, 148–149
  shortening of, 162
  see also global value chains (GVCs); value
    chains

T
taxonomy building *see* manufacturing countries:
    taxonomy
trade balance, normalized
  and degree of trade openness, 53–54, 57–59
  and industrialization rate, 105–106
  and international integration, 51–54
  as variable used to build taxonomy, 100–101,
    105–106
trade in tasks, 16–19, 22, 34–35, 61, 116, 166–167
trade openness, 52–55, 57–59, 74–75, 101

U
Ukraine war, 24, 33, 138, 148–149, 162, 168
unbundling, 16–17, 20, 25, 61, 116, 159, 166
United Nations Conference on Trade and
    Development (UNCTAD), 22–23,
    28, 31–32, 91–92, 160–161, 162 n.29,
    163–164

United Nations Industrial Development Organi-
    zation (UNIDO), 17–19, 29 n.35, 46–47,
    98–100, 101 n.7, 106–107
United States-Mexico-Canada Agreement
    (USMCA), 153 n.21, 157

V
value chains
  control of, 25–26
  European, 87
  fragmentation of, 54, 118, 137, 158, 166
  international, 17, 34, 134–135, 145, 146, 167
  length of, 154–155
  supportive, 64
  unbundling, 17, 159, 166
  see also global value chains (GVCs); supply
    chains

W
Washington Consensus (WC)
  decline of, 12, 14–15
  dissatisfaction with provisions of, 11–12
  East Asian economies not following, 85 n.36
  economic policy principles, 10, 165
  effects of, 1, 12
  export-led development strategies advocated
    by, 28
  formulation of new system of rules, 10
  globalization process as driven by logic of
    comparative advantages, 37
  idealism of, 12
  idea of desirable state intervention, 111
  performance of countries accepting rules
    of, 2–3, 10–11, 29, 30
  performance of countries following strategy
    opposite to, 165–166
  radical change in logic of economic
    policy, 14–15
  rules of, 2
WTO (World Trade Organization), 1, 13, 54,
    76–77, 94, 98 n.3, 151–152, 154, 169–170